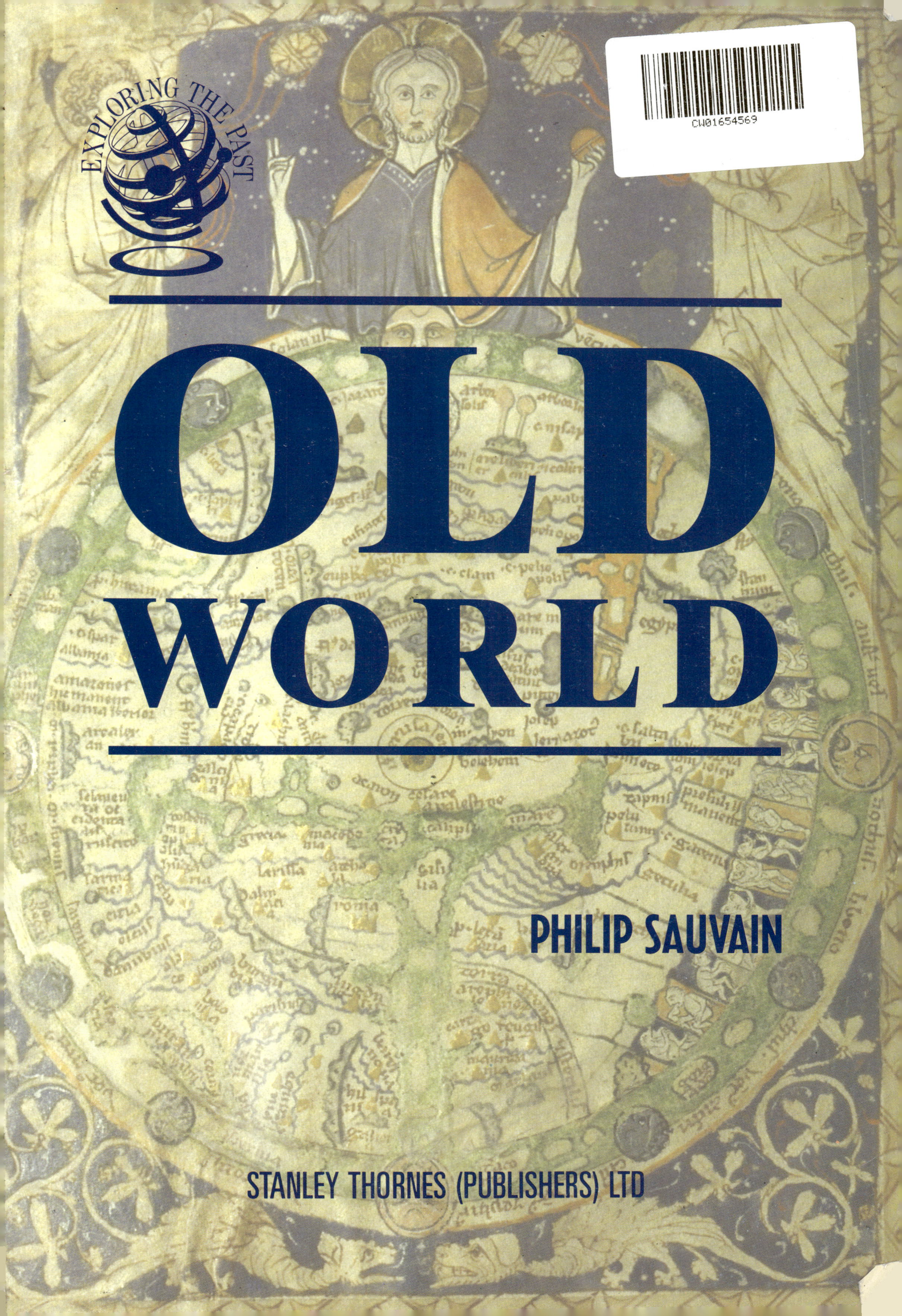

EXPLORING THE PAST

OLD WORLD

PHILIP SAUVAIN

STANLEY THORNES (PUBLISHERS) LTD

First published in 1991 by:
Stanley Thornes (Publishers) Ltd
Old Station Drive
Leckhampton
CHELTENHAM GL53 0DN
England

British Library Cataloguing in Publication Data

Sauvain, Philip
Exploring the past: Book 1. Old world.
I. Title
909

ISBN 07487-1184-8

Typeset by Florencetype Ltd, Kewstoke, Avon
Printed and bound in Great Britain
Designed by Simon Borrough

Acknowledgements

Most of the written sources printed in this book are translations of documents which were originally written in Latin, Arabic, Norman-French or Middle English. I have adapted them where necessary to improve the clarity and readability of the text while fully retaining the flavour and intent of the originals.

Many come from the classic collections of historical documents, such as the *Loeb Classical Library*, *Bohn's Antiquarian Library*, *Everyman's Library*, the *Reports of the Historical Manuscripts Commission*, H.T. Riley's *Memorials of London and London Life*, etc. A number of short extracts have also been taken from modern translations as well. Grateful acknowledgements are due, therefore, to the authors and publishers of the following books which have been invaluable in the research and preparation of this book. The forgiveness is begged of anyone whose rights may have been overlooked.

Cato the Censor on Farming, by Ernest Brehaut, New York, 1939.
Citizens of Rome, By Simon Goodenough, Hamlyn, 1979.
Roman Britain: A Sourcebook, by S. Ireland, Croom Helm, 1986.
Roman Civilization: Sourcebook I: The Republic, edited by Naphtali Lewis and Meyer Rheinhold, Columbia University Press, 1951.
Roman Civilization: Sourcebook II: The Empire, edited by Naphtali Lewis and Meyer Rheinhold, Columbia University Press, 1955.
The Histories, by Polybius, translated by Mortimer Chambers, edited by E. Badian, Washington Square Press, 1966.
The Roman Empire: Augustus to Hadrian, edited and translated by Robert K. Sherk, Cambridge, 1988.
The Roman Republic, by T.R. Holmes, Oxford, 1923.
The Satyricon, by Petronius, translated by William Arrowsmith, Mentor Books, 1960.
Chronicles of the Crusades, edited by Elizabeth Hallam, Weidenfeld and Nicolson, 1989.
History of the Arabs, by Philip K. Hitti, Macmillan, 1937.
Istanbul and the Civilization of the Ottoman Empire, By Bernard Lewis, University of Oklahoma Press, 1963.
Medieval and Renaissance Medicine, by Benjamin Lee Gordon, Peter Owen.
Social Life under the Abbasids, by Muhammad MoManazir Ahsan, Longman.
Tales from the Thousand and One Nights, translated by N.J. Dawood, Penguin, 1973.
The Great Documents of Western Civilisation, by Milton Viorst, Bantam Books, 1967.
The Travels of Ibn Jubayr, by R.J.C. Broadhurst, Jonathan Cape.
'De Gest is Mirabilibus' by Robert of Avesbury, in *Everyone a Witness: The Plantagenet Age*, compiled by A.F. Scott, White Lion Publishers, 1975.
Domesday Book: Suffolk, edited by Alex Rumble, Phillimore, 1986.
English Hisorical Documents, Vol II, edited by David C. Douglas and George W. Greenaway, Eyre Methuen/Oxford 1981.
Life on the English Manor, by H.S. Bennet, Cambridge, 1937.
Sussex Record Society: Volume LX, 1961
The Chronicle of Jocelin of Brakelond, translated by H.E. Butler, Nelson, 1949.
The Chronicle of Walter of Guisborough, edited by H. Rothwell, Royal Historical Society, 1957.
The Decameron of Giovanni Boccaccio, by J.M. Rigg, Dutton, 1930.
The Vision of Piers Plowman, translated by H.W. Wells, Sheed and Ward, 1935.
Life in a Medieval Castle by Joseph and Frances Gies, Abelard, 1975.
Memoirs of Usamah Ibn-Munqidh, translated by P.K. Hitti, Columbia University Press.
Readings in English Social History, edited by R.B. Morgan, Cambridge, 1923.
Social Life in Britain, by G.G. Coulton, Cambridge, 1918.
The Damascus Chronicle of the Crusades, translated by H.A.R. Gibb, Luzac, 1932.
The History of the King's Works, edited by H.M. Colvin, HMSO, 1963.
The Medieval Castle, by Philip Warner, Weidenfeld and Nicolson, 1971.
The Portable Medieval Reader, edited by James Bruce Ross and Mary Martin McLaughlin, Viking Press, 1949.
Visitations of Religious Houses in the Diocese of Lincoln, translated by A. Hamilton Thompson, Lincoln Record Society.

The author and publishers would like to thank the following for permission to reproduce copyright photographs in this book:

Aerofilms, pages 22 (left), 164 (bottom left), 172, 180; Ancient Art and Architecture Collection/R. Sheridan, pages 39 (left), 61; Arxiu Mas, Barcelona/Biblioteca del Monasterio de el Escorial, Madrid, page 66 (left); Bayerische Staatsbibliothek, Munich, page 143 (bottom left); Bibliothèque de Genève, pages 138 (top left), 166 (top); Bibliothèque Nationale, Paris, pages 52 (bottom), 56, 64 (top), 68, 70, 71 (top), 73 (top right), 77 (bottom right), 109 (bottom), 131 (top), 155, 163 (top), 176 (top); Bibliothèque Royale, Brussels, pages 152 (top), 181 (right); Bodleian Library, Oxford, pages 105 (middle right), 106–7 (top), 128–9; British Library, pages 60, 38 (right), 72–3, 78, 88, 104, 105 (left, top and bottom), 112 (top left and bottom), 116–17, 130, 132–3, 145 (right), 146, 148, 149 (top left), 150, 154, 156–7, 160, 166 (bottom), 171, 181 (left); British Museum pages 16 (right), 42–3, 45; Camerapix, page 53 (top); Trustees of the Chester Beatty Library, Dublin, pages 62 (left), 73 (bottom left); Viscount Coke/Trustees of Holkam Estate, page 106 (left); G. Dagli Orti, page 74; C.M. Dixon, pages 31 (right), 41 (bottom), 44 (top); Giraudon, pages 32 (top), 36, 63, 66 (right), 97 (bottom), 100, 138 (top right), 139 (top right), 176 (bottom); The Green Studio, Dublin, page 125; Sonia Halliday, pages 58 (bottom), 79, 80 (left), 81, 110, 112 (top right); Robert Harding, page 58 (top); Michael Holford, pages 29, 82–3, 83 (top right), 84–6, 87 (top); Hutchison Library, pages 57, 59; Institute of Archaeology, University College, London, page 34 (middle right); Istanbul University Library, page 69 (bottom); John Work Garrett Library, John Hopkins University of Baltimore, page 67; Magnum/Bruno Barbey, page 75; Mansell Collection, pages 5 (right), 13, 17, 23 (bottom), 24 (left), 31 (left), 34 (bottom right); Musée d'Art et d'Histoire, Geneva, pages 53 (bottom), 69 (top), 73 (bottom right), 76 (top left); Museum of London, page 39 (right, top and bottom); National Museum of Wales, page 126 (bottom); New York Public Library (Spencer Collection)/Astor, Lenox and Tilden Foundations, page 140–1; Osterreichische Nationalbibliothek, page 177; Pierpont Morgan Library, New York, pages 122 (bottom), 162 (bottom); Public Record Office, pages 98, 119 (bottom); Rheinisches Landesmuseum, Trier, pages 24 (right), 41 (top and middle); Roger Viollet, page 8; Scala, Florence, pages 15, 28, 47 (left), 50–1, 151 (top); J.R. Thoumine/Dean and Chapter of Worcester Cathedral, page 115 (top); Trinity College Library, Dublin, page 124; Universitatsbibliothek, Heidelberg, page 136 (right); University Library, Ghent, page 159 (left); Vatican Museums, pages 10 (left), 32 (left); Dean and Chapter of Westminster, page 129 (bottom); Windsor Castle, Royal Library © 1990/Her Majesty the Queen, page 123; Roger Wood, page 37.

All other photographs and engravings were supplied by the author from his own collection.

(38)

Contents

THE ROMAN EMPIRE

The Islamic Civilisations

MEDIEVAL REALMS

Castles & Cathedrals

THE ROMAN EMPIRE

1 ROME AND THE ROMANS

▶ *HOW and WHY did Rome become the centre of an important empire?* ATIB ■

▶ *HOW did the Romans govern Rome as a republic?* ATIC ■

The Romans were the masters of the ancient world for well over 500 years. Their empire began as groups of mud huts built by the Latins in about 800 BC. They chose a site on the hills above the river Tiber where the river was easily crossed. This settlement became a prosperous trading centre.

In 616 BC their land was seized by the Etruscans, a more advanced nation than the Latins. At Rome they built a town of houses and streets in place of mud huts. They drained the marshes to build the Forum (market place), recruited an army of citizens and built a town wall. They also built a huge temple to the god Jupiter on one of the hills. A council of leading men, the Senate, advised the Etruscan king. Rome became a strong fortress town. Ships could sail up the river Tiber as far as Rome. The city grew in wealth, importance and size.

Map of the Roman World in 509 BC

This Etruscan statue of the god Mars was made in about 300 BC. This means 300 years before the birth of Christ. Years after the birth of Christ are either shown with the letters AD in front (as in 'AD 1992') or on their own ('1992').

1.1 How can you tell that Mars was the god of war? AT3/L3

1.2 Write a sentence to describe the Roman Empire in 509 BC.

1.3 Did the year 509 BC come before or after 616 BC?

This is a relief—a sculpture in stone or metal which stands out from a flat or rounded surface—in which you can see some Roman senators. Reliefs like this tell us a lot about what Romans wore and the exploits of their soldiers. ▶

How Rome was governed

The year 509 BC was important to the Romans, since this was the year in which they overthrew their Etruscan king, the tyrant Tarquin. The rich families of Rome—the *patricians*— ruled in his place. They made Rome a *republic*. This is a land ruled by the people and not by a king or queen.

At first only the patricians had a say in how Rome was governed. A government controlled by a small group like this is called an *oligarchy*. The patricians met in the Senate to make laws. Here they debated the pros and cons of each new law. Some of the senators were brilliant orators (people who speak well in public). Many of the laws made by the Senate were copied by other countries hundreds of years later.

1.4 How did the *fasces* demonstrate the power of the consuls and the praetors? What punishments could be carried out with an axe and rods?

1.5 Look at the senators in the picture. What are they wearing? Do the men have beards? Write a sentence to say what they look like.

The daily work of government, however, was done by two consuls elected by the citizens of Rome. The consuls ruled with the advice and support of the Senate. One led the army, the other ruled Rome. They were assisted by *praetors* (judges) and *quaestors* (who collected taxes). *Lictors* walked in front of them carrying the *fasces* as a symbol of their power. This was a bundle of rods with an axe in the middle.

To stop them gaining too much power, consuls were only allowed to hold office for one year at a time. After this they were sent to govern a Roman province. If Rome was attacked, however, the Senate could give a consul the powers of a dictator for a short time.

Over the years, the poor people (called *plebeians* or *plebs*) wanted a greater say in the way they were governed. They were eventually granted the right to hold an assembly like the Senate to make laws. An elected *tribune* looked after their interests. He could stop a new law simply by saying *veto* ('I forbid'). In 367 BC the plebeians were at last given the right to be elected consul. They later gained the right to be elected to other offices as well, such as quaestor, praetor, *aedile* (in charge of games and public buildings), and *censor*.

Wall painting showing Samnite warriors

The wealth of Rome was envied by other people living close by. For two hundred years the Romans had to defend their city against attack. To do this they made alliances with other cities and built a powerful army. Bit by bit they gained control of much of the rest of Italy. They fought and defeated the Etruscans to the north and the Samnites to the south. As their empire grew, they came into conflict with Carthage. This was a city in North Africa with colonies in Sicily and Sardinia. In 264 BC the Romans invaded Sicily.

Hannibal and the Punic Wars

Map of the Roman World in 264 BC

The invasion of Sicily sparked off a long series of wars between Rome and Carthage. We call them the Punic Wars. At one stage Rome was nearly defeated by a brilliant general called Hannibal. In May 218 BC he marched the Carthaginian army through Spain and France until he came to the river Rhône. The Romans had every reason to think he would try to reach Italy by sea, but Hannibal took them by surprise. He crossed the Alps instead. As the Carthaginians climbed the mountains, they were harassed by fierce tribes. There were other dangers as well.

We know about this crossing from the writings of a historian called Polybius. He lived at a time when he could have talked to old soldiers who had fought with, or against, Hannibal as young men.

Source 1.A

The enemy did not dare to come near. They were frightened by the startling size of the elephants. Because of the surface of the ground and the snow, Hannibal lost nearly as many men going down as he had lost during the ascent. The snow made the path invisible to everyone. Any man or beast that stepped off the path and fell was hurled down the heights. When the men trod through the soft fresh snow, they stepped on hard ice below. As they fell and tried to use their hands and knees to regain their footing, they slid even more rapidly because the ground was so steep.

Hannibal crossed the Alps in fifteen days. He reached Italy with about 20 000 African and Spanish foot soldiers and 6000 cavalry. In a valley near Lake Trasimene in Italy, he laid a trap for the Roman army led by Flaminius. You can read what happened next in Source 1.B.

1.6 Why were some of the tribesmen in the Alps afraid to come too close to the Carthaginians? AT3/L3

1.7 Why were the Romans defeated (a) at Lake Trasimene (b) at the battle of Cannae? AT1B ■

1.8 Why do you think that some experts say Hannibal was the greatest general who ever lived? Is this a fact or an opinion? AT2/L3

1.9 How did Hannibal make good use of the fact that the Roman soldiers were highly disciplined? AT1C/L5

1.10 What were the advantages and disadvantages to Hannibal in crossing the Alps? AT1B ■

Source 1.B

Hannibal led out his slingers [they hurled stones from slings] *and spearmen and concealed them in a long line under the hills on the right side of the valley. In the same way he led out his cavalry and stationed them on the left.*

The day was very misty. As soon as the Roman army entered the valley, Hannibal gave the signal for attack. His men fell upon the enemy from all sides at once. They took Flaminius by surprise. At the same time the weather made it hard for the Romans to pick out the enemy pouring down and attacking from the higher ground. Nearly 15 000 Romans fell. They found it hard to fight back but refused to run or leave their ranks.

Hannibal defeated an even larger Roman army at the battle of Cannae. Before the battle he arranged his soldiers in the shape of a new moon. Facing them were the highly disciplined Roman soldiers. The Romans fought close together and joined their shields to make a solid wall of iron as they advanced. They were elated when Hannibal's front line began to give way in the centre. But it was a trap (Source 1.C).

The Romans were afraid that Hannibal would march on Rome itself, but the city was strong and well defended. Hannibal attacked the rest of Italy instead and devastated the south. This gave the Romans time to recover their strength. They built a fleet and sent an army to Africa to attack Carthage. Hannibal had to go back to defend his homeland. But in 202 BC Scipio, a young Roman general, defeated him at the battle of Zama. Afterwards the Romans gave Scipio the title 'Africanus'.

Map of the Roman World in 201 BC

Source 1.C

As they thrust their way forward into the place where the line had given way, the heavily-armed African soldiers on the right wing of Hannibal's army turned in to their left. Those on the left turned in to their right. As Hannibal had foreseen, the Romans were trapped. Now they were forced to fight not in close formation but alone or in small groups as they turned to face the Carthaginians attacking them from the sides.

1.11 Compare the two maps on these pages. What big difference was there between the Roman World in 264 BC and 63 years later in 201 BC?

AT1A/L3 AT1C/L3

1.12 Why did the Romans need a strong navy?

1.13 Who had the stronger claim to Sicily? Was it Rome or Carthage?

War elephant depicted on a plate from the time of the Punic Wars

The Roman Army

The Roman army made victory over Carthage possible. Its soldiers were very tough. They thought nothing of marching thirty kilometres in a day. In fact the army moved so rapidly it often took enemy forces by surprise. What is more, each Roman soldier was an expert builder of roads and bridges as well as a fighting man.

This relief on a column in Rome shows soldiers attacking a fort. This way of fighting was called the 'tortoise'.

We know about the Roman army at the time of Hannibal from the works of Polybius. He tells us about the weapons the soldiers carried and the armour they wore.

Source 1.D

The youngest soldiers carry a sword, javelins and a light round shield. The javelin is wooden, about a metre long and as thick as a finger. Its spearhead is about 20cm long and sharpened to a fine point.

From each unit they choose 10 centurions [company commanders] *according to ability. They also choose the two bravest soldiers from each unit as standard-bearers.*

The sword was short and had a sharp point. This was more useful than a sharp blade since the soldiers used it to thrust rather than to cut. They wore metal or leather armour and a helmet to protect the head. They also carried a shield. However, the type of armour they wore and the weapons they carried depended on their rank and whether they fought

1.14 What was the 'tortoise'? How did it get its name? Why was it a good defence against missiles? AT3/L3

1.15 When do you think the relief of the 'tortoise' was made? Was it (a) before the battle of Zama in 202 BC (b) before the death of Caesar in 44 BC (c) after the death of Augustus in AD 14? (Clue: Look at the shields) AT3/L4

1.16 Describe the armour and weapons of the soldiers in the picture above. What do you notice about the Roman cavalry?

Source 1.E

They always pitch camp in the same way. The spot best suited for issuing orders is taken by the general's tent and marked by a flag. A 60-metre square is measured off with this flag at the centre. The streets of tents make it look like a town. They build the wall of wooden stakes 60 metres away from the tents on all sides.

1.17 Why do you think they left a gap of 60 metres between the wooden fence round the camp and the tents where they slept? AT3/L3

1.18 Why did they always pitch camp in the same way?

1.19 Why did they choose the bravest soldiers as standard-bearers? AT3/L3

Marble relief of Roman soldiers in about AD 150

1.20 Compare the map below with the one on page 7. What changes took place in the Roman World between 201 and 133 BC? AT1A ■ AT1C/L3

1.21 Why did the Roman World expand? What effect did this have on Rome and on the people who were conquered? AT1B ■

Time Line

BC

509 Rome becomes a republic

290–275 Rome gains control of most of Italy

218 Hannibal crosses the Alps

217 Battle of Lake Trasimene

216 Battle of Cannae

202 Scipio defeats Hannibal at the battle of Zama

197 Defeat of Philip of Macedon

148–146 Macedonia and North Africa become Roman provinces

on foot or on a horse. It also changed over the years. The armour and weapons of a soldier in the Punic Wars was different from that of a Roman soldier 300 years later. For instance, they did not use long oblong shields until the first century AD.

Each centurion commanded a company or *century* of about 100 soldiers. The different centuries had their own barrack blocks or groups of tents. Each of these was divided, in turn, into about ten rooms.

In Source 1.E Polybius describes the way in which the Romans pitched camp after a day's marching.

The provinces

After the defeat of Carthage the Romans fought many wars. They completed the conquest of Italy. They invaded Macedonia. Bit by bit they conquered and occupied all the lands around the Mediterranean. They often treated the people of these conquered lands badly. After a revolt in Carthage they destroyed the city in 146 BC and sold all its citizens into slavery. Many of the other people captured by the Romans were taken back to Rome as slaves. Crops and other farm produce were taken to feed the soldiers. Ships took the surplus back to Rome. Metals and minerals provided raw materials for Roman industries.

The wealth gained by these conquests made it possible to abolish some of the taxes paid by the citizens of Rome. Becoming a citizen of Rome was now a very great privilege indeed. In about 49 BC Caesar granted it as a right to some of the people of Gaul and to every eligible Italian living south of the Alps. In AD 212 it became the right of almost everyone in the empire except the slaves.

Map of the Roman World in 133 BC

2 JULIUS CAESAR

FOCUS

▶ *WHY did the Roman republic collapse?* AT1B ■

▶ *WHY was Julius Caesar assassinated?* AT1B ■

The dictators

In the first century BC, about 2100 years ago, the Roman system of government began to break down. The army had become too successful. Many of its leaders had accumulated great riches, taking treasure from the lands they conquered. Governors and generals treated the legions under their command as if they were their own private armies.

Some commanders, such as Marius, Sulla and Julius Caesar, seized power as dictators. Their commands were law, not those of the Senate. What was worse, they fought against each other. Conflict like this, between soldiers of the same country, is called civil war.

The most successful dictator was Julius Caesar. He was a brilliant general. As governor of Gaul, he invaded Britain in 55 BC and again in 54 BC to teach the British tribes a lesson. They had been helping the people of Gaul in their fight against the Romans. Caesar told the story in his book *The Gallic Wars*.

Source 2.A From *The Gallic Wars* by Julius Caesar

The barbarians sent their charioteers to stop our men landing. This was proving difficult. Our huge ships could only be anchored in deep water. This meant that our soldiers, weighed down with heavy armour, had to leap into the sea to face the enemy. Our men were hesitating because the water was deep. Then the standard bearer of the Tenth Legion, after praying to the gods, cried out. 'Jump for it fellow soldiers, unless you want to let the enemy take the Eagle. I, for my part, will do my duty to my country and to my general.' After he shouted this out, he leapt over the side. At this the rest of our men did likewise and advanced on the enemy.

Sign at Deal in Kent

2.1 Why did the Romans find it hard to land their troops? What was 'the Eagle'? Why was it important to the Romans? AT3/L3

2.2 Are there any reasons for wondering if Julius Caesar's story of the landing is accurate or not? AT2 ■ AT3/L5

2.3 Why did the people of Deal celebrate the 2000th anniversary of Caesar's landing in 1946 and not in 1945?

2.4 How can you tell that this Roman galley (left) was a warship? How did it move through the water? AT3/L3

2.5 Did the sculptor make the people too small, too big, or about the right size for the size of the ship?

2.6 What creature is shown at the front of the ship? Why might a historian use this as a clue to suggest that the carving may have been made *after* Julius Caesar went to Egypt in 47 BC? AT3/L5

Julius Caesar

Julius Caesar was born in 100 BC. He first became a soldier in 81 BC and served in the army in Asia and Spain. He became an aedile (see page 5) in 65 BC. Two years later he bribed people to become high priest. To get further power he made an alliance with a successful general called Pompey and with Crassus, the richest man in Rome.

In 59 BC he was elected consul but made many enemies when he forced laws to be passed against the wishes of the Senate. In 58 BC he became governor of Gaul and used his power there to become very rich indeed. He also built a powerful army of over 50 000 loyal soldiers.

He used them to conquer northern and western Gaul. This was the area we know today as France, Switzerland and the Low Countries. Caesar greatly enlarged the Roman World. For the first time it extended far away from the warm lands of the Mediterranean.

His rise to power was challenged by his enemies. Roman soldier fought Roman soldier when he fell out with Pompey, his former ally. These years were dreadful years of civil war and ended, for Caesar, when he was assassinated in 44 BC.

Civil war

The quarrel between Julius Caesar and his enemies in Rome came to a head in 49 BC when he was told to hand over his armies to the Senate. He refused. Instead he advanced towards Italy but paused for a while at the river Rubicon on the frontier. Roman law said a governor must not leave his province. But Caesar was determined to confront his enemies. He said: 'The die is cast.' Then he crossed the Rubicon and advanced on Rome. His enemies, including Pompey his former ally, treated this as treason.

Pompey sailed to Greece to muster an army. But Caesar followed him. In 48 BC he defeated him at the battle of Pharsalus. Pompey fled to Egypt but was killed by the Egyptians soon after he landed. Caesar invaded the Nile region himself. There he fell under the spell of Cleopatra and made her Queen of Egypt. In the next few years he pursued and defeated his other enemies in battles fought in Turkey, North Africa and Spain.

2.7 What did Caesar mean when he said, 'The die is cast'?

2.8 What is meant today when someone says, 'I've crossed the Rubicon'?

The Ides of March

Caesar returned to Rome in 45 BC as dictator. He allowed the Senate to do its work but appointed many of his own supporters as senators. Unlike other dictators, however, he did not put his enemies to death. Many of them kept their wealth and position in Rome. This was a mistake. They decided to get rid of him. You can see how they did it in Source 2.B. This was written by a Roman historian called Plutarch in about AD 100.

Source 2.B The Ides of March — 15 March 44 BC

The Romans made him dictator for life. This was indeed a tyranny. A soothsayer warned him to be on his guard against a great danger on the Ides of March. When this day was come Caesar, on his way to the senate, greeted the soothsayer with these words, 'Well, the Ides of March are come.' The soothsayer replied, 'Aye, they are come, but they are not gone.'

When Caesar entered, the senators stood up. Some of Brutus's fellow plotters stood behind Caesar's chair. Others stood round. As they pressed upon him, he began to get angry. Casca struck the first blow in his neck but Caesar turned about, seized the dagger and held it fast. 'Vile Casca, what does this mean?'

Each of those who had come prepared for the murder took out his dagger and closed in on Caesar in a circle. Whichever way he turned he met blows and weapons.

When Caesar had been killed, Brutus came forward as if to say something. The senators would not hear him, but burst out of doors. Their flight filled the people with confusion and helpless fear. Some shut up their houses. Others left their counters and shops. All were running about.

Nearly 1500 years later, the playwright William Shakespeare wrote *Julius Caesar*. Compare his account of the murder (Sources 2.C and 2.D) with the one written by Plutarch.

2.9 Read Source 2.B. How long after the event did Plutarch write his account of the assassination? Why is it important to know this? Give a reason for thinking that Plutarch did not fully approve of Caesar. AT2/L4

2.10 Why were the people of Rome filled 'with confusion and helpless fear'?

2.11 Give a reason for thinking that Shakespeare had probably read Plutarch before he wrote his play. How does his version of the murder differ from that of Plutarch? AT2/L4

Source 2.C

Caesar: *The ides of March are come.*
Soothsayer: *Aye, Caesar; but not gone.*

Source 2.D

Casca: *Speak, hands, for me! (They stab Caesar)*
Caesar: *Et tu, Brute?* [You too, Brutus?] *Then fall, Caesar! (Dies)*
Cinna: *Liberty! Freedom! Tyranny is dead!*
Run hence, proclaim, cry it about the streets.

After the assassination the Romans debated whether it had been right to kill Caesar. This is what a famous writer called Cicero said:

Source 2.E

Our tyrant deserved to die. Here was a man who wanted to be king of the Roman people and master of the whole world. Those who agree with an ambition like this must also accept the destruction of existing laws and freedoms. It is not right or fair to want to be king in a state that used to be free and ought to be free today.

Cicero

2.12 Read Sources 2.E and 2.F. How did Cicero and Gaius Matius differ in what they said about Caesar? What reasons did Cicero give for hating Caesar? Why did Gaius Matius take a different view? AT1C/L6

2.13 Look at the picture on the right. Why do you think the Praetorian Guard was founded by Augustus? Describe the footwear, tunics, armour and headwear of the Praetorian Guard. What weapons did they carry? AT1C/L4

2.14 The members of the Praetorian Guard were the finest and best-paid soldiers in the Roman army. They were the only soldiers allowed in Rome. Could you guess any of this just by looking at the sculpture? AT3/L5

2.15 Give a modern example of an army unit like the Praetorian Guard.

Time Line

BC

100 Julius Caesar born
82 Sulla's reign of terror
60 Caesar forms an alliance with Pompey and Crassus
58 Caesar begins to conquer Gaul
55–54 Britain invaded
49 Caesar crosses the Rubicon
48 Pompey defeated at Pharsalus
45 Caesar is dictator in Rome
44 Caesar assassinated

Others took a different view. Gaius Matius, one of Caesar's friends, said this:

Source 2.F

People blame me for mourning the death of my friend. They say my country should be preferred to my friends, as if they had proved that killing him was good for the state. I did not abandon him as a friend, however much I disapproved of what he was doing. When my friend was triumphant, I was not tempted by high position or by money—even though others, who had less influence with him than I, grabbed at these prizes with unrestrained greed. Most of those who now are glad he is dead kept their position in the state.

The Praetorian Guard (shown on this relief) was formed in 27 BC to guard the Emperor Augustus

3 THE ROMAN EMPERORS

Map of the Roman Empire in AD 14

Octavian

After Julius Caesar's assassination, his great-nephew Octavian avenged his death. Together with Mark Antony and Lepidus he became a joint ruler of Rome. They punished those who had opposed Caesar. Even Cicero, the great orator, was put to death. In 42 BC they defeated Brutus and Cassius (the murderers of Caesar) at Philippi. Afterwards they divided the Roman Empire between them. Mark Anthony governed the East, Octavian the West.

They quarrelled, however, when Mark Anthony fell under the spell of Cleopatra in Egypt. In 31 BC a fleet of ships commanded by Octavian defeated Mark Anthony and the Egyptians at the battle of Actium. Anthony and Cleopatra committed suicide and Egypt became part of the Roman Empire. Octavian returned in triumph. In effect he was now Emperor of Rome. There was no one left to challenge him.

The first emperor

In 27 BC the Roman Senate gave Octavian a new name. He was called Augustus—meaning someone greatly revered and highly respected. As emperor he made many changes in the way Rome was governed. He reorganised the army and made himself its commander-in-chief. He appointed clerks and other officials to help rule the empire. He gave the Senate the job of governing peaceful provinces but kept those with large armies under his own control.

FOCUS

▶ *HOW and WHY did the government of Rome change?* ATIB ■

▶ *WHO were the Roman emperors and what did they achieve?* ATIA ■

▶ *HOW were the provinces Romanised and HOW did this affect Rome?* ATIA ■ ATIC ■

Augustus Caesar

Augustus Caesar was born Gaius Octavius in 63 BC but was later known as Octavian. In 27 BC, after his victories at Philippi and Actium, the Roman Senate gave him the name Augustus ('the respected one'). Later still they made him a god.

Augustus brought lasting peace to the Roman Empire for the first time in its history. In time most Romans forgave him for the crimes he had committed in order to seize power. This was because Rome flourished under his rule. The Romans were happy to have him as their leader.

During his 44-year period as emperor, Augustus brought in many reforms. He changed the system of coinage used in Rome. He brought in a better way of administering justice, collecting taxes and running the government.

He was also the first emperor. His reign brought an end to the Republic which had become unmanageable. He succeeded because he was efficient and because he still respected the Senate and the laws and customs of Rome. Later emperors were not so lucky or so wise.

Source 3.A

It is said he wore a coat of mail [iron armour] *under his tunic as he presided over the Senate. He had a sword by his side. Ten of the toughest of his friends among the senators stood round his chair. Even then the senators were only allowed to come forward one by one after the folds of their robes had been carefully searched.*

3.1 What precautions did Augustus take?

3.2 Why? What was he afraid of?

3.3 Compare this map (right) with a modern map of Europe. Make a list of countries where Roman remains might be seen today.

3.4 Compare the two maps on these pages. What changes to the Roman Empire took place between AD 14 and AD 116? AT1A/L3 AT1C/L3

3.5 Compare the six maps showing the growth of the Roman World on pages 4, 6, 7, 9, 14, and 15. Between which two dates did the empire grow at its fastest? AT1A/L4

3.6 Look at the photograph below. Why do you think Trajan's Column was erected? Suggest a possible event from Roman history depicted in these scenes. When do you think work on the column might have begun?

3.7 What differences were there between Rome under Augustus Caesar and Rome under Julius Caesar? AT1A ■

Trajan's Column in Rome ▶

Augustus ruled with the advice and consent of the Senate but he first made sure the senators were on his side. He cut their numbers down from over 1000 to 600. In future only rich men could become senators. The others had to leave. Some went of their own free will. Others were told to go by Augustus himself. The Roman historian Suetonius described what happened in the Senate in Source 3.A.

The expansion of the Roman Empire

The Roman Empire expanded still further under Augustus and under succeeding emperors, as you can see from the maps on these pages. Claudius was responsible for the conquest of Britain from AD 43 onwards. Trajan completed his conquest of Dacia (now part of Romania) in AD 106.

Map of the Roman Empire in AD 116

The Emperor Caligula

The Emperor Nero

The Emperor Hadrian

Octavia, sister to Augustus, and Mark Anthony's second wife

Livia, second wife of the Emperor Augustus

The first emperors

Augustus ruled the empire for 44 years, After he died the Romans were ruled by ten emperors within the short space of only 67 years. Tiberius followed Augustus. He was the only one among the first seven to die a natural death. The first four were all related to Augustus Caesar. After Tiberius, Caligula, a cruel tyrant, was assassinated. Claudius may have been poisoned by his wife. Nero committed suicide after murdering his mother and former wife. The new emperor in AD 68, Galba, was killed by the Praetorian Guard. Otho committed suicide and Vitellius was murdered in the street by supporters of Vespasian, a leading general. Vespasian was later adopted as emperor by the Senate.

In general, the best emperors were those who were chosen by either the Senate or by the previous emperor. Since so many died a violent death, however, it is not surprising that human life meant so little to them. In fact, no fewer than four emperors were killed in one year alone (AD 238).

At first the emperors treated the Senate with respect, as the place where laws were made. However, bit by bit its powers decreased as the emperors ruled more and more by decree. This angered Romans, who wanted the laws of Rome to be obeyed by everyone, including the emperor.

The 'Roman Peace'

Under Trajan (98–117), Hadrian (117–138), Antoninus Pius (138–161) and Marcus Aurelius (161–180), the empire expanded once more. As you have seen, Trajan conquered Romania. He also conquered Armenia and Mesopotamia in the east. Hadrian made the borders of the empire secure and built the wall in northern England which bears his name. Antoninus built another, less effective wall in central Scotland.

This was the period known as the *Pax Romana* ('Roman Peace'). Thirty legions, each with about 5000 men, patrolled the frontier regions. They made it safe for the remaining 100 million people who lived well within the frontiers of the empire. This was an area of peace with towns, fine roads, prosperous farms and country villas. Most of the local people soon adopted the Roman way of life and benefited from its trade with the provinces. They could drink French wine in a Syrian glass and eat African food from pottery made in Italy.

3.8 How did the growth of the Roman Empire affect the people of Rome? How did it affect people living in the provinces? AT1A ■

3.9 What is meant by the phrase 'the Romanisation of the Empire'? How was it achieved? AT1C ■

3.10 Complete the Time Line below up to the year AD 180.

The influence of the Romans was felt in other ways as well. For hundreds of years the chief language of Italy, Britain, France, Spain, Algeria, Egypt and Romania was Latin, as used in Rome. There was only one monetary system—the same as that used in Rome, hundreds of kilometres away. Many superb roads were built. Again, all of them led to Rome. The same buildings were built by the same methods throughout the Roman Empire. This is why the remains of a Roman town or fort in North Africa look much the same as the Roman remains found in England, France or Germany. In addition, all laws were made in Rome. We call this the Romanisation of the Empire.

It had a bad effect on Rome itself. Taxes, raw materials, food, pottery and other goods poured into Rome. The rich in Rome became even richer. Many of them preferred to spend their money on pleasure, and not earn it, or spend it for the public good. The plebeians were discontented, since they lived in overcrowded and squalid slums and got little benefit from the growth of the empire. In fact, they were often poor because no one needed their work any more. Goods were often cheaper from the provinces of the empire. A writer called Juvenal said the plebs only wanted two things out of life—'bread and circuses'. The bread was free. So, too, was admission to the games.

Bronze statue of the Emperor Marcus Aurelius erected in Rome shortly after his death in AD 180

Time Line

BC

63 Augustus Caesar born
44 Julius Caesar assassinated
43 Octavian allied with Mark Anthony
42 Battle of Philippi; Brutus and Cassius commit suicide
31 Mark Anthony defeated at the battle of Actium
30 Anthony and Cleopatra commit suicide; Egypt annexed
27 Octavian becomes Emperor Augustus

AD

14 Death of Augustus
98 Trajan becomes emperor
106 Trajan conquers Romania
117 Death of Trajan

4 THE ROMAN CONQUEST OF BRITAIN

FOCUS

► *HOW did the Romans conquer Britain?* ATIC ■

► *HOW did the Romans defend Britain against attack?* ATIC ■

The invasion of Britain

Aulus Plautius, a leading senator, led the Roman legions sent by the Emperor Claudius to conquer Britain in AD 43. His soldiers landed at Richborough in Kent without a fight. Britain at that time was not ruled by a single king or queen. There were many tribes, such as the Iceni and the Atrebates. They were no match for the well-armed Roman legions. This is why they took refuge in marshes and forests. They may have hoped the Romans would go away, as Caesar did a hundred years earlier.

When Plautius at last met them in battle he defeated two important tribal leaders called Caractacus and Togodumnus. Despite defeat, the Britons did not give in. They got together to muster a larger army. Plautius was alarmed at this. He sent a message to Claudius seeking help. A Roman historian called Dio Cassius described what happened next (Source 4.A).

Source 4.A

Claudius set out for the front. He crossed over to Britain, where he joined the Roman legions waiting for him near the Thames. Taking over command, he crossed the river, and met the barbarians in battle. He captured Camulodunum [Colchester], *the capital of Cunobellinus. Many tribes went over to the Roman side. Some did so by agreement, others by force. Claudius was acclaimed emperor several times.*

◄ *Look at this tombstone of a soldier called Flavinus. He was killed at the age of 25, fighting in the Roman army against the Britons.*

4.1 Write a sentence describing Flavinus from this photograph. What type of soldier was he?

4.2 Who is lying on the ground? What does this tell you about the attitude of the Romans to the Britons they defeated in battle? AT1C/L6

▲

4.3 How do you think metal bolts were fired by a ballista?

4.4 What is the modern equivalent of a war machine like this?

4.5 Look at the photograph on the right. How has the sculptor depicted Boudicca in her chariot? Is she shown as a heroine or as a murderess?

4.6 Why is it most unlikely that Boudicca and her daughters looked like this? AT2/L5

4.7 Boudicca is shown driving a war chariot with blades fixed to the wheels. Experts say there is no evidence that this was the case. What would they need to see before changing their minds? AT3/L5

4.8 How does this statue differ from the one of Marcus Aurelius on page 17 which was created by a Roman sculptor shortly after the emperor's death in AD 180? Which statue is of use to a historian wanting to find out about the Roman period? AT3/L6

The Roman legions made Colchester their headquarters in southern England. Another legion commanded by Vespasian, a future emperor of Rome, marched towards the west. They defeated British tribesmen at Maiden Castle in Dorset.

We know about this battle because the remains of some of the Britons killed in the fighting were found there. They were dug up during an excavation. The wounds on these skeletons showed they had been struck by iron arrowheads. Experts worked out that these had been fired by a *ballista*. This was a large and powerful catapult. You can see a modern replica of a *ballista* in the photograph on the left.

By the year AD 47 the Roman legions had successfully conquered the whole of the south-eastern half of England. They controlled the land from Devonshire in the south and west, to Lincolnshire in the north and east. But their hold on the country was not yet secure.

Boudicca's rebellion

Thirteen years later the Romans nearly lost Britain. Boudicca (sometimes known as Boadicea), Queen of the Iceni, sacked Colchester, St Albans and London. Her warriors looted treasure, set houses on fire and slaughtered thousands of the inhabitants.

This statue of Boudicca and her daughters was erected in 1902 near the Houses of Parliament

We know about Boudicca's rebellion from an account written by a Roman historian called Tacitus in about AD 100. In Sources 4.B (below) to 4.G (on page 20), he explains why Boudicca led her people, the Iceni, into battle.

Source 4.B

When Caesonius Paetus and Petronius Turpilianus were consuls, a dreadful disaster happened to the army in Britain.

Source 4.C

Prasutagus, the old king of the Icenians [in East Anglia] *had had great wealth. When he died he left it in equal shares to his two daughters and to the Roman Emperor. He hoped in this way to guarantee peace for his kingdom and his family. Instead his lands were looted by Roman centurions. His wife Boudicca was flogged. His daughters were raped. His relatives became slaves.*

Source 4.D

Angered by these acts of violence and dreading worse to come, the Iceni took up arms. What chiefly angered them was the conduct of the Romans living in the colony for retired soldiers at Camulodunum [Colchester]. *These men treated the Britons with great cruelty, driving them from their homes and treating them as slaves.*

The Iceni attack on Colchester and London

The Britons prepared for war, so the soldiers in Colchester asked for reinforcements.

Source 4.E

Two hundred men were all that could be spared. As a result, only a handful of soldiers defended the town. Since the temple was strongly fortified, they hoped to make a stand there. But no other precautions were taken. They didn't dig a ditch or build a spiked fence. Nor were the women and the elderly sent out of the town. They were unguarded and unprepared.

Source 4.F

At last the attack came. The Romans were taken by surprise. The barbarians overwhelmed them. They set fire to the town and laid it waste. The temple held out at first but after a siege of two days was taken by storm. The ninth legion tried to come to the rescue but the Britons cut the legion to pieces.

Source 4.G

Suetonius decided to abandon London to make sure of controlling the rest of Britain. Londoners who chose to follow him were given protection. Of those who remained behind, not one escaped the rage of the barbarians. The people of Verulamium [St Albans] *were likewise put to the sword.*

London was set on fire. However, Boudicca gained nothing but revenge. Suetonius had had time to build up his forces. He defeated her in battle. Boudicca, in despair, took poison and ended her life.

Written accounts by people who lived at the time of the events they describe often give us a vivid picture of what life was like in the past. But they are not always accurate. The writer may not have been in a good position to know what happened. Some copied stories from people who were not to be trusted. Some told lies. Some were biased. This is where archaeologists can help, if they find evidence which helps to confirm that an event really did take place.

Source 4.H sums up, in a simplified form, just a few of the Roman remains found in London. Study it carefully.

Source 4.H Roman remains in London from the 1st century AD

Top Level
Roman pottery made between AD 70 and AD 400.

Middle Level
A thick layer of ash. Tiny pieces of painted wall plaster. Tiles from a roof. Pieces from a burnt red clay wall. Charred pieces of wood. Burnt pieces of pottery known to have been used in Rome at the time of the Emperor Claudius. A heap of Roman coins from the time of the Emperor Claudius—some badly burnt, some partly melted.

Bottom Level
Pieces of broken pottery from the time of the Emperor Claudius and the Emperor Nero.

4.9 Why was Colchester not prepared for an attack? What preparations should have been made by the defenders?

4.10 Write two or three sentences explaining why Boudicca attacked the Romans. AT1B ■

4.11 Write down statements made by Tacitus (in Sources 4.B to 4.G) where he sympathises (a) with the Romans (b) with the Iceni. AT3/L4

4.12 When archaeologists dig up objects from the past, are the older remains likely to be found above or below the most recent finds?

4.13 How do we know there was a fire in London? How do we know a number of houses were burnt down? Write a sentence to say what these houses were built of. AT3/L3

4.14 How do we know that the fire *definitely* took place *after* the Roman invasion in AD 43? AT3/L3

4.15 How do we know the fire probably took place at some time *after* AD 54 but *before* AD 70? AT3/L3

4.16 Which of the sources B, C, D, E, F, G refers to this disaster? What phrase did Tacitus use to describe it? AT3/L4

Source 4.1

The Romans had little further trouble in southern England after the defeat of Boudicca. Many of the Britons living there welcomed the Romans and the luxuries they brought with them. It was a different matter, however, in northern England, Wales and Scotland. The hills and mountains there made it easier for tribesmen to harass and hinder the Romans. Even so, Roman troops marched as far north as Inverness in northern Scotland. They defeated the tribesmen there at the battle of Mons Graupius.

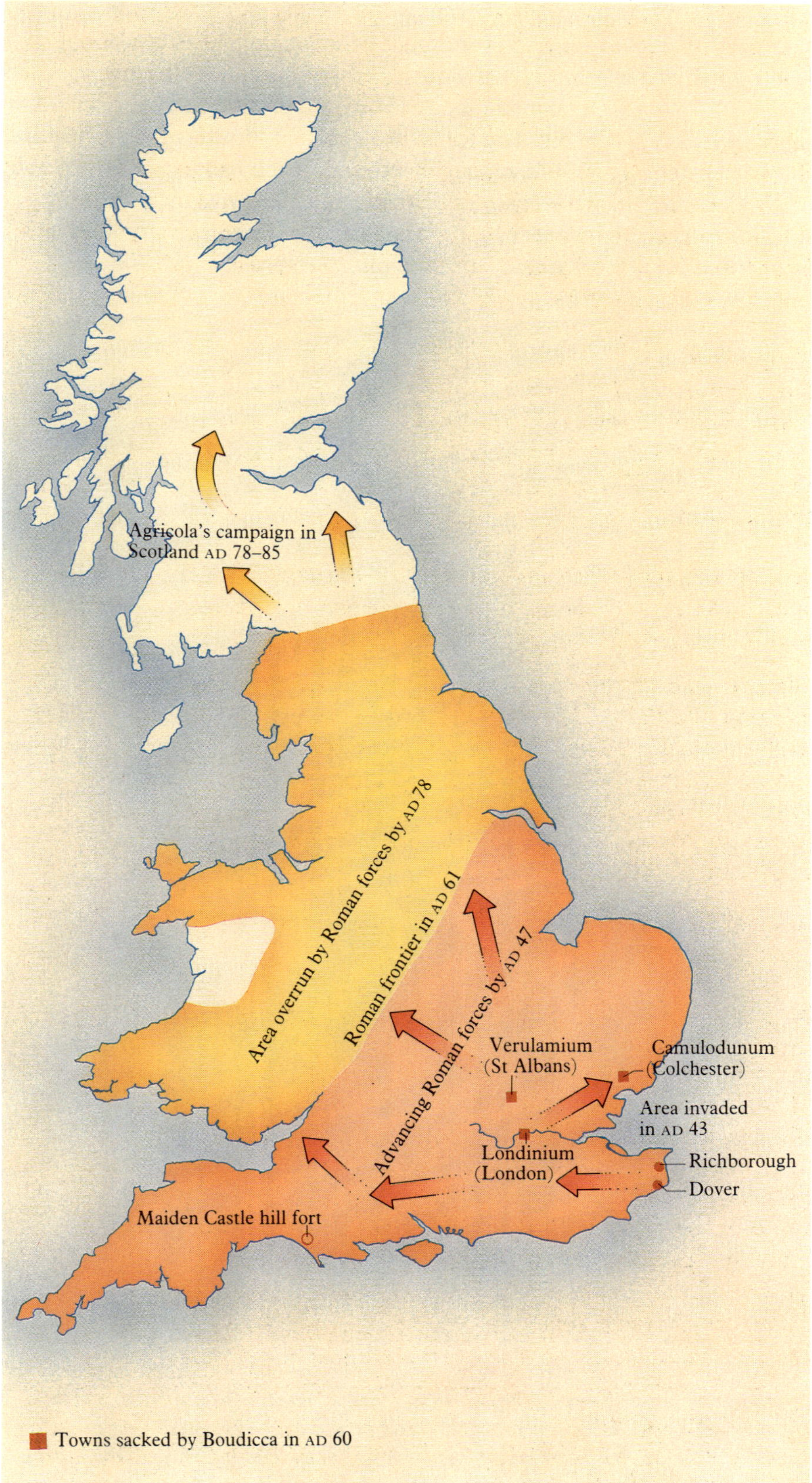

Map of the Roman conquest of Britain

Time Line

BC

41 Claudius becomes emperor

43 Roman invasion of Britain

54 Death of Claudius. Nero becomes emperor

61 Caesonius Paetus and Petronius Turpilianus become consuls

68 Death of Nero

4.17 Look at the map. From which part of Europe did the Roman invaders come? What was the importance of London and Colchester to them?

4.18 Find the position of your home town or village on this map. Write a sentence to say from which of these dates—AD 43, AD 61, AD 78, AD 85—you might expect to see Roman pottery or coins in your local museum. If you get the chance, visit the museum and see if you are right or wrong.

Defending Hadrian's Wall

The tribes of Wales and Scotland continued to menace Roman Britain. This is why the Romans stationed their legions in three great garrison towns. The Sixth Legion was based at York. The Twentieth Legion was based at Chester. The Second Legion was based at Caerleon (near modern Newport). Later still (after AD 122) they built Hadrian's Wall and a string of forts across northern England to keep out the fierce tribes from Scotland.

Hadrian's Wall is 117 km long and built of stone. In places it is about six metres high and three metres wide. Milecastles defended by twenty men were built every Roman mile (about 1500 metres) and turrets manned by guards every 500 metres. The forts, like those at Housesteads, Chesters and Corbridge, were built at longer intervals. Each had a garrison of 500 to 1000 men. A military road, called the Stanegate, was used to bring supplies to the soldiers serving on the Wall. You can get some idea of what these forts looked like from the photographs.

4.19 Write a sentence to describe the fort at Housesteads when seen from the air. What shape are the corners of its four walls?

The Roman fort at Housesteads was built on the south side of Hadrian's Wall. The headquarters building was in the centre near the grain stores (granaries), workshops and hospital. Barracks for the soldiers were situated to the east and west of the main buildings. The fort was surrounded by a high wall with four gateways in the middle of each wall. Local people built shops and taverns outside one of the gates. The wash-house and toilet block was in the south-eastern corner of the fort.

4.20 Identify Hadrian's Wall on the aerial photograph. In which direction was the camera pointing when the photograph was taken?

This is what is left of the water tank or reservoir at the Roman fort at Corbridge.

Columns like these at Corbridge are usually a sign of an important building, such as the headquarters at the centre of the fort.

Long, rectangular barracks where the soldiers lived can often be seen. These barracks are at Chesters, a cavalry fort, on Hadrian's Wall.

4.21 The fort had four entrances—the North, East, South and West Gates. Which of these gates is shown in the middle of the wall nearest the camera?

4.22 Near which gate were the shops and taverns built?

4.23 Find out if you live near a Roman fort. Do you live in a Roman town? Towns built by the Romans often end in –CASTER, – CESTER, –XETER or – CHESTER. They all come from the same Latin word—*castra*—meaning camp or fort. Look at a map of your county and make a list of any town names which end like this.

4.24 Describe what is happening in the relief below from Trajan's Column (see photograph on page 15)? Who are these workers? What are they building? What tools are they using?

This is the washroom and toilet block at Housesteads. Seats were placed above the drains here. These were flushed by a stream of running water. Fresh water on the stone table was used to rinse the sponges on sticks which the soldiers used instead of toilet paper.

The soldiers defending a Roman fort needed a source of water they could always rely on. This is why you can often see a well within the walls of a fort.

A typical Roman fort always had enough grain in store to last a year. It was kept dry by means of an ingenious heating system called a hypocaust. The granary, like this one at Housesteads, was built with a stone floor resting on pillars. Warm air flowed into the space below the granary floor from a furnace nearby.

Time Line

AD

41 Claudius becomes emperor

43 Conquest of Britain begins

61 Boudicca leads revolt against the Romans

71–78 Conquest of Wales and northern England

78–85 Roman campaigns in Scotland

122 Hadrian's Wall built

140 Antonine Wall built

5 TRANSPORT IN ROMAN TIMES

Ostia

Transport by sea

As you can see, we don't have to guess what Roman ships looked like. We have pictures and carvings like the cargo ship above and the Roman warship on page 10. We can even study evidence from the sea itself. Sunken ships tell us about the type of goods carried to and from Roman ports.

In 1962 the remains of a Roman merchant ship were found buried in mud on the bed of the River Thames. The ship was about 20 metres long. It had been used to carry building stone from Kent to London. We know it was Roman because a coin from AD 88 was found there. It had been wedged under the mast of the ship for luck. There was also Roman pottery on board.

London was an important port in Roman times. Ships took skins, lead, tin, woollen cloth and grain to Rome and to other parts of the Roman Empire. They brought back goods for the soldiers stationed here, such as German wine in casks or in huge containers called *amphorae*, olive oil from Spain, and pottery from France. There were other ports in Britain, too, such as Dover and South Shields at the mouth of the Tyne.

Rome itself had a problem as you can see from Source 5.A. The Roman writer Dio Cassius tells us how it was solved.

Source 5.A

Most of the grain used by the Romans came by sea. Yet the region near the mouth of the Tiber had no safe landing places or suitable harbours. This is why Claudius decided to build a harbour. He enclosed a large area of water by erecting two long sea walls on either side of the harbour entrance. In the middle he constructed an island. He built a tower on it with a beacon light.

The relief in the picture above shows us what this new port, called Ostia, looked like.

FOCUS

▶ *WHY was transport by sea important in the Roman Empire?* ATIB ■

▶ *HOW and WHY did the Romans build an extensive system of roads?* ATIB ■ ATIC ■

5.1 What do you think the archaeologists found which enabled them to say the Roman merchant ship discovered in the Thames mud was carrying building stone from Kent to London?

5.2 What type of cargo do you think was carried in a Roman boat like the one shown above? This is a stone carving of a boat which traded on the River Moselle in Germany. How did it move in the water? AT3/L3

5.3 How does this boat differ from the galley shown in the picture on page 10? AT3/L4

5.4 What type of ship is shown in port at Ostia? Write a sentence to say how it differs from the Moselle ship shown above. What other boats are shown in the harbour at Ostia? AT3/L4

5.5 Use the Time Line on page 21 to say roughly when the port of Ostia was built.

5.6 Look at the photograph on the right. What was the Roman tower in Dover used for? See if you can find a similar building in the relief showing Ostia harbour. How did it work? Which sentence in Source 5.A refers to this building? AT3/L4

5.7 Write one or two sentences to describe the vehicles you could have seen on a Roman road. Study Sources 5.B, 5.C and 5.D.

5.8 What special use did Augustus make of the Roman road system? Use the Time Line on page 17 to say when it was introduced.

5.9 What do you think was the reason for Julius Caesar's decree? What traffic problem did Rome have at that time?
AT3/L3

5.10 What connection is there between Source 5.B and Source 5.D? AT3/L4

This tower was built on a rocky headland overlooking the harbour at Dover. In Roman times the tower was nearly twice as high as this. A similar building stood on the other side of the harbour.

Transport by road

Carvings, reliefs, sculptures and paintings also show us how the Romans travelled on land. Travellers described their journeys on these roads. Even the laws of Rome tell us about transport problems and how they were solved.

Source 5.B Decree of Julius Caesar

No person shall be allowed to lead or drive a heavy wagon after sunrise or before the tenth hour of the day [when it was nearly dusk].

No person shall block a street, path or entrance with any construction which stops people freely using these places.

Source 5.C How Augustus used the roads (by the writer Suetonius)

Augustus kept in close touch with the provinces by relays of runners. These were strung out at short distances along the roads. Later on, he used chariots, based on posting stations [where the horses were changed].

Source 5.D Traffic noise in Rome (by the writer Juvenal)

Only the rich can sleep in Rome. All night long wagons rumble through the narrow winding streets. The way the drivers swear at traffic jams would rob even the heaviest sleepers of their rest.

Building a Roman road

One of the reasons why the Roman Empire remained intact for hundreds of years was because the army built an extensive network of roads to link the provinces. They used them to make sure supplies and soldiers could reach the frontier as quickly as possible. There were over 10 000 kilometres of roads in Britain alone. Roads as good as these were not built again until about two hundred years ago.

Many modern roads often follow the course of an old Roman road. One clue to this is where a road is very straight. The Romans built their roads chiefly for use by an army marching on foot. To cut down the distance travelled, they made them as straight as possible. This also helped to save time and money since there was less road to build. In fact, one of the ancient laws of Rome even specified that a straight road had to be at least 2.5 metres in width. But on a bend it had to be twice as wide (5 metres).

This map of Roman Britain shows Hadrian's Wall and some of the most important roads and towns

5.11 Find your nearest town on this map. Is it on, or close to, one of the Roman roads shown in the map on the left?

5.12 Compare this map with a modern road map showing motorways and other main roads today. What similarities and what differences are there to the system of roads built by the Romans? AT1A ■

Roman road on Wheeldale Moor, North Yorkshire ▼

When they built roads, the Romans used an instrument called the *groma* to line up poles to ensure the line of the road they were building was straight. They used local building materials for the foundations. Paving stones were used to surface roads in towns (and in the countryside) which got a lot of wear, such as the Appian Way in Italy. This was the most famous of all the roads built by the Romans. Roads in more isolated areas were surfaced with layers of gravel or pebbles.

We know how the Romans built their roads from two main sources. There are written accounts (such as the one written by Claudius Galen in Source 5.E) and there are sections of Roman road which can still be seen today.

5.13 Read Source 5.E. What improvements did Trajan make? Why were they needed? Use the Time Line on page 17 to say roughly when these improvements were made.

5.14 Compare the two sections of Roman road shown in the photographs below. What is the main difference between the two roads? What do you think has happened to the surface of the Wheeldale Moor road? What was the purpose of the ditch? Why is the road higher than the surrounding moorland? Why was the surface of a Roman road slightly curved so that it sloped down towards the ditches on either side?

AT1C/L5

Source 5.E

Since all the roads in Italy were in such poor condition, Trajan began a programme of road improvements. In wet and muddy areas he paved the roads with beds of stones or raised them up above the level of the land on high embankments. He cleared the rough and thorny ground and built bridges over rivers difficult to cross.

Where a road was too long, he built one that was shorter. If it was a difficult road because of the height of some hill, he changed its direction and made it go through land which was easier to cross. If a road went through an area which was full of wild animals or deserted, he closed it and built a new road instead in a populated area.

You can see the methods the Romans used in the diagram below. A writer in AD 95 said the first task when making a road was to clear the site of trees, stones and buildings. The next job was to dig a deep trench for the foundations. Road building materials, such as blocks of stone, gravel and sand, were kept in place on the road by rows of kerbstones.

Building a Roman road

Roman road in Lyon, France

6 A ROMAN TOWN

▶ *WHAT was it like to live in a Roman town?* ATIC ■

▶ *HOW did a Roman town differ from a town today?* ATIA ■

▶ *HOW were the skills of the Roman engineer used to build towns?* ATIC ■

6.1 How many basilicas and temples can you see in the Forum?

6.2 Write two or three sentences describing the Forum in Rome from these pictures. Can you think of any modern squares as splendid as this?

6.3 Which buildings in the picture drawn by the artist can be easily recognised on the photograph? Which buildings can only be identified from clues on the ground, such as a column or pillar?

6.4 How did the Roman engineers use arches when they built the Pont du Gard (below)? Why were so many arches needed? AT3/L3

6.5 How many different types of arch can be seen in the Forum in Rome? AT3/L4

The Forum in Rome

The centre of any Roman city was the *forum*. This was the market place and main square. It was here that most of the chief buildings of the city were built. On one side stood the *basilica*. This was like a town hall. It was where the town was governed and where taxes were collected. It was also a court of law where disputes could be settled and where people accused of crimes were tried. In addition, the basilica was used as a trading centre where merchants met to do business.

On another side of the square stood a temple, dedicated to the emperor or to one of the other Roman gods. Sometimes there were statues, triumphal arches or columns here as well. There were also many shops, taverns and market stalls.

The oldest and most important forum was in Rome, of course. This was the centre of the Roman Empire for hundreds of years. You can see what is left of it in the photograph on this page. Compare this with the picture which the artist has drawn showing how the Forum might have looked nearly 2000 years ago.

▼ *The Pont du Gard*

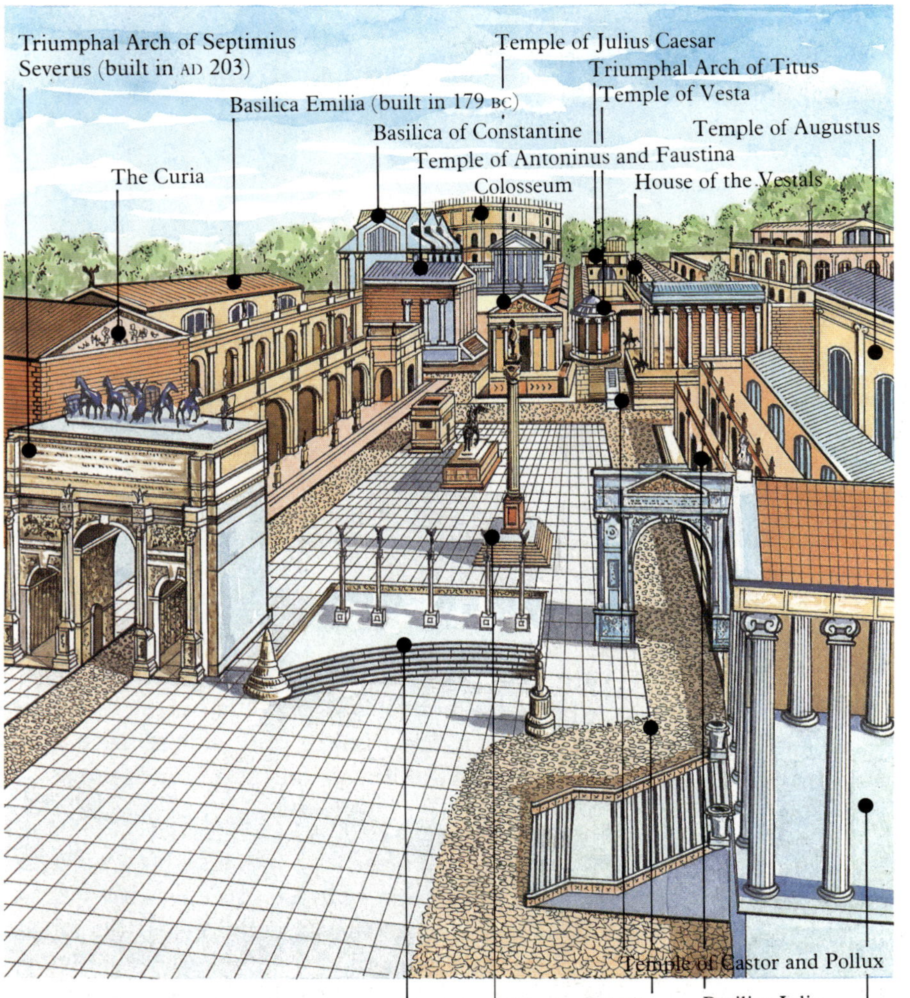

6.6 Look at the photographs on page 30. What use did Roman builders make of the arch when they built the basilica and Porta Nigra in Trier? AT3/L4

6.7 Look at the shape of the arches on the Pont du Gard, the Porta Nigra and the basilica in Trier. What do they all have in common? What are the typical features of a Roman building? AT1C/L4

6.8 Draw a diagram to show how an arch can be made using wedge-shaped stones and a central keystone.

Roman architecture

As you can see, the Romans had many clever engineers and architects. They were particularly skilled at building round arches. They used them to support the roofs of large buildings, such as a dome, and to build bridges. They built the arch by cutting each building stone so that it was shaped like a wedge. When the stones were laid on either side of the arch, they had to be supported by scaffolding as they curved round to meet in the middle. The last stone, the keystone, was slotted into place in the centre. It held them all firmly in place without the use of cement or mortar.

Roman engineers used arches like these to help bring water to the cities. The water came from wells, springs and rivers. It was brought to the towns along special channels called *conduits*. Engineers built special bridges, called *aqueducts*, to take these channels across valleys. You can see how they did it in the photograph of the Pont du Gard. This huge aqueduct, 50 metres high and nearly 300 metres long, took water across the River Gard to the Roman city of Nîmes in France.

Roman towns in the provinces

This was the main gateway, the Porta Nigra ('Black Gate'), to the Roman city of Trier in Germany

6.9 How many storeys high is the Porta Nigra?

6.10 What does the size of the basilica and the Porta Nigra tell you about the town of Trier in Roman times? AT3/L3

The remains of Roman towns have been found in many parts of Europe and North Africa. They were often better designed and better built than Rome itself. Roman towns in Britain, for instance, had wide streets, good drains, a piped water supply, public bath-houses and sometimes public lavatories as well.

A typical Roman town in the provinces was surrounded by high walls. It usually had four gateways. Just outside one of these gates was the Roman equivalent of a football stadium. This was the town's amphitheatre where wild beast shows were held. Inside the walls, close to the main gateway, was an inn where travellers could rest for the night and visit the public baths or go to the theatre. The streets of the town were almost always straight. They crossed each other at right angles to form a grid like a chessboard. At the centre, as you have seen, was the forum with its basilica, temple and shops.

The basilica in Trier is one of the best preserved Roman buildings in Western Europe

The eruption of Vesuvius has even enabled us to see what bread from a Roman baker's oven looked like

6.11 How do the photographs prove that the inhabitants of Pompeii had little warning of the eruption? AT3/L3

6.12 Find a phrase in Source 6.A which may explain why the dog was writhing on the ground when it was covered with ash. AT1B/L3

6.13 How do we know that some people, at least, managed to get away from Pompeii alive?

Source 6.B Election Slogans in Pompeii

Numerius Barcha is a fine man. I ask you to elect him duovir [an official]. *If so, may Venus of Pompeii, holy goddess, be kind to you.*

Numerius Veius Barcha! Let him rot!

Anyone who refuses to vote for Quinctius should be carried through the town on a donkey!

6.14 Who was Numerius Barcha? What was his middle name? Was he popular? What did the supporters of Quinctius think about their opponents? What are the modern equivalents of these messages? AT1C/L6

6.15 What is the value of slogans and messages like these to someone finding out about life in Roman times? AT3/L6

Pompeii

Much of what we know about Roman towns comes as a result of excavations made at Pompeii. This was an important town to the south of Rome. In AD 79 it was covered by ash when the volcano Vesuvius erupted. Pompeii was not seen again until parts of the city were uncovered about 250 years ago. The amazing discoveries found there, such as streets, homes, taverns, shops and theatres, helped to start the study of archaeology as a scientific way of finding out about the people who lived long ago.

In Source 6.A you can read what happened. This extract is taken from a letter by Pliny the Younger. In it he describes how his uncle died near Pompeii.

Source 6.A

The courtyard was choked with cinders and pumice stones. The walls of the house rocked and shook all the time, as if the foundations were shaking. The servants were afraid of the constant shower of pumice stones. They tied pillows to their heads to protect them against the storm of volcanic ash.

My uncle struggled to his feet, supported by two slaves, but fell down suffocated by clouds of ash and dust. His body was later found intact, uninjured. He was still wearing the clothes he wore when he fell. He lay like a man asleep rather than a dead man.

The body of this dog at Pompeii kept its shape because it was buried deep below a thick layer of ash

Pompeii had been built with streets in straight lines to form a grid. Their surface tells us a lot about traffic in Roman towns. Deep ruts about a metre apart show that heavy carts regularly brought goods into the city. A raised pavement on either side tells us which roads were also used by pedestrians. Large stepping stones across a street indicate they were often muddy and dirty.

The people of Pompeii wrote or painted hundreds of messages on the walls of their shops and buildings. You can read a few of these messages in Source 6.B.

6.16 What types of shops are shown in these pictures? Write one or two sentences to describe the goods on sale in each shop. AT3/L4

6.17 How do they differ from shops selling the same goods today? AT1A/L4

At work in a Roman town

The streets of a Roman town were very noisy. Many workers were employed there in small workshops. They made goods such as pottery, furniture, cutlery and metal tools. Some of these industries were well in advance of their time. Potters used the same mould, for instance, to mass-produce thousands of identical pots, such as the pottery called Samian ware. There were factories as well as workshops, such as the imperial weaving sheds in Winchester or the dyeing works in Silchester.

The Romans mined tin ore in Cornwall, iron ore in Kent, gold in Wales and lead ore in the Pennines. They used wood and charcoal for fuel. Clues tell us about the work people did in these and other industries.

Clues

A roof tile in the Roman museum in St Albans with the paw marks of a large dog clearly imprinted in the clay as it was drying in the sun. Just behind the paw marks a stone is embedded in the clay.

Large Roman grindstones (to grind corn) found on the bed of a river flowing into the Thames.

6.18 Look at the clues. What do they tell us about women in Roman times? AT3/L4

6.19 How do we know from these clues that some Romans: (a) knew that coal can be used as a fuel, (b) locked the doors to their houses, (c) used water wheels to turn grindstones, (d) employed their slaves to do important jobs, (e) took a pride in the work they did? AT3/L4

6.20 How do you account for the stone embedded in the St Albans roof tile? AT3/L5

6.21 Listed below are some of the problems which people living in towns sometimes have to face today. For each one find a Roman source (6.C to 6.H) which shows they had a similar problem. AT1A/L4

- risk of being mugged
- crowded streets
- badly lit streets
- risk of fire
- rudeness in the street
- lack of proper drains
- high cost of living
- dirty streets

6.22 Have we always made progress since Roman times? Give examples. AT1A/L6

A mixing bowl in the Museum of London stamped with the name of a potter called Doinus.

Coal found on a Roman site in Wiltshire, a long way from a coalfield.

Names of Romans on memorials: Flavia Sabina (midwife), Nicon (secretary and slave), Aulus Hertius Felix (locksmith), Terentia Thisbe (nurse), Extricata (needlewoman), Hippocrates (slave and farm manager).

Town problems in Rome

Before the great fire in AD 64, the city of Rome was a maze of narrow winding streets. Although some buildings, such as the homes of the rich, had a fresh water supply, the tenements where most people lived did not. Nor were there adequate drains. Plague (see page 152) spread through the city on several occasions killing many people.

We know a lot about the problems of people living in Rome from the complaints of Roman writers at the time (Sources 6.C to 6.H). The first five were written by Juvenal in about AD 100. The sixth extract (Source 6.H) is taken from a novel written by Petronius in about AD 60.

Source 6.C

I prefer to live where fires and panic at midnight are not quite such common events. By the time the smoke gets up to your third-floor apartment (with you still asleep), your heroic neighbour downstairs is shouting for water and moving his bits and pieces to safety.

Source 6.D

In Rome everything costs money. A high price has to be paid for poor lodgings, the upkeep of a slave, even a simple meal.

Source 6.E

However fast we try to get there on foot, we get blocked by the crowds ahead while those behind us tread on our heels. My legs are thick with mud. I'm trodden on by people with big feet and stamped on by soldiers in hobnailed boots.

Source 6.F

What a great height are the rooftops from which a tile can fall! You'll be lucky to escape with a wash basin emptied over you!

Does your local museum have a collection of Roman pottery? ▶

Source 6.G

Watch out for other dangers at night! When the houses are shut and all the shops are quiet, there will always be someone around to rob you.

Source 6.H

We had no torch to light us on our way. For nearly an hour we stumbled about in the pitch blackness. We dragged our bleeding feet over broken crockery scattered along the streets. At last we reached the inn.

7 ROMAN LEISURE TIME

▶ *HOW did the Romans spend their leisure time?*

ATIC ■

The Roman bath at Bath is fed by water from a natural spring at a constant temperature of 49°C

At the baths

There was a time when bath-houses were few and far between. They were never luxurious. Why should they have been? They were designed for use, not for pleasure. There were no showers in those days. People washed their arms and legs each day and bathed all over only once a week on market day.

This complaint was written in about AD 50, although it could have been written today! The writer, a man called Seneca, was right. People still went to the baths to wash all over, since only the rich had bathrooms, but going to the baths had become one of the chief pleasures of the Romans. Seneca tells us more about Roman bath-houses in Source 7.B.

Source 7.A
By Petronius

We quickly undressed, went into the hot baths and after working up a sweat, passed on to the cold showers. There we found Trimalchio again. His skin was glistening all over with perfumed oil. He was being rubbed down, not with ordinary linen, but with cloths of the purest and softest wool. He was then wrapped in a blazing scarlet robe, hoisted into a litter [a carriage on poles carried by slaves] *and trundled off.*

The changing room at the baths at Chesters on Hadrian's Wall

The Roman baths at Leptis Magna in Libya

Source 7.B

I live over a public bath-house. You can imagine the noise. First there are the tough guys exercising and swinging heavy weights about in their hands, grunting and groaning. Second, there are the less-energetic types having a massage. I hear the slap, slap, slap of the masseur's hand on their shoulders. On top of that there's the ball-player yelling out the score, the drunk picking a fight and the bloke who sings in the bath or splashes in the pool.

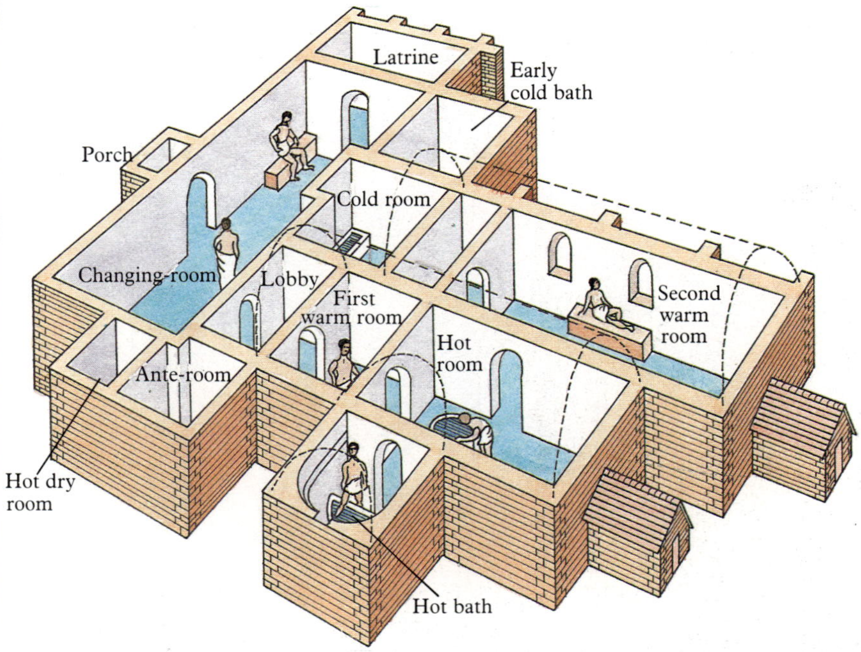

Layout of a small bathhouse ▶

7.1 Make a list of the different activities and people you might have seen on a visit to the baths in Roman times. Write a short account of your visit. AT1C ■

7.2 How would you recognise the changing rooms if you were taken to the ruins of a Roman bathhouse today?

7.3 What do you notice about the roof of the baths at Leptis Magna? Why do you think the Romans chose this type of roof for a bath-house?

7.4 Why did Seneca complain?

7.5 Write a sentence to describe the type of entertainment shown in the Roman mosaic below. AT3/L3

7.6 What shape was the auditorium (where the audience sat) of a Roman theatre? What type of seats did the audience sit on?

Some went there to soak up heat in the hot room and hot bath and to tingle all over in the cold. Afterwards slaves massaged them with olive oil, using a curved *strigil* to scrape off the surplus. Many Romans used the baths to keep fit through exercise or by playing games. Others went there chiefly to drink and talk with friends.

Entertainment

Roman toys, games and entertainments often seem surprisingly modern. A board game with counters discovered at Silchester and toy soldiers from Essex tell us about Roman children at play. A clay mould found at a site in Northamptonshire even shows a player with a curved stick and a ball in his hand.

Roman theatre in Lyon, France ▶

Roman theatres were massive in size. Some could hold as many as 30 000 people. The audience sat in the open air with canvas canopies on poles (called awnings) to protect them against rain or sun. The stage itself had a permanent roof. The plays performed there were comedies and violent thrillers. Actors and actresses could make a lot of money on the Roman stage. Some were treated like our present-day film stars.

At one time the Romans had no fewer than 200 public holidays a year. This gave them a lot of leisure time. On most of these days there were festival plays in the theatres, chariot races at the circus and spectacular shows in the amphitheatre.

The circus

Mosaic of a Roman chariot race at Lyon in France

The chariot races in Rome were held in a huge stadium called the Circus Maximus. It wasn't a circus like those we know today, although during the intervals between races the crowds were entertained by acrobats, jugglers, fire-eaters and clowns. There were also animal acts, such as an elephant using its trunk to spell out words (in Latin) in the sand.

The top charioteers were great heroes in Rome. They raced for one of the four great racing clubs. Each of these was known by a colour and had its own fans. A slave in a story by Petronius even 'bet his master that the Greens would win the next race in the Circus.' We know about one of these charioteers from a marble tablet listing his exploits. His name was Appuleius Diocles. He started racing with the Whites in AD 122 at the age of 18 but joined the Reds nine years later. His racing career lasted 24 years. In that time he won 1462 of his 4257 races earning 36 million sesterces—a very considerable sum of money indeed.

At the Games

The Romans also built amphitheatres where they held wild beast shows and staged bloody contests between gladiators. The most famous was the Colosseum in Rome but there were amphitheatres in most towns. The following graffiti appears on a wall in Pompeii, advertising a forthcoming spectacle.

7.7 Look closely at the mosaic. What were the colours of the four racing clubs? How many chariots did each enter in a race? How many horses were there in a chariot team? Which chariot teams crashed? Make a list of the different features shown in the mosaic. How are they related to each other?
AT1C/L5

7.8 What is the value of this mosaic to someone studying chariot racing in ancient Rome?
AT3/L5

7.9 Find the following: (a) a slave throwing water over the chariot wheels to cool them down (b) a horseman setting the pace (c) the *agitator* whipping the horses to make them go faster.

7.10 Do you think the mosaic shows an actual chariot race?
AT2/L5

A troop of gladiators will fight in Pompeii on 31 May. Wild beast hunts. Awnings.

Most shows involved the slaughter of many people and many wild animals. Men and women were thrown to the lions. Elephants fought rhinoceroses. There were even competitions with slaves as prizes. So many wild beasts were used that animal hunts had to be organised in Africa to keep the crowds happy back in Rome. Mosaics and written accounts tell us much of what we know.

Source 7.C From a novel written by Petronius in about AD 60

Don't forget, there's a big gladiator show coming up the day after tomorrow. Not the same old fighters either. They've got a fresh shipment in. There's not a slave in the batch. Just wait. There'll be cold steel for the crowd, no quarter and the amphitheatre will end up looking like a slaughterhouse. There's even a girl who fights from a chariot.

Source 7.D Letter written by Cicero in about 50 BC

The wild beast hunts, two a day for five days, are magnificent. There is no denying it. But what pleasure is there in seeing a puny human mangled by a powerful beast or a splendid animal killed with a hunting spear?

Source 7.E Written by Seneca in about AD 50

I went to the Midday Games expecting to relax and see some fun. Not a bit of it. It was just murder. The gladiators were fighting without armour. In the morning men are thrown to the lions and bears. At midday they are thrown to the spectators. They shout for the killer to be thrown to those who will kill him in turn. The outcome for the contestants is always death. 'Kill him! Whip him! Burn him! What a coward!' And when the show stops for the interval? 'Let's have some more killed while we're waiting! We can't sit here doing nothing!'

7.11 Write an account of a chariot race as if the Lyon mosaic is a picture of a real race you have actually seen. AT1C/L5

7.12 How many different wild animals can you identify in the mosaic on the right?

7.13 What parts of Source 7.D are facts rather than opinions? AT2/L3

7.14 What was Cicero's point of view? AT2/L3

7.15 What difference would it make if you chose Source 7.C instead of Source 7.E to show to someone who wanted to know what the Romans thought about the Games? AT2 ■

7.16 One of the more horrible Roman punishments is illustrated in the mosaic. What was it? Write out the phrases in Sources 7.D and 7.E which are illustrated by the mosaic. AT3/L4

7.17 How do Sources 7.C, 7.D and 7.E differ in their attitudes to the Games? AT1C/L6

8 A ROMAN VILLA

▶ *WHAT were the main features of a Roman villa?* ATIC ■

▶ *HOW did a Roman family differ from a family today?* ATIA ■

▶ *HOW did the farmers of the Roman Empire farm the land?* ATIC ■

A villa by the sea

Source 8.A

You seem surprised I like my seaside villa at Laurentum so much. The house is big enough for my needs and not too expensive to look after. There is an entrance hall which leads through to a small but pleasant courtyard. Opposite is a cheerful inner hall and a splendid dining room with superb views of the sea.

Wall painting from Pompeii depicting a villa by the sea

The owner of this villa was Pliny the Younger. He wrote this letter to a friend in about AD 100. His villa had a summer bedroom with east and west windows. The winter bedroom was heated by a hypocaust central heating system. He also had a library, sun lounge with a couch and two easy chairs, bathhouse, swimming pool, ball court and large garden. It was also close to Rome. Pliny found this very convenient.

Source 8.B

It is only seventeen miles [about 25 km] *from the city. This means that after getting through with business you can be here with the day's work safely out of the way.*

Most country villas were farms. You can see an artist's impression of such a villa on page 42. This is why archaeologists excavating the site of a villa often find storerooms and granaries there as well as dining rooms and living areas. A writer called Columella advised owners to keep the different parts of their villas separate.

Source 8.C

The villa should be divided into three areas—the manor house, the farmhouse and the storehouse. The manor house should be divided into winter and summer apartments. The baths should face the northwest so they are light from midday to evening.

◀ *This Roman villa at Sirmione in Italy was built on land jutting out into a large lake*

8.1 What do the Roman villas shown here and described by Pliny all have in common? AT1C/L4 AT3/L4

8.2 Write one or two sentences to say how Roman architects built villas in Italy to make the most of the weather and the direction of the sun. AT1C/L5

8.3 How might the painting of the villa and Pliny's letter be of use to an archaeologist studying the villa at Sirmione? AT3/L5

8.4 Why did Columella advise farmers to keep their storehouses and farms separate from their homes?

8.5 How would you have advertised Pliny's house if you had wanted to sell it 1900 years ago?

Inside a villa

Inside a rich man's villa you would almost certainly have seen some very striking pictures. There were paintings on the walls and mosaics on the floor. The mosaics were made by laying thousands of tiny cubes of coloured stone or glass on a flat surface to create a design. A thin cement was poured on top and brushed into the cracks between the cubes to make it set hard. The designs are often very beautiful and tell us there were many talented artists in the Roman Empire.

As you can imagine, mosaics were very expensive to lay. Only rich people could afford to have them. Even then they were normally only laid in the rooms which visitors to the villa would see, such as the bathhouse and the dining room.

You can sometimes get a very good idea of what it was like to live in a Roman house if you go to a museum. At the Museum of London, for instance, the reconstructed Roman rooms (below) are based on genuine Roman finds, carvings and pictures.

8.6 The mosaic you can see in the picture greeted people when they entered a Roman villa in Pompeii. What do you think the Latin words *CAVE CANEM* meant?

8.7 How do you think a mosaic like this was designed and planned?

8.8 Which of the rooms in Pliny's villa do you think would most likely have had a mosaic floor?

8.9 Which types of room are shown in the photographs on the right? Write two or three sentences to say (a) how they differ from (b) how they are similar to the rooms at home today. AT1A ■

8.10 What do these rooms tell you about the daily life of the Romans? AT3/L4

8.11 Which of the pictures overleaf (pages 40–1) could have been used as a source of information by the Museum of London? AT3/L4

Entertaining guests

Young man in about AD *150*

Young woman in about AD *70*

People visiting a Roman villa expected to eat well. In a novel (Sources 8.D, 8.E and 8.F), the writer Petronius described a meal given by a rich man in about AD 60. His guests were first taken to his private baths.

Source 8.D Before the meal

After a generous rubdown with oil, we put on dinner clothes. We were taken into the next room where we found three couches drawn up and a table, very luxuriously laid out, awaiting us. Hanging from the ceiling on a long chain was a two-bracket lamp.

Source 8.E At the meal

We were invited to take our seats. Immediately Egyptian slaves came in and poured ice water over our hands. Now that the guests were all in their places, the starters were served. On a large tray stood a donkey made of bronze. On its back were two baskets, one holding green olives, the other black. On either side, in dishes shaped to look like little bridges, were dormice, dipped in honey and rolled in poppyseed. Nearby, on a silver grill, piping hot, lay small sausages. As for wine, we were fairly swimming in it.

Many other courses were served as the meal progressed.

Source 8.F After the meal

Meanwhile the oil lamps had burnt low and gave out only a feeble dying flutter. A servant refilled the flickering lamps. Then with a great crash of cymbals a girl musician with cymbals went marching around the room banging away.

8.12 Write a brief description of the young man and young woman shown in the pictures above. What is this type of painting called?

8.13 How were the homes of the wealthy lit at night? How were they furnished? How many couches were there in the dining room?

8.14 The poor in Rome lived on a cheap diet of olives, bread, fruit and grapes. Why do you think there are many pictures and descriptions of the lives of rich Romans but very few which tell us how ordinary people lived? AT2 ■

8.15 What were the duties of the slave in the mosaic (right)? How old would you say he was?

8.16 How can you tell that some girls were educated as well as boys? AT3/L3

8.17 What does the relief at the top of the next page tell you about the life of a rich Roman woman? What are her attendants doing? Why are there so many of them? AT3/L4

Roman women took a great pride in their appearance

Family life

Living together as a family was important to all Romans. By law, the father was the head of the household, not the mother. The Romans called him *paterfamilias*. *Pater* meant father and *familia* meant family or household.

In the early days, when Rome was still a republic, the *paterfamilias* had the legal right to punish the members of his household—his wife, children, and any others who lived in his home. It was almost as if he owned them. He even had the power of life and death over his newly-born children. At that time there was nothing to stop him leaving an unwanted baby outside to die of hunger or cold. Over the years, the power of the *paterfamilias* diminished. He no longer got, or expected, the unquestioning obedience of his wife and children. Some did not even get it from their slaves.

A woman got married when she was about 14 or 15 years old. Her marriage was usually arranged by her parents. They gave the husband a sum of money, called a *dowry*, when she got married. A wife could not take part in politics or public affairs. Only men could become senators or officials. The only way she could exert influence was through her husband. One Roman writer said sarcastically:

We who rule all men are ruled by women.

A rich woman like this led a life of leisure with scores of slaves at her command. Some learned to paint, play music and write poetry. She planned the decorations in the house and ordered the furnishings. She also had a lot of power in her own right, controlling the work of the slaves and educating the children.

8.18 Give a reason for thinking that the stone carving below shows a teacher and pupils at school and not in a private home.

◄ *At one stage nearly one Roman in every three was a slave. Even ordinary people owned one or two slaves to do their manual work. Most were well treated, although there were some cruel owners. In practice, many slaves gained their freedom and became prosperous citizens in their own right.*

▲ *Roman children were often taught by a Greek slave called* paedogogus. *The Romans admired the Greek writers, philosophers and scientists. Educated Greek slaves, therefore, were highly prized. Sometimes the children went to a school run by a freed slave.*

A Roman farm

A Roman villa and country estate

This picture has been based on finds made by archaeologists. It shows a country villa surrounded by fields in the Rhine Valley. Villas like this could be seen all over Europe—in France, Spain and England as well as in Italy.

As you have seen, the Romans made good use of the provinces they conquered to grow grain, fruit and other farm products to feed and clothe the army and the huge number of people in Rome itself. At the time of Augustus, 2000 years ago, Egypt and Roman Africa together supplied enough grain each year to feed a million people. Even farms in England, which the Romans thought of as cold and wet, produced enough corn to feed the army in Britain and send the surplus to other parts of the Roman Empire as well. We know, for instance, that 600 barges of grain were sent to Germany in AD 359.

In about 60 BC, a writer called Varro said that almost all the old country families had gone to live in Rome.

Source 8.G

They have abandoned the sickle and the plough. They would sooner go to the theatre or circus than work in the grain fields and vineyards. Nowadays we hire men to bring us the grain to fill our stomachs from Africa and Sardinia. The wine we store in our cellars comes in ships from the islands of Greece.

Farming methods

The Romans did not make any startling changes to the way in which the land was farmed. However, their farming methods often helped to increase the amount of food produced. In Britain, for instance, they used teams of oxen to pull iron ploughs. These were often stronger than the ploughs used by local people. This meant they could cultivate difficult land which had not been farmed before.

8.19 What did Varro mean in Source 8.G when he said 'They have abandoned the sickle and the plough.'? What was he complaining about? AT1B/L3

8.20 Describe the villa and the farmland shown in the picture above. What were the main features of a country villa in a province of the Roman Empire? AT1C ■

Statuette found near Piercebridge in County Durham ▼

8.21 Many of the farms in the provinces of the Roman Empire were farmed by local people. What problems do you think Roman settlers must have had when they first started to farm there? AT1C/L6

8.22 What can you learn about Roman farming from the statuette? AT3/L5

8.23 Why was it an advantage to the farmer to be near a busy town? What did all the other sites have in common? AT1C/L5

8.24 Which of the monthly jobs on the Roman farm are still done today on many British farms? AT1A/L4

8.25 Make a list of the different changes made by the Romans to the countries they conquered. AT1A ■

8.26 Which of these changes brought advantages to the people they conquered? Which brought disadvantages? AT1A/L6

We know a lot about Roman farming from different writers. You can see some of these in the sources which follow.

In about 160 BC, Cato advised anyone buying a farm to make sure it had good soil.

Source 8.H

If possible, choose a farm at the foot of a mountain looking toward the south. It should be in an area where there is plenty of labour available. It should have a good water supply. It should also be near a busy town, or near the sea, or near a river reached by ships, or next to a good and well-used road. See that it has good buildings. The vineyard is of first importance if the wine is good and the yield is great. The irrigated garden is next in importance.

Two hundred years later, Columella gave this advice.

Source 8.I

There should be stables for the cattle used for work. For other animals kept on the farm there should be sheds partly covered over and partly open to the sky. They should be surrounded by high walls to protect them against wild animals. The huts for the herdsmen and shepherds should be next to their animals so they can easily run out to care for them.

We even know what jobs were done each month on a typical farm in Italy in about AD 50. The farming calendar below is based on details found on a marble block in Rome.

Source 8.J

January	*mend fences*
February	*weed crops*
March	*prune grapes; sow spring wheat*
April	*lambing time*
May	*weed corn; shear sheep*
June	*make hay; hoe in between grape vines*
July	*harvest barley and beans*
August	*harvest wheat*
September	*gather fruit*
October	*pick grapes to make wine*
November	*sow winter wheat and barley*
December	*manure vineyard; sow beans; gather olives; cut wood*

9 DECLINE OF THE ROMAN EMPIRE

Roman temple in Nîmes, France

Religion in the Roman Empire

Many gods were worshipped by the Romans as part of their religion. They included Mars, the god of war, and Diana, the goddess of the moon. Most Romans had favourite gods. They hoped their gods would look with favour on them. Instead of church services, there were sacred rituals. These were carried out by priests. At some of the ceremonies they sacrificed animals. This was because the Romans were very superstitious. They thought the insides of an animal could be used to foretell the future.

Source 9.A

In the corner at the entrance to the house was a huge cupboard with a small built-in shrine. Inside the shrine were silver statuettes of the household gods, a Venus in marble and a golden casket.

The Vestal Virgins took a leading part in the Roman religion. They guarded the sacred flame of Vesta, goddess of fire. Like the Olympic flame, it was never allowed to die out. You can see their temple on page 29. The Romans also worshipped the emperors as gods. Augustus was made a god shortly after his death in AD 14. Later emperors, like Claudius, were sometimes treated as if they were living gods.

Other religions were usually tolerated by the Romans. The cult of the Persian sun god Mithras, for instance, appealed to Roman soldiers. Mithraism tested the courage of new worshippers to see how strong and brave they were.

Temple of Mithras at Carrawburgh on Hadrian's Wall ▶

FOCUS

▶ *WHAT part did religion play in the Roman Empire?* AT1C ■

▶ *HOW and WHY did Christianity spread throughout the Roman Empire?* AT1B ■

▶ *WHY did the Roman Empire collapse in the West?* AT1B ■

▶ *WHY did it survive in the East?* AT1B ■

9.1 Source 9.A comes from a story written in about AD 60. What does it tell us about the Romans and the part played by religion in their lives? AT3/L3

9.2 What clues are there in the relief below to suggest that a sacrifice is about to take place? AT3/L3

9.3 Look at the Roman temple in Nîmes (above) and the temple in Rome (below). Make a list of things which are the same in both pictures. How are they different? AT1C/L4 AT3/L4

9.4 Why do you think the worship of Mithras was popular with soldiers?

9.5 Describe the Temple of Mithras at Carrawburgh. Is there any evidence that it was once a temple? AT2/L4

Relief showing priests in front of a temple in Rome

Roman Mosaic of Christ. The cross in the middle is made up of two Greek letters Chi *and* Rho. *These were the first letters of the Greek word for Christ.* ▶

9.6 Write down the words or phrases in Source 9.B which tell us that Tacitus was not a Christian. Did he approve or disapprove of Nero's actions?
AT1C/L6

9.7 How did Diocletian's soldiers persecute the Christians?

The first Christians

After the Crucifixion, in about AD 30, the number of Christians grew. The new religion even spread to Rome itself. It appealed to the poorest people and to slaves because it gave them hope. But in AD 64 a great fire destroyed a large part of Rome. A rumour spread that the Emperor Nero had set the city on fire so that he could build a new palace. The writer Tacitus tells us what happened next.

Source 9.B

In order to squash this rumour, Nero punished a race of men who were hated for their evil practices. These men were called Christians. He got a number of people to confess. On their evidence a number of Christians were convicted and put to death with dreadful cruelty. Some were covered with the skins of wild beasts and left to be eaten by dogs. Others were nailed to the cross. Many were burned alive and set on fire to serve as torches at night.

At length the cruelty of these proceedings appalled everyone. The crimes of the Christians, no doubt, called out for punishment. It was clear, however, that they were being sacrificed, not for the public good but to satisfy the anger and cruelty of one man.

So began the persecution of the Christians by the Romans. This went on for many years. In about AD 303, the Emperor Diocletian ordered further persecutions. Two Christian writers, Eusebius (Source 9.C) and Lactantius (Source 9.D), tell us about them.

Source 9.C

We saw with our own eyes the houses of prayer pulled down and the sacred Scriptures burned in the middle of the market places.

Source 9.D

While it was hardly light, the prefect and the military came to the church. When the doors had been broken down, they looked for an image of God. Scriptures were found and burned. Treasure was given to all. The Praetorian Guard poured in from all sides with axes and other iron tools. In a few hours they levelled that sacred shrine to the ground.

The Roman Empire divided

As you saw on pages 16–17, the Romans enjoyed a long period of peace called the *Pax Romana*. It began to break down in about AD 200. The new emperor, Septimius Severus, had little respect for the Senate. He told his sons, 'Stick together. Give money to the army. Ignore everyone else.' In other words, the emperor wanted power for himself, not justice for the people. This weakened Rome. It was the start of a time when Roman leaders took the law into their own hands. Generals fought against each other for power. In less than fifty years (AD 238–284) there were no fewer than twenty different emperors. Most of them died violent deaths.

At the same time, warlike tribes (called the *barbarians* by the Romans) attacked the frontiers of the empire, seizing goods and treasure. This unsettled the people who lived in the frontier lands. However, thanks to the squabbling generals, there was no longer a strong Roman army to push the barbarians back. Britain, like other parts of the Roman Empire at this time, also suffered from these attacks. Saxon pirates raided the shores of England, looting towns and villages. This is why the Romans built a string of forts along the coast for protection. They were commanded by the Count of the Saxon Shore.

The slow decline of the empire was halted for a period when the Praetorian Guard installed Diocletian as emperor in AD 284. He divided the empire between East and West to make it easier to govern. He ruled the East himself from Nicomedia in Turkey, while Maximian ruled in the West. Both emperors were given the title of 'Augustus'. Two other men junior to them each became a 'Caesar'. They were given half a territory to govern, one in the West and one in the East. Maximian ruled Italy, Spain and Roman Africa, while Constantius as the Caesar ruled Gaul and Britain. Diocletian ruled in the East (Turkey), with Galerius as the Caesar governing the lands along the Danube. Together the four leaders were called the *Tetrarchs* or *Tetrarchy*.

The four quarters of the empire were further divided into 14 smaller areas called *dioceses*. These in turn were divided into 117 provinces each ruled by a provincial governor.

Gold coins issued by Diocletian and Maximian in AD 287

9.8 How are the barbarians shown in the relief below?

9.9 How is this similar to the Roman tombstone on page 18?

AT3/L4

Roman relief showing Roman and barbarian soldiers ▼

This statue in Venice shows the four men in the Tetrarchy. Galerius and Constantius are on the left. Diocletian and Maximian are on the right. ▶

Diocletian and Maximian brought a period of welcome peace to the empire. In AD 305 they retired so that Galerius and Constantius could succeed them. But further civil war followed after Constantine took power in AD 306. He was acclaimed emperor by the Roman soldiers in Britain after his father, Constantius I, died at York. Constantine went on to defeat his rivals in battle. He became emperor of both East and West after the battle of Chrysopolis in AD 323.

Constantine the Great

Constantine the Great was born in AD 280. In AD 310 he had a religious experience the night before a crucial battle. Some said he saw a fiery cross in the sky. Underneath was written: 'By this sign you will conquer.' When he won the battle of Milvian Bridge the next day, he took this as an omen from God and became a Christian.

A year later, in AD 313, he issued the Edict of Milan. In future all people could follow their own religions. This brought an end to the persecutions. It also gave the Christian Church the powerful backing of the Roman leader. It helped to make Christianity the main religion of Western Europe.

In AD 323 Constantine defeated the last of his rivals at the battle of Chrysopolis in Turkey. He was so impressed with the site of the old city of Byzantium, he decided to build a new city there. It was called Constantinople and became the capital of the eastern empire.

9.10 Describe the uniform of a Roman general in about AD 300.

9.11 What does the statue on the left at the bottom of page 46 show? How does it symbolise the way in which Diocletian changed the government of the Roman Empire?

9.12 What differences are there ▶ between this Triumphal Arch for Constantine erected in AD 325 and the arch you can see in the Roman forum on page 28? AT1A ■

Christianity was now the official religion of the Roman Empire. It was strong in the East. The Church was made exempt from having to pay taxes. This helped it to become rich. It was soon highly organised, like the Roman Empire. The strength of the Church in Rome later helped it to survive even after the Roman Empire itself had fallen. It is also the main reason why Rome was for a long time the centre of the Christian world (and still is for Roman Catholics).

The barbarian invasions

For a hundred years the Romans tried to keep the barbarians at bay. But a new threat appeared in about AD 370. A fierce people, the Huns from Central Asia, began to attack the barbarians in the east, such as the Goths and Alans. This forced the barbarians, in their turn, to look to the frontier lands of the Roman Empire as a place where they could settle and take refuge from the fury of the Huns.

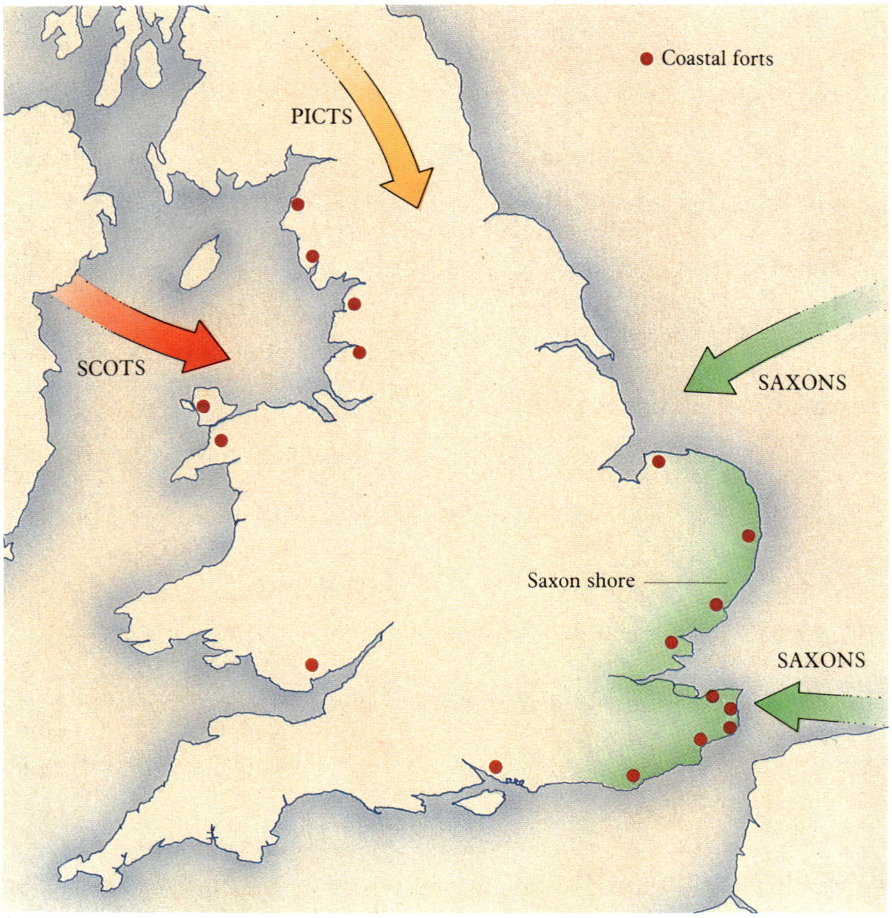

As you can see from this map, barbarians invaded Roman Britain in AD 367 from three different directions: the Saxons came from the east, the Picts from the north and the Irish (the *Scotti*) from the west. Britain would have fallen if a general called Theodosius had not come to the rescue with more troops and forced the invaders out.

In AD 396–8 an able commander called Stilicho took charge of Britain's defences. For a time it looked as if the Romans in Britain might be able to fend off a new attack. But Rome itself was under threat from the barbarians. Stilicho went back to Italy in AD 401. Britain was doomed. Gildas, a monk writing over a hundred years later, described what happened next.

Source 9.E

As the Romans went home, the vile hordes of Scots and Picts came back again. When they learned that the Romans had gone for good, they grew more daring than ever. They seized the whole northern part of the country as far as the wall.

The miserable people left behind sent a letter to Rome in AD 446. 'To Agitius, consul, come the groans of the Britons. The barbarians drive us to the sea. The sea drives us back to the barbarians.'

The Roman coastal fort at Richborough near Dover. It was built to defend the coast of Kent against attack from the Saxons.

9.13 What was 'the wall'?

9.14 Who said: 'The barbarians drive us to the sea. The sea drives us back to the barbarians.'? What do you think they meant by this?

9.15 Was Gildas living at the time of these events? What difference does this make to the way in which we look at his account of 'the groans of the Britons'?

AT3 ■

The end of the Roman Empire

Towards the end of the fourth century AD a new Roman emperor called Theodosius took steps to make Christianity the only religion of the Roman peoples. He banned the old Roman religion and ordered the destruction of its temples and images of the gods.

The Emperor Theodosius presiding over the Games in Constantinople in about AD 390 ▶

9.16 Write one or two sentences comparing the actions taken by Theodosius against the Roman religion with those described in Sources 9.C and 9.D on page 45. AT1C ■

9.17 Make a list of the short-term and long-term causes and consequences of the fall of the Roman Empire. AT1B/L5

9.18 Why did the Byzantine Empire survive? AT1B ■

When Theodosius died in AD 395, the Roman Empire was divided between his two sons. This time the division was for good. The West was left to fend for itself and lasted only eighty years. It was badly led by weak emperors, poorer than the East and less able to support a strong army to defend its long frontier. As a result, the Romans were no longer able to keep back the barbarian tribes.

Even Rome itself was weak. On 24 August AD 410 the Visigoths from Germany, led by their king Alaric, sacked Rome. To Romans everywhere it was a catastrophe. Alaric had demanded gold from the Emperor Honorius in Ravenna (in Italy). When this was refused, he let his soldiers go on the rampage through the streets of Rome. It was the worst disaster in Roman history.

Other calamities soon followed. Gaul and Spain fell to the Visigoths. Africa fell to the Vandals. Britain was colonised by the Angles and Saxons. Bit by bit the empire was split into separate states, each ruled by different tribes of barbarians. Sometimes they fought with the Romans and sometimes against them. Visigoths, Franks and Burgundians, for instance, joined with the Romans to defeat Attila the Hun in AD 451. Only four years later, however, Rome was sacked again, this time by the Vandals. Only the intervention of the Pope stopped them from burning the city to the ground. By AD 476 the barbarians had overrun the empire in the West. The last emperor, Romulus Augustulus, had been overthrown.

Time Line

- **64** Great Fire of Rome; Nero persecutes Christians
- **70** Destruction of the Temple in Jerusalem
- **284** Diocletian becomes emperor and founds the Tetrarchy
- **303** Persecution of Christians
- **312** Constantine becomes a Christian; Christianity now the state religion of Rome
- **330** Constantine makes Constantinople his capital
- **395** Roman Empire divided between East and West
- **410** Alaric and the Visigoths sack Rome
- **419** Visigoths seize part of Gaul
- **429** Vandals seize Roman Africa
- **451** Defeat of Attila the Hun
- **455** Vandals sack Rome
- **476** Odoacer deposes Romulus Augustulus

The Byzantine Empire

In the East, however, the empire survived. For one thing it was richer than the West. It also had a much shorter frontier, so it was easier to defend. Its people were more prepared to fight than the Romans, who preferred free bread and circuses to war. The soldiers of the East were also better led. As a result, the Roman Empire in the East was able to withstand the onslaught of the barbarians. It survived and became the Byzantine Empire with Constantinople at its centre.

Incredibly, the Byzantine Empire outlived the Roman Empire by nearly a thousand years. It was only overthrown when another great empire, that of the Ottoman Turks (see pages 78–81), captured Constantinople in 1453.

10 WHAT WE OWE TO THE ROMANS

▶ *WHAT features of our life today do we owe to the Romans?* ATIA ■

Many things today remind us of the Roman way of life. We call this the *legacy of Rome.*

Roman law

The Roman system of justice was much admired. Roman law gave a free person many rights. After the fall of the Roman Empire in the West, the Eastern Empire continued to use Roman laws. In AD 529 the Byzantine Emperor Justinian brought these laws together in a series of books called the *Justinian Code.* Many of these ideas still form part of our own system of justice today, such as that a person is innocent until proved guilty.

The Church

The Christian Church has also kept alive many Roman traditions. Church services were held in Latin in Catholic churches until about thirty years ago. The Roman Catholic Church is still run like the Roman Empire itself. It is controlled from Rome by the Pope or *Pontiff.* The word 'Pontiff' comes from the Latin *Pontifex Maximus*—the name of the High Priest of the Roman religion.

Latin

Latin continued not only as the language of the Church, but it also became the main subject studied in many schools in the Middle Ages. Even today some people still need to know Latin as part of their everyday work. Scientists use Latin names to distinguish between different animals and plants. In the dog family, for instance, *Canis lupus* means wolf and *Canis familiaris* means pet dog. Words like *opera, veto, consensus* and *bus* (from *omnibus*) come directly from Latin. There are many other words in English and in other European languages that are based on Latin. The Latin word for green, for instance, is *viridis.* In French it is *vert* and *verde* in Italian, Spanish, Portuguese and Romanian.

Roman writers

The great Roman writers wrote poems, plays and stories which are still enjoyed today. Some, such as Tacitus, Juvenal, Seneca and Cicero, have already been quoted in this book. Other great Roman writers included Virgil, Terence, Ovid and Livy. We call their works the *classics.* In Latin, *classicus* meant the highest *class* of all. As you can see in the panel below, some of the phrases of these writers have become everyday expressions.

Julius Caesar: (100–44 BC)	*Veni, vidi, vici*—'I came, I saw, I conquered'
Virgil: (70–19 BC)	'Fortune assists the bold' 'There's a snake hidden in the grass'
Cicero: (106–43 BC)	*Civis Romanum sum*—'I am a Roman citizen'
Ennius: (239–169 BC)	'No sooner said than done'
Seneca: (BC-AD 65)	'It's quality not quantity that matters'
Terence: (190–159 BC)	'Fortune favours the brave'

10.1 Two writers used the same phrase. Who said it first?

10.2 In 1963 President Kennedy of America visited Berlin at a time of crisis. To reassure the people there, he told them: 'Ich bin ein Berliner' ('I am a Berliner'). Which Latin author had he read?

10.3 Which months of the year get their names from Julius Caesar, Augustus Caesar, the gods Mars and Janus?

Latin inscriptions in the Temple of Mithras on Hadrian's Wall

Roman art

We still enjoy the work of Roman artists today. As well as telling us about their way of life, Roman wall paintings, portraits, mosaics, sculptures and statues are admired as things of beauty.

The Romans had a great influence on art. Sculptures, like the one of Marcus Aurelius (page 17), were copied much later by the artists and sculptors who lived in Italy in about 1500.

Roman engineering and architecture

The Romans also left behind many great works of engineering, such as their warm air central heating system (page 23), aqueducts like the Pont du Gard (pages 28–9), and the Roman road network in Britain (page 26). As you have seen, they perfected the art of using an arch to bridge gaps and spaces. Their buildings inspired many architects and builders. This is why a lot of our own buildings today have been based on those of Rome.

10.4 On these pages you can see buildings built within the last two hundred years. Find a matching picture in this book showing a similar building built in Roman times. Are there any buildings like these in your home town?

10.5 Write a paragraph saying what features of our life today we owe to the Romans. AT1A ■

The Arc de Triomphe du Carrousel (above) and the Vendôme Column (below left) were erected in Paris to celebrate Napoleon's victories in 1805

The Pantheon, built in Rome in 27 BC, is as high (42 metres) as it is wide. It is roofed with a massive dome. At the front are three rows of columns. The large triangular structure above is called a pediment. *These features are typical of the* Classical *style of architecture. This refers to the buildings of ancient Greece and Rome.*
▼

The Corn Exchange in Bury St Edmunds, Suffolk, was built in 1862

The Islamic Civilisations

11 The rise of Islam

► *HOW and WHY did the religion of Islam begin?* ATIB ■
► *What effect did Islam have on the world between AD 610 and AD 660?* ATIA ■
► *HOW and WHY did the Umayyads seize the Caliphate in 660?* ATIB ■
► *WHAT are the five great Pillars of Islam?* ATIC ■

The Prophet Muhammad

The Prophet Muhammad was born in AD 570, less than a century after the fall of the Roman Empire. The Islamic religion he founded grew rapidly. By 750 it controlled much of the area which had once been Roman. The word *Islam* means submitting to the will of God. A Muslim, therefore, is one who has submitted to the will of God.

Muhammad was born in Mecca in what is now Saudi Arabia (see map on page 60). He was an Arab. At that time, most Arabs lived in tents and wandered from place to place with their goats and camels, living on a diet of dates and milk. Muhammad, too, spent part of his early life looking after sheep. Later he worked for a woman called Khadija who became his wife.

Mecca, about 80km inland from the Red Sea, was at a meeting point of important trade routes. One linked Yemen in the south with Syria in the north. The other linked the Red Sea with Iraq to the north-east. Caravans followed both routes. These were long processions of camels carrying packs filled with luxury goods such as silks and spices from the Indian Ocean. These caravans brought wealth to the merchants of Mecca, who came from a leading tribe called the Quraysh which controlled Mecca and its trade.

Arabs at that time worshipped many gods. Allah, the Creator of the Universe, was the main one. Even then, Mecca was a holy place because it was the site of a sacred shrine called the Kaaba. The Kaaba was guarded by the Quraysh. Pilgrims helped to bring trade and wealth to their city.

A camel caravan entering a town

The Kaaba, in the courtyard of the Great Mosque in Mecca, is a stone building about 15 metres high, 12 metres long and 10 metres wide. It contains the Holy Black Stone revered by Muslims. To a Muslim, this is the centre of the world. This is why Muslims always face Mecca when they pray. They circle the Kaaba when they come to Mecca as pilgrims. ▶

11.1 Look at the Muslim picture below. Describe this scene. What does it show? AT1C/L5

11.2 What is the value of a picture like this in history? AT3/L5

11.3 The Muslim year has about 354 days and 12 lunar months. This is why the year AH 1409, for instance, began on 14 August AD 1988 according to the Western (Gregorian) calendar. What do the letters AD stand for? What do you think the letters AH stand for?

11.4 When, approximately, did AH 1410 begin? What is the current Muslim year?

In AD 610 Muhammad had a religious experience which changed the world. He saw a vision and heard the message

Oh Muhammad! You are the Messenger of God and I am Gabriel.

This, and other visions, inspired Muhammad to preach that there was only one god, Allah. Everyone who submitted to the will of Allah and lived a good life on earth would have a life of glory after death.

Muhammad's first converts were his wife Khadija, his close friend Abu Bakr and his cousin Ali. He soon gathered together a group of followers who listened to what he taught. Muhammad's later religious experiences and visions added to his teaching. These words were seen as revelations direct from God which were passed on to mankind through his Messenger, Muhammad. They were memorised and recited. One of his followers, Uthman, later set these thoughts and instructions down in writing before the Faithful could forget what they had learned. This collection of writings became the Muslim holy book. It is called the *Qur'an* (or Koran).

The migration from Mecca to Medina

Muhammad's preaching annoyed the Quraysh. They denounced him, thinking that if the new religion spread, fewer pilgrims would visit the Kaaba. However, the people of Yathrib, about 300km to the north, thought differently. They invited Muhammad to come to their city instead. This is why Muhammad left Mecca in 622 with a handful of his followers. He made his new home in Yathrib. It later became known as *al-Madinah*—'The City [of the Prophet]'. It is usually known in the West as Medina.

Muhammad's migration from Mecca to Medina in 622 is called the *Hegira*. It became the starting point of the Muslim calendar. During his period at Medina, Muhammad encouraged his growing number of supporters to attack the rich caravans from Mecca which passed close to Medina. He soon built up a powerful army of warriors. In 630 the Quraysh people of Mecca agreed, at last, to make their peace with him. They accepted him as the Prophet.

Muhammad returned in triumph. All the religious idols in the Kaaba were removed. Instead, a *muezzin* (prayer leader) climbed to the top. He called on the Faithful to say prayers. Ever since, the Kaaba has been the most sacred shrine in the Islamic world.

In 651 the words of the Qur'an *(Koran) were set down in Arabic on parchment on Uthman's orders. The Qur'an is generally regarded as an outstanding piece of writing. Notice the exquisite lettering. Muslim teaching prevented artists from showing human beings in religious books like this. They used their skills instead to perfect the art of writing. This is called calligraphy.* ▶

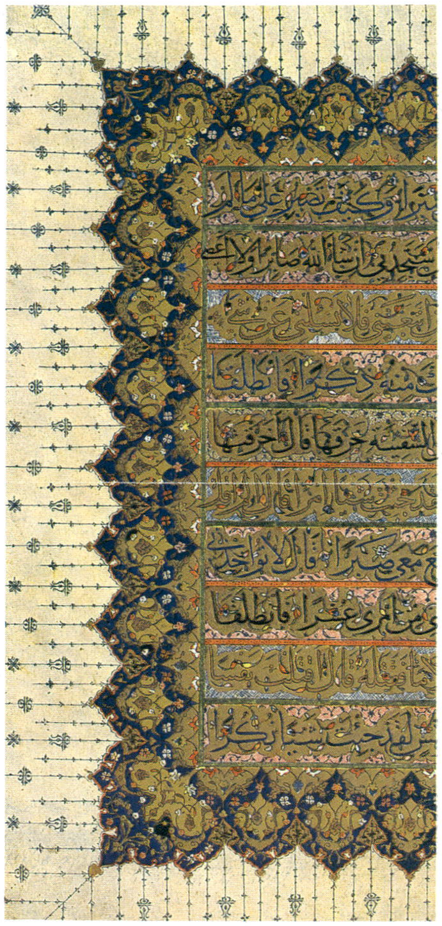

The first four Caliphs

Muhammad died in 632. By that time, Islam had already spread down the coast to Yemen and to most of the other towns of the Arabian peninsula. Although Muhammad had several children, he had no son to succeed him as leader of the new religion. In any case, to many Muslims it was not quite the same thing as a king's son succeeding his father.

Muhammad had not named a successor to follow him. This meant the elders of the religion had to choose. They followed the traditional Arab practice when choosing a sheikh. They picked an elder who they thought would have the support of the different tribes. They chose Abu Bakr, one of Muhammad's first converts. He was called the *caliph*. This meant 'Successor of the Prophet'.

Abu Bakr only ruled for two years. In that time, however, he had to deal with a serious crisis. A number of tribes refused to accept his leadership and would not pay their taxes. An outstanding commander called Khalid ibn-al Walid ('the sword of Allah') soon brought them into line.

Before he died, Abu Bakr named Umar, another of Muhammad's oldest friends, as the next caliph. Umar continued the same policy of fighting for the cause of Islam. His armies, led by outstanding leaders such as Khalid ibn-al Walid, were highly successful. First, Iraq fell to the conquerors in 637. Then Syria fell in 640. In 642 Persia (now Iran), Egypt and eastern Libya were all converted to Islam.

Umar was revered as the ideal caliph, or ruler, but was assassinated in 644. A council of elders then picked Uthman as his successor instead of choosing Ali, Muhammad's son-in-law. Uthman was a member of the Umayyad clan and the most senior of Muhammad's remaining friends.

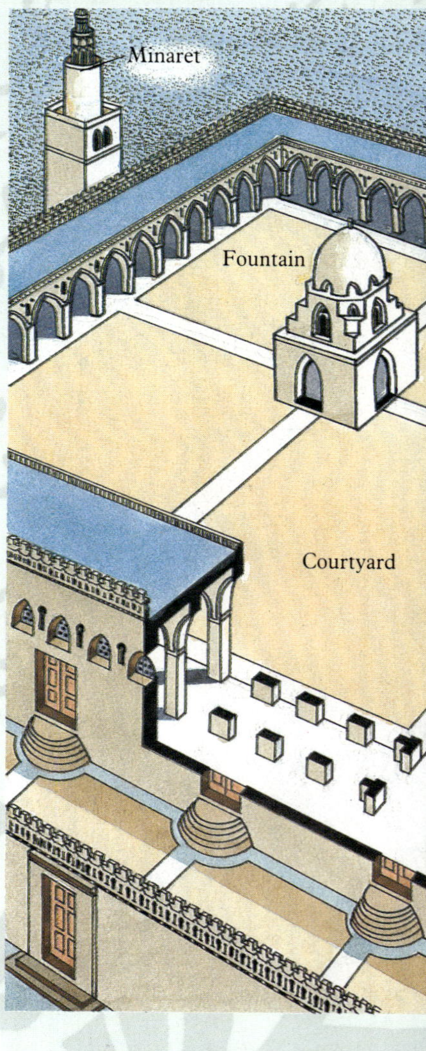

Under his control the power and influence of Islam continued to grow. By 647 Muslim soldiers had entered Tunisia in North Africa. In less than twenty years the Muslim empire had become nearly as wide in extent as that of the Romans.

In 656 Uthman, too, was assassinated. Some of his followers, led by the governor of Syria, Mu'awiyah (one of Uthman's kinsmen), objected strongly when Ali was made caliph in his place. Ali had a strong claim. He was Muhammad's cousin, husband of his daughter Fatima, and one of the very earliest of his converts. Indeed, Ali's supporters thought he should have been made caliph in 632.

But Mu'awiyah set out to avenge Uthman and challenged Ali to hand over the caliph's assassins. The dispute between the two men led to war. Mu'awiyah was proclaimed caliph in 660, the year before Ali was assassinated at Kufa in Iraq. Mu'awiyah later took steps to keep the Caliphate in the hands of the Umayyads. Before he died he named his son Yazid as his successor.

Ali's supporters did not forgive Mu'awiyah. They supported the claims of Ali's younger son, al-Husayn, when Mu'awiyah died in 680. Al-Husayn was Muhammad's grandson. However, the hopes of Ali's supporters were dashed once more when al-Husayn was killed at the Battle of Kerbela in 680.

The followers of Ali and his family (*Shi'at Ali*) were later known as Shi'ite or Shia Muslims. The disagreement with the Umayyads led to a permanent split in Islam between the Shi'ites and the Sunnites. The Sunnites followed the customs and tradition (*Sunnah*) of the Prophet. Unlike the Shi'ites, they believed the Caliph or imam could only act as leader of Islam. He could not inherit Muhammad's religious powers.

The five great Pillars of Islam

All Muslims were commanded to follow the five great Pillars of Islam. These were as follows.

1 Faith *There is no God but Allah, and Muhammad is His Prophet.* To the followers of the new religion, faith was the first of the five great Pillars of Islam. What this meant could be found in the Qur'an.

2 Prayer Muslims were told to face Mecca and say prayers five times a day. They were called to prayer by the muezzin from a high tower or *minaret* in the mosque. They worshipped in the sanctuary facing the *qibla* wall. In the middle of this wall was a niche or hollow called a *mihrab*. This indicated the direction of Mecca.

Each day they washed to purify themselves before prayer. This is why most mosques were built with a fountain in the courtyard. Once a week, on Fridays at noon, they prayed together in the mosque. These Friday prayers were led by an imam who delivered a sermon or message to the Faithful. Women also attended the Friday prayers, but had to wear a headdress and stand away from the men.

11.5 Draw a flow chart showing Muhammad and the first five caliphs. AT1C ■

11.6 Why was the minaret necessary in a mosque? What do you think the elders in the mosque looked for when they appointed a muezzin? AT3/L3

11.7 Write one or two sentences describing a medieval mosque. AT1C ■

11.8 How did it differ from a medieval church (see page 174)? AT1C ■

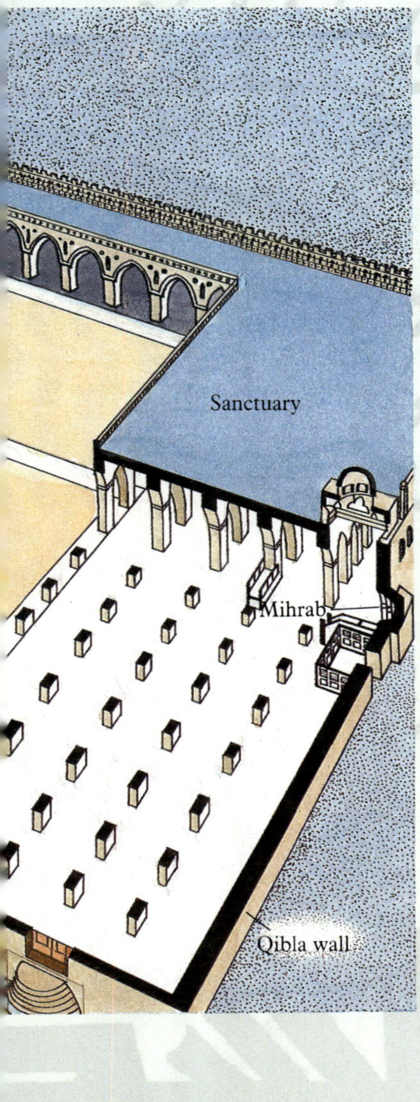

In this diagram you can see the chief features of a medieval mosque. This was a place of prayer for all the community. It had a tower, or minaret, from which the muezzin called the Faithful to prayer. There was a fountain where worshippers could wash before prayer. It had a qibla wall with a niche, or mihrab, facing Mecca. Worshippers prostrated themselves in the sanctuary in a sheltered arcade next to the qibla wall.

3 Alms The third great Pillar of Islam was the requirement that every Muslim should give *alms* to the poor. This was compulsory. A certain sum of money, or a contribution in kind (such as corn, dates or animals), had to be paid according to a person's wealth.

4 Fasting It was also required that every Muslim should fast during the daylight hours throughout the month of *Ramadan*. From sunrise to sunset the Faithful were not allowed to eat or drink. At night, when it was too dark to see without a light, they ate their main meal of the day. They celebrated the end of Ramadan with a period of feasting for anything up to three days.

5 Pilgrimage The last great Pillar of Islam was the compulsory pilgrimage, or *hajj*, to Mecca. All the pilgrims dressed in the same clothes. The *hajj* united Muslims from all over the world.

◀ *This miniature painting shows the trumpeters and flag-bearers of a medieval Caliph of Baghdad. The trumpets sound the end of Ramadan and the start of the festivities which will follow.*

Time Line

570	Birth of Muhammad
610	Muhammad begins to preach
622	The Hegira
630	Muhammad returns to Mecca
632	Death of Muhammad
632–634	Caliph Abu Bakr
634–644	Caliph Umar
637	Iraq conquered for Islam
640	Syria conquered
642	Persia and Egypt conquered
644–656	Caliph Uthman
651	Qur'an set down in writing
656–661	Caliph Ali
680	Battle of Kerbela

The Sharia

Islam also gave its followers clear instructions how they should live. These were contained in a set of laws called the *Sharia*. They were based on the Qur'an and on the Hadith, the traditions and customs of Islam. They made some practices compulsory, such as saying prayers. They forbade crimes, such as murder and theft, and also prohibited the Faithful from eating certain foods. Some acts, such as freeing slaves, were praised but not made compulsory. Other practices were permitted, such as marrying more than one wife. A number of acts were frowned upon but not forbidden, such as gambling.

There were also laws governing the relations between men and women. Divorce was simple for a man but difficult for a woman. *Jihad* (a holy war) was made the duty of every Muslim. This was a war against unbelievers. Soldiers killed in battle during a *jihad* were guaranteed a place in Paradise.

The Tales from the Thousand and One Nights

We can find out something about medieval Islam from a book called *The Tales from the Thousand and One Nights*. This famous book contains stories which were written over a thousand years ago. They include familiar tales such as 'Aladdin' and 'Sinbad the Sailor'. Words and phrases from these stories tell us a lot about the Muslim way of life at that time. You can see some of these phrases in the sources which follow.

Source 11.A

They were directed by the passers-by to the house of a Jewish doctor.

Source 11.B

'My son,' said the old woman, 'the hour of Friday prayers is almost past, and I have not yet made the necessary ablutions.' Al-Ashar brought her a large jug of water and a basin.

Source 11.C

A Christian, who was the king's broker, passed through the lane on his way to the public baths.

Source 11.D

The hour of prayer had come and the imams had already begun their sermons when at long last the barber finished shaving my head. The muezzins had now intoned their blessings on the Prophet from the minarets of the city.

We can also learn about the early years of Islam from medieval travellers. Ibn Jubayr was a Spanish Muslim. He went on a pilgrimage to Mecca in 1183. When he returned, he wrote this:

Source 11.E

When the pilgrims returned to Damascus, a vast crowd of people went to meet them, giving dinars [coins] *to the poor and offering them food. Many women gave them bread which if the pilgrims bit, they snatched from their hands and hastened to eat it in order that they might be blessed since the pilgrims had tasted it first.*

The Great Mosque at Yazd in Iran ▶

11.9 Which of the five Pillars of Islam are illustrated in Sources 11.A to 11.E? AT3/L4

11.10 How can we prove that other religions were tolerated in Baghdad over a thousand years ago? AT3/L4

11.11 How can a book of stories like *The Tales from the Thousand and One Nights* help us to find out about Baghdad in the Middle Ages? AT3/L5

11.12 Write an account of what it was like to be a Muslim pilgrim about a thousand years ago.

11.13 What features can you see in the photograph of the Great Mosque at Yazd? Trace or draw a picture of this mosque and mark and name a minaret.

12 The Caliphate at Damascus and Baghdad

▶ *HOW, WHY and WHERE did Islam grow so rapidly by 750?* ATIB ■

▶ *WHAT did the Umayyad and Abbasid caliphs achieve?* ATIA ■

▶ *WHAT was life like at the court of a caliph or sultan?* ATIC ■

◀ *The Dome of the Rock in Jerusalem is one of the most beautiful mosques in the world. It was built in 691. The dome and walls of the mosque are covered with mosaics made from glass.*

The Caliphate at Damascus

Mu'awiyah, the Governor of Syria, became caliph in 660 (page 55). He kept all the power in the hands of the Umayyad clan. He made Damascus his capital city and named his own son Yazid as his heir. This was the first time the position of caliph had been handed on from father to son.

Many of Mu'awiyah's subjects in Syria were Christians or Jews. He allowed them to follow their own religions. However, they had to pay a special tax because they were not members of the Muslim faith. Even so, they stayed loyal to their Muslim ruler.

Mu'awiyah's reign as caliph began the period known as the Umayyad Dynasty. The first Umayyads were very able and talented rulers. They built many fine mosques. These included the Dome of the Rock in Jerusalem and the Great Mosque in Damascus.

Caliph Abd al-Malik (685–705) was one of the ablest of the Umayyad caliphs. He did two things which helped to unite the Muslim lands: he made Arabic the language of the government instead of Greek or Persian or Coptic (in Egypt), and he also brought in a common system of coinage.

◀ *Some of the Umayyads built castles, palaces and hunting lodges in the desert. They preferred life in the desert to life in the town. Desert castles, like this one at Qasr-al-Kharana in Jordan, were often heavily fortified. Some had machicolations, or 'murder holes' (see page 163), above the gatehouse. Defenders dropped stones or boiling liquid through them on to the enemy below. The Crusaders who went to the Holy Land with Richard the Lionheart in about 1190 copied this idea when they built their own castles.*

12.1 Compare the photograph of the Dome of the Rock with the Great Mosque in Yazd on page 57. Write one or two sentences saying what both mosques have in common.
AT1C/L5

12.2 What scenes from nature can you see in the mosaics of the Great Mosque at Damascus?

12.3 What do you notice about the shape of the walls of the desert castle in the photograph? Castle walls like these were not built in Britain until the thirteenth century (as you can see on page 164). By how many years, roughly, were the Arab castle builders ahead of those in Britain? Make a list of the similarities and dissimilarities between the two castles.
AT1A ■ AT1C/L3

12.4 Why did the author of Source 12.A describe the arrival of Musa in Damascus in 715 as a triumph for Islam?
AT1B ■

12.5 What is the modern name for the place where Tariq landed in Europe in 711?
AT3/L3

The conquest of Spain

The Umayyad caliphs not only united their vast empire, they expanded it still further. Islam made great gains under the Umayyads. By 698 they had conquered North Africa. In 711 Musa ibn-Nusayr, the Muslim governor of North Africa, sent one of his leading commanders, a former slave called Tariq ibn Ziyad, to attack Spain. Tariq sailed with 12 000 soldiers. He took the shortest sea route and landed at a place with a rocky hill which his troops called 'Mount of Tariq' or *Jabal Tariq*.

On 19 July 711 Tariq defeated the Visigoth king Roderick in southern Spain, even though the Spanish ruler had an army of twice the size. After this, Tariq and his army marched through southern Spain. They met little opposition. They took Granada and Cordoba and then Toledo in central Spain. Tariq's master, Musa, was jealous. He invaded Spain himself in 712. He captured much of the rest of Spain and punished Tariq for going too far.

News of this reached Caliph al-Walid I in Syria. He ordered Musa to return. Musa came back slowly. He brought with him a long line of princes, slaves and prisoners, as well as jewellery, gold and many priceless treasures. He reached Damascus in February 715.

This is how a modern writer, Philip K. Hitti, writes about Musa's arrival at the Great Mosque.

Source 12.A

The official reception, held with great dignity and pomp in the courtyard of the magnificent Umayyad Mosque, is one of the high-water marks in the history of triumphant Islam. For the first time hundreds of Western royalty and thousands of European captives were seen offering homage to the commander of the believers.

Caliph al-Walid I ordered work to begin on the Great Mosque in Damascus in 705. Skilled Indian and Persian, as well as Syrian, craftsmen worked here. They made these fine mosaics in about 715.

The growth of Islam

In 732 the Muslim armies marched as far as the Loire Valley in France. Then they were defeated at the Battle of Poitiers. Meanwhile, the march of Islam in the East went at a similar pace. In 664 Muslim soldiers took Afghanistan. In 712 an army led by Muhammad ibn al-Kassim conquered Sind in what is now Pakistan. Other Muslim armies further to the north seized much of what is now Soviet Central Asia. In 751 the forces of Islam even defeated a Chinese army at the Battle of Talas in Central Asia.

Much later, Islam spread peacefully into other parts of South-East Asia as well, such as Indonesia, Borneo and the Philippines. It also spread southwards across the Sahara into Nigeria, Mali and other West African states. You can see the full extent of the Islamic Empire in 750 on the map below. All this had been achieved in only 120 years.

Arab cavalry ▼

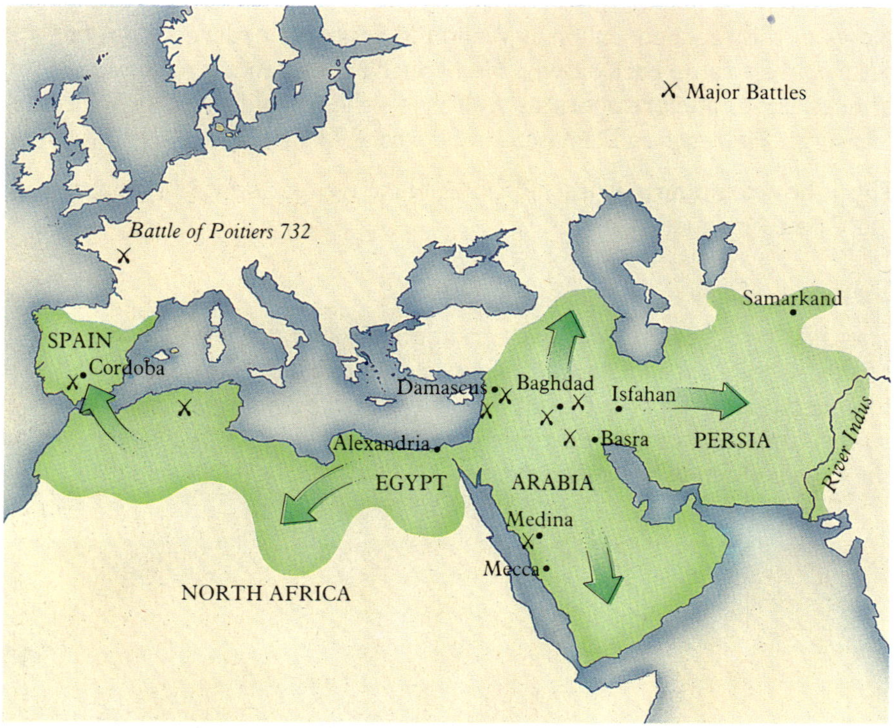

◀ *This map shows the rapid growth of the Islamic world from* AD *630 to* AD *750*

Reasons for the rise of Islam

There were several reasons why Islam grew so rapidly in such a short time. Firstly, there was the spirit and power of the new religion. Islam appealed at once to many of those who met it for the first time. Its main message—*There is no God but Allah, and Muhammad is His Prophet*—was easy to understand. It appealed to poor people in particular. It taught that all people were equal before Allah. It made the rich aid the poor.

Another reason was military strength. On the battlefield, the Arab cavalry on camels or horses were fierce foes. What is more, they were fired with the idea of *Jihad*. This was a holy war against the infidels or non-believers. Soldiers who were true believers were told they would go to Paradise if they were killed in battle.

The ease with which the Muslim armies made their conquests was also aided by the fact that many of the provinces they conquered were badly ruled and highly taxed. From the earliest raids on caravans leaving Mecca, the Islamic armies also made a point of seizing great quantities of booty from the peoples they defeated. This was an incentive for the soldiers.

12.6 Look at the picture of Arab cavalry in action. What weapons did they use? What armour did the Arab cavalry have? Write a paragraph describing the Arab cavalry after studying the picture.

The Caliphs of Baghdad

The later Umayyad caliphs were weak and ineffective. They were challenged by Abu al-Abbas. He claimed descent from Muhammad's uncle who was also called al-Abbas. Al-Abbas became caliph in 749 with the support of many Shi'ite Muslims. Once in power he ignored the Shi'ites. What is more, all but one of the remaining members of the Umayyad family were put to death.

In the ninth and tenth centuries the Abbasids created the greatest civilisation in the world at that time. Caliphs, like Harun-al-Rashid were great princes and very wealthy. They owned thousands of slaves and lived in superb palaces guarded by well-trained soldiers.

Very little now remains of the Abbasid capital of Baghdad. We have to use pictures of Islamic buildings in other places to get some idea of what the caliph's palaces might have looked like. This palace is in Granada in Spain. It shows the Court of the Myrtles in the Alhambra Palace. ▶

The first of the great caliphs was al-Mansur who succeeded al-Abbas in 754. He moved his capital city from Damascus to Baghdad. You can read more about this city on pages 68–9. It took 100 000 workers four years to build it.

The Abbasid caliphs were famed for their enormous wealth and for the money they spent on learning and on the arts. They enjoyed beautiful things. Muslim craft workers created many exquisite objects for them, such as jewels, textiles and carpets.

They were also learned men. Many of the finest scientists and doctors of the Middle Ages lived and worked in Baghdad or in other Islamic cities such as Cordoba, Damascus and Cairo. Caliph Al-Mamun, for instance, who ruled from 813 to 833, even founded a House of Wisdom in Baghdad. He employed scholars to translate Greek, Latin and Persian books into Arabic. In this way he kept alive the ideas and thoughts of people like the Greek philosophers Plato and Aristotle.

12.7 Write a paragraph saying how and why Islam as a religion changed history.

AT1B ■ AT1A ■

12.8 Compare the Islamic Empire in 750 with that of the Roman Empire shown in the map on page 15. Which areas were once Roman but not Muslim? Which areas were once Muslim but not Roman?

AT1A ■ AT1C/L3

An Islamic palace

You can get some idea of the wealth which surrounded the Abbasid caliphs and the sultans of medieval Islam from the sources and pictures on these pages.

For instance, a list of the contents of the Caliph Harun al-Rashid's palace in about 809 gives some idea of the luxury in which he lived. There were 4400 carpets, 6000 pillows, 9000 cushions and 5300 curtains on the list. In about AD 925 a writer called Abul Qasim compared the luxurious lifestyle of a rich man in Baghdad with that of a Persian in Isfahan. He said the house of the rich man in Baghdad had the following:

Source 12.B

Public rooms furnished with carpets from the Mahgrib, Khurasani carpets, carpet-strips from Andalusia and Cordoba, Armenian carpets and Byzantine velvets, Tustari cushions, gold-embroidered pillows of Dabiq, square carpets from Cyprus and cushions.

Saman or Abbadani mats which fold in two as cloth does, lovelier than carpets and softer than silk, of fine workmanship, perfect craftsmanship picked out with gold. Cushions mixed with Iraqi gold, and embroidered with pictures of elephants and horses; carpets stuffed with feathers of the Indian bullfinch and Tustar brocade embroidered with gold.

There are similar descriptions in *The Tales from the Thousand and One Nights* (see Sources 12.C and 12.D).

A writer called Ibn al-Qalanasi described the wealth of a Muslim princess in about 1100 (see Source 12.E).

This unusual painting shows the Caliph Al-Mamun's toilet arrangements. It is rather like a strip cartoon, since the caliph is shown in three different rooms at the same time.

Source 12.C

An impressive company of nobles and mighty sheikhs were seated according to rank at tables spread with the daintiest meats and richest wines, and gaily decked with flowers and fruit. On one side of the hall sat beautiful slave girls who sang and made music; and in front reclined the host, a distinguished old man, whose beard was touched with silver.

Source 12.D

A spacious and nobly vaulted hall. The ceiling was wondrously carved in patterns of elaborate design, and the walls were hung with tapestry of silk and rich brocade. In the centre of the hall a fountain played in a pool of crystal water.

Source 12.E

The princess, the sultan's daughter and wife of the caliph, arrived at Baghdad from Persia in such magnificence and with such quantities of jewellery, moneys, utensils, carriages and riding beasts of all kinds, furniture, varieties of gorgeous raiment, attendants, guards, slave-girls, and followers, as exceeds all reckoning.

A Sultan being entertained in his palace

12.9 How did the Caliph Al-Mamun's shower work? How did he have his hair trimmed?

AT3/L3

12.10 Use the information in the pictures and written sources on these pages to write a paragraph describing the things you might have expected to see on a visit to an Islamic palace about a thousand years ago.

AT3/L4

12.11 Which pictures and sources help you to know what an Islamic palace actually looked like? Which pictures and/or sources are most useful?

AT3 ■

Time Line

661–680	Caliph Mu'awiyah
664	Afghanistan conquered
680	Battle of Kerbela
685–705	Caliph Abd al-Malik
691	Dome of the Rock built
705–717	Caliph al-Walid I
705	Great Mosque of Damascus
711–714	Conquest of Spain
712	Conquest of Sind
732	Battle of Poitiers
744	Caliph al-Walid II murdered
749–754	Al-Abbas becomes Caliph
751	Battle of Talas
754–775	Caliph Al Mansur
762	Baghdad founded
786–809	Caliph Harun-al-Rashid
813–833	Caliph Al-Mamun
832	House of Wisdom in Baghdad
969	Cairo founded
1055	Seljuk Turks seize Baghdad

A Persian monarch in front of his palace

The end of an era

Although much of the Islamic world was ruled by the Abbasid caliphs, other lands took a much more independent line. The Moors in Morocco and the Umayyad rulers of Spain refused to take orders from the Abbasid caliphs. A number of other Muslim groups also broke away from Baghdad in this way.

One of the most important was the Fatimids. They conquered Egypt in the tenth century. The Fatimids claimed descent from Muhammad's daughter Fatima. In 969 they founded the city of Qahira (Cairo) and built a university there long before universities were founded in Britain or Europe. Cairo became one of the greatest of all the Muslim cities. By the time of the Norman Conquest it had 20 000 shops, a palace with over 10 000 servants and houses for well over 100 000 people. Its streets were lit by lamps.

The end of Abbasid control of Islam came in 1055 when the Seljuk Turks entered Baghdad. The Seljuks were fierce Muslim warriors. Their attack on the Byzantines and Christians in Palestine was largely responsible for the start of the Crusades (pages 64–7).

13 Islam at the time of the Crusades

Destruction of the Holy Sepulchre in Jerusalem in 1009

FOCUS

▶ *WHAT were the Crusades?* AT1C ■

▶ *HOW and WHY were they fought?* AT1B ■

▶ *HOW did Muslims and Christians see each other during these wars?* AT2 ■

The Crusaders

Ever since the Romans, Christian pilgrims had visited the Holy Land. Even when Palestine became Muslim they could still visit Jerusalem. However, this changed in the eleventh century. On 4 October 1009 Caliph al-Hakim of Egypt ordered the destruction of the Church of the Holy Sepulchre in Jerusalem. Four years later he expelled both Christians and Jews from Egypt. This angered Christians, but when Al-Hakim died in 1021 pilgrims were allowed to visit Jerusalem once more, and the Church of the Holy Sepulchre was rebuilt.

In 1085, however, the Seljuk Turks seized Jerusalem and attacked the Byzantine Empire (page 49). The Byzantines were Christians. They appealed to the Pope to help. At a meeting in France in the year 1095 Pope Urban II urged the knights and princes of Europe to fight a crusade.

Source 13.A

An accursed race has violently invaded the lands of the Christians. They have destroyed the churches of God or taken them for their own religion. Jerusalem is now held captive by the enemies of Christ, subject to those who do not know God—the worship of the heathen. He who makes this holy pilgrimage shall wear the sign of the cross of the Lord on his forehead or on his breast.

Pope Urban's speech was so effective that kings and knights at once made plans to sail to the Holy Land. They wore a cross on the front of their armour as they went and on the back when they returned.

Most of the Crusaders were Franks (from France and Flanders). They were led by Robert of Normandy and Godfrey of Bouillon. They set off on this, the First Crusade, in 1096. In 1099 they captured Jerusalem. The Crusaders also captured other cities in the Holy Land, including Acre, Sidon and Beirut.

13.1 Look at the picture below showing Crusaders setting off for the Holy Land. Write a paragraph saying what you can see in this picture. Describe the ship which took them to Palestine. What stores were put on board? How did the soldiers reach the ship? AT1C/L5

13.2 Has the artist drawn the ship to scale? Do you think it is an accurate picture? What use is a picture like this in history? AT3/L5

Crusaders setting off for the Holy Land ▼

To the Muslim leaders, these were minor defeats. They affected only a tiny part of the Islamic Empire. Even so, they could not let Christians occupy Muslim cities, and in Jerusalem holy shrines such as the Dome of the Rock (page 58). The Crusaders were attacked and many of the cities they had taken were recaptured.

Muslim writers tell us what they thought of the Crusaders. Ibn al-Qalanisi lived in Damascus from about 1070 to 1160. In Source 13.B he describes a battle fought near Aleppo on 28 June 1119. The Crusaders had been ambushed between two hills.

Source 13.B

Roger, lord of Antioch marched out of his city with an army of twenty thousand horse and foot soldiers. It was an immense army indeed. The soldiers were well armed. But the Muslims charged down upon them. They attacked them on all sides with blows of swords and hails of arrows. God Most High, to whom be the praise, granted victory to the party of Islam against the infidels.

The Franks were on the ground, horsemen and foot soldiers alike, with their horses and their weapons. Not one man of them escaped to tell the tale. Their leader Roger was found stretched out among the dead.

Roger of Antioch's secretary, however, also wrote about the same battle. He gives the Christian point of view.

Source 13.C

Suddenly the flags and standards of the heathens appeared from the mountain sides among the olives. When he saw them, Prince Roger declared 'Let us serve today as soldiers for God in a successful battle, whether we end up alive or dead'.

Then, at once and all together, a hundred thousand infidel fighting men attacked our army very fiercely. Some of our men (of whom there were said to be seven hundred knights and three thousand foot soldiers) were wounded. Some were killed. Some who were mutilated were put to death on the battlefield. Others were taken captive.

13.3 Read Sources 13.B and 13.C. How big were the two armies? How many were killed? Why are there so few facts on which both writers agree? AT2 ■

13.4 If Source 13.B was accurate in *every* detail (which it is not), why would that make it difficult to believe anything in Source 13.C? AT2/L5

13.5 Why do we have to treat both of these sources with caution? AT2 ■

13.6 What can we believe? Write a paragraph about the battle, but only use facts which are not contradicted by the other source. AT2/L6 AT3/L6

13.7 What does Source 13.D (below) tell us about the effects of the Crusades on the people living in Syria and Palestine? AT1A/L4 AT1B/L4

Ibn Jubayr, another Muslim writer, wrote this in about 1183:

Source 13.D

Although Muslim and Christian armies meet in battle, yet Muslim and Christian travellers can come and go between them without interference. We saw Salah-al-din depart with all the Muslim troops to lay siege to the fortress of Kerak, one of the greatest of the Christian strongholds. Long the siege lasted, but still the caravans passed continuously from Egypt to Damascus, going through the lands of the Franks without interference from them.

The capture of Jerusalem

Salah-al-din's secretary described the capture of Jerusalem on Friday 2 October 1187.

Source 13.E

The Muslims took the city at the time when the noon Friday prayer was due. The al-Aqsa mosque, and the mihrab in particular, was a den of pigs and filth. It was occupied by all manner of infidels, evildoers, oppressors and criminals.

The Sultan Salah-al-din held court in the camp outside Jerusalem. The Qur'an reciters sat reading and repeating parts of the Book. Tears filled everyone's eyes. Hearts were overcome by the joy of victory. Lips whispered God in prayer.

An English priest took a different view when he wrote this in about 1220.

Source 13.F

Salah-al-din laid siege to the city, and broke into the holy places. A muezzin climbed the high mount of Calvary. There, on the site of the Crucifixion, the cry of a different religion rang out. Another shocking deed was to pull down the cross on the church of the Hospitallers. They smashed it and spat upon it, then dragged it through the city dungheap as an insult to our faith.

Christians and Muslims in Spain ▼

Salah-al-din (Saladin)

Salah-al-din was one of the outstanding leaders of medieval Islam. He was a Kurd, born in 1138, and was brought up in what is now Iraq. He joined the army of Nur al-Din, ruler of Syria, and was sent to Egypt where he rose to become the Sultan's vizier (Prime Minister). In 1171 he himself became Sultan of Egypt. This was the beginning of the Ayyubid dynasty. They controlled Egypt and Syria for about a hundred years.

Salah-al-din united much of the Muslim world. He built up a powerful army and seized Syria and part of Iraq. He defeated the Crusaders at the Battle of Hittin on 3–4 July 1187. On 2 October 1187 he took Jerusalem (Sources 13.E and 13.F). He seized other Crusader cities and castles as well.

The Crusaders respected him as an outstanding leader. He behaved with great chivalry towards his captives and his enemies. He was also much admired as a ruler. He built hospitals and schools and founded a college for the study of Islamic laws.

13.8 How and why do Sources 13.E and 13.F differ in describing the capture of Jerusalem? AT2 ■

13.9 What did the Christian writer say about the Muslims? What did the Muslim writer say about the Christians? How are their accounts similar, even though they disagree? AT1C/L6

13.10 What had Albert of Aachen (right) tasted? AT3/L3

13.11 Look at the pictures below. Which picture do you think was painted by a Muslim artist? Which was painted by a Christian? Give reasons for your answers. AT2 ■

13.12 What story do you think the sequence of pictures tells? How do you know which soldiers are Crusaders and which are Muslims? AT3/L4

13.13 Write one or two captions for each picture in this strip. AT1C ■

13.14 Why were the Crusades fought? AT1B ■

13.15 What did they achieve? AT1A ■

Time Line

1056	Seljuk Turks stop pilgrimages to the Holy Land
1095	Pope calls for a Crusade
1096	First Crusade
1099	Crusaders capture Jerusalem
1148	Second Crusade
1187	Battle of Hittin
1188	Third Crusade
1202	Fourth Crusade
1217	Fifth Crusade
1228	Sixth Crusade
1248	Seventh Crusade
1270	Eighth Crusade

The news of the fall of Jerusalem came as a shock to Christians in Europe. Three great kings—Richard the Lionheart (of England), Philip (of France) and Frederick Barbarossa (the Holy Roman Emperor)—formed armies to seize the Holy Land. However, only Richard played a major part in this, the Third Crusade. He captured Acre and Jaffa, but failed to take Jerusalem. However, he did reach an agreement with Salah-al-din which gave Christian pilgrims the right to visit Jerusalem unharmed.

The later Crusades (see Time Line) achieved very little. Soldiers of the Fourth Crusade (1202–4) did not even reach the Holy Land. They disgraced themselves by sacking the Byzantine capital of Constantinople. This was a Christian, not a Muslim, city.

The effects of the Crusades

The Crusades affected the people of Europe in many ways. They had to pay extra taxes to pay for the armies. Many of their soldier relatives were killed or maimed in battle. They even had to pay the ransoms demanded for the safe return of a king or great lord captured in battle. But there was one great benefit: trade between East and West increased. The Crusaders also brought back new goods and ideas from the East. Albert of Aachen, for instance, said that the Arabs sucked 'little honeyed reeds which they call sukkar'. It was crushed and filtered into containers. When hard it looked like 'snow or white salt'. It tasted sweeter than honey.

Muslim knights attacking a Crusader fortress in Turkey ▼

14 Everyday life in an Islamic town

▶ *WHAT were the typical features of an Islamic town?*
▶ *WHAT was it like to live there?*
▶ *HOW was trade and commerce carried on in an Islamic town?*
▶ *WHAT public services were provided?* ATIC ■

◀ *Boys were sent to school at the age of six or seven. Up to that time they were brought up exclusively by the women in the house. Schools were run by the elders of the mosque. The children learned to read and write from the Qur'an. If they were clever they could go on to study at one of the great mosque-universities, such as al-Azhar in Cairo.*

Islamic towns

The first Islamic towns were built to house soldiers in military camps. They soon attracted other settlers as well. The soldiers were well paid. They had money to spend. They shared in the booty taken from the people they conquered. This is why traders came to town to sell them goods. The profits they made in the markets meant that they, too, had money to spend. This attracted even more settlers to the town. Services were provided for the townspeople, such as baths, schools and street-cleaning. As a result, towns grew very rapidly in size.

Baghdad

Baghdad itself was a new city. It grew up around a circular town planned by Caliph Al-Mansur in 762. His palace, a mosque, the treasury (where his wealth was kept) and the barracks for his most trusted soldiers were built inside a round town surrounded by thick sloping walls. This was futher protected by a huge deep ditch filled with water from the River Tigris. Most Islamic towns had a strongpoint or citadel like this, surrounded by a wall and moat.

The round town had four main gates and four main streets criss-crossing the centre. Each street had shops on either side under arcades which provided shelter from the sun.

The caliph chose this flat site for his city for a number of reasons. It was on the River Tigris and close to the River Euphrates. Overland caravan routes crossed the rivers at this point. There were canals to supply water for drinking and for the city's baths and fountains. Farmland nearby grew food for the inhabitants.

14.1 How was the school-room in this picture kept cool? Where did the teachers and pupils sit? AT3/L3

14.2 Look at the picture on the right. What shape were the town walls? How many mosques were there? Which feature helps to identify them? Which was the biggest mosque? Which mosque had a large courtyard? Where did the richer merchants live in this town? Where would you have expected to see the markets and main shops? Write a description of this town from the point of view of a traveller like Ibn Jubayr. AT1C/L5

14.3 Why do you think a town grew up on this site? AT1B ■

14.4 Draw a sketch map or a picture outline of this town. Mark and name the features you can identify. AT3/L4

Persian metalworkers in 1482

It soon became clear, however, that the caliph's round town was too small. Baghdad's suburbs grew and grew. By 800 the city's houses and streets covered an area over six miles (10 km) wide and its population was between one and two million. Other great cities of medieval Islam were huge but not as big as this. Cairo, Samarkand (Central Asia) and Cordoba in Spain all had about half a million inhabitants each. This was at a time when London had less than 25 000 inhabitants!

The business centre of an Islamic town was in the *souq* or market where traders and merchants met. The Muslim writer Ibn Jubayr said that in Aleppo

the large markets were in long adjacent rows so that you passed from a row of shops of one craft to that of another.

The weavers' district of Baghdad, for instance, was called the *Attabiya*. They made a cloth with a wavy pattern. This is why cats with striped fur are called 'tabby' cats today.

The great mosques were built close by. Other important town-centre buildings included the public baths, the governor's home and government offices. Rich merchants also built their homes near the town centre. Poorer people had further to travel from their homes. They lived in more distant suburbs outside the protection of the city walls.

This picture was drawn by Nasuh al-Silahi al-Marraki. It shows a town in Iraq or Iran at the time when Suleiman the Magnificent (page 80) was campaigning in that region in 1534–5.

Trading centres

Many towns became rich and wealthy because they were ports, like Basra and Alexandria. Some prospered because they were trading centres, like Baghdad and Mecca, where overland caravan routes met (see picture on page 52).

Trade routes criss-crossed the Sahara and Central Asia. The overland route to China was always busy with caravans of laden camels and horses. By 800 the merchants of Baghdad were already trading with Sri Lanka, Madagascar, India, China, Russia, Scandinavia and Indonesia.

Merchants travelling by sea took cargoes of grain or iron from Iraq and exchanged them for ivory and incense in the Indian Ocean. These were sold, in turn, to Chinese merchants for fine pottery (chinaware) and silk which they brought back to Baghdad or Cairo and sold in the markets. A merchant described this trade in *The Tales from the Thousand and One Nights.*

A group of merchants on an Arab dhow. When they got to port, they moored the boat at the quayside, put out the landing planks and unloaded the cargo under the watchful eye of the controller of shipping at the port.

14.5 How was the Arab dhow steered? How did it move in the water? AT3/L3

14.6 Our modern word 'traffic' comes from the Arabic word *tafriq*. The French word *magasin* for shop or store comes from the Arabic word *makhazine*. We have adopted other words used by traders from the Middle East:

Source 14.A

I bought a large quantity of merchandise and made preparations for a long voyage. Then I set sail together with a company of merchants in a river-ship bound for Basra. There we put to sea and voyaged many days and nights from isle to isle and from shore to shore, buying and selling and bartering wherever the ship anchored.

You can get some idea of the extent of this trade from the list of imports in Source 14.B. It was compiled from a list made by a merchant of Basra in about 850.

Source 14.B

Arabia	*pedigree camels and horses, hides and skins*
Central Asia	*slaves, paper, sugar, grapes, fur*
China	*fine pottery (china), silk, paper, ink, drugs*
Egypt	*papyrus, balsam (oil used in perfumes and medicines)*
India	*ebony wood, rubies, elephants, tigers, panthers*
North Africa	*hawks (used in hunting), panthers, oils*
Oman	*pearls*
Persia (Iran)	*fruit, salt, saffron and indigo (dyes), carpets, linen, zithers, honey, nuts, clothes, minerals, fragrant scents*
Russia	*carpets, wool, rugs, mats, saddles*
Yemen	*giraffes, scents, dyes*

The slave market was a familiar sight in most Islamic towns. The luxurious life of the rich merchants of a city like Baghdad depended on the hard work of thousands of slaves. They worked on the plantations, in the mines, and as servants in palaces and mansions. Many were captured slaves from Eastern Europe (the Slavs). Some were Blacks seized by raiding parties or purchased from African kings. They were bought and sold as if they were household goods.

Arab slave market ▶

al-henna a dye
al-kohl strong drink
al-manakh a calendar
al-qutun a cloth made from a flowering plant
amir-al-bahr commander of a fleet of ships
bazar a market
laimun a citrus fruit
mawsim a seasonal wind used by sailing ships
sakk a written promise to pay a sum of money
sharab a sweet drink
tarifah a customs duty
zarafah an animal with a long neck AT3/L3

14.7 Show how the picture on the right can be used to write a description of a merchant's house. How many floors or storeys did it have? How was it decorated? What materials were used to build this house? AT3/L5

14.8 Use these sources to describe the life of a Muslim merchant in medieval Baghdad. AT3/L4

Letters from merchants in Muslim cities tell us about their work. A Syrian merchant in the eleventh century wrote to Cairo to ask if there was any news of the Spanish ship he was expecting. When Nasir-i-Khosrau visited Tripoli in 1046 he noted how trade was carried on in the port.

Source 14.C

There is a custom house where ships pay a tax to the sultan. The garrison is paid for out of this money. The sultan also keeps ships here, which trade with Byzantium [Constantinople], *Sicily and the West.*

Merchants who travelled overland by caravan could stop the night in a *khan* or *caravanserai*. This was a two-storeyed, mudbrick building built around a courtyard. Merchants slept on the first floor and kept their camels and other pack animals in the stables below. Some were fortified against attack. According to the Muslim writer Ibn Jubayr, Aleppo had a large suburb on the fringe of the city with a number of khans where travellers could stay.

In this picture an artist called Yahya ibn Mahmud al-Wasiti drew three slaves greeting a merchant on his return to his palatial home in Baghdad in 1237

Daily life

There is very little evidence today of the huts and hovels in which the poor lived. These were made of baked mud and were only one storey high. They soon crumbled away to dust without leaving a trace. The houses of the very rich, however, have been excavated by archaeologists. Some palatial houses at Samarra, in central Iraq, had as many as 50 rooms. These surrounded one or more courtyards. Some of the rooms were used to store food. Some were for summer use only, when the weather was very hot.

They were kept cool with *punkas*. These were canvas panels which were raised and lowered by a slave to create a current of cool air. The canvas was usually kept moist to make the atmosphere of the house more comfortable. The very rich even bought huge slabs of ice from the mountains and put them in a dome inside the roof. Slaves with punkas fanned the ice to cool the rooms below. Keeping warm in winter was not usually a problem. Portable braziers burning charcoal were sufficient to raise the temperature on a chilly night.

Water came direct from a river, from a canal, from a well or from a small reservoir called a *cistern*. Water-carriers took water in skins to people living some distance away from sources of water like this. Water was also brought by channels or conduits to the public fountains, mosques and public baths in the city.

The homes of the well-to-do had baths and a system of drainage. Rainwater was caught by pipes and taken away into drainage pits underground. They also had lavatories built well away from the house. Some were deep pits like wells. They were covered over with stones and earth when full. Others were cleaned out with water at regular intervals by people who earned their living this way.

The streets were often very narrow. Some were only wide enough for two camels to pass. They were sometimes kept clean by road sweepers or by the inhabitants on either side. They threw water down to stop the dust flying in dry weather.

Inside a house, you would have seen very little furniture. Instead there were pillows, cushions, rugs, carpets, curtains and other soft furnishings.

Every town had a public bath-house, called a *hammam*. It was similar to a Roman bath-house (page 34). There were changing rooms, cool, warm and hot rooms, swimming pools, massage rooms, a furnace to supply heat, and rest rooms. Men and women used the hammam on different days. Like the Roman baths, they were popular because they were places to meet friends. They were healthy and people could cleanse themselves thoroughly before prayer.

The people of medieval Baghdad could enjoy a number of sports and entertainments. These included board games (such as chess and backgammon), going to the races in the hippodrome, wrestling, weight-lifting, swimming, running, cock-fighting, archery, horse-riding and polo using wooden polo sticks and leather balls.

Damascus had two walled racecourses close to a river. They were shaded by poplar trees. Ibn Jubayr said they were, 'so green as to seem to be rolls of silk brocade'. The sultan, Salah-al-din, played polo and raced his horses there.

This picture was painted by a Persian artist called Bihzad in 1494. It shows workers building a castle.

14.9 How can we use the picture above to find out more about the tools, machines, scaffolding and building methods used in an Islamic town? AT3/L5

14.10 Compare this picture with the one on page 167 showing building workers in Europe at about this time. Make a list of the similarities and differences between the two pictures. AT1C/L5

14.11 What sports are shown in the pictures on these pages? Why do you think they were popular with Muslim soldiers? AT3/L4

Every mosque had a library like this. Some were huge. Mosques in Baghdad and Damascus had up to half a million books apiece. There was a great demand for learning at the time of the Abbasids. One doctor even gave up the idea of moving house because he would have needed 400 camels just to carry his books! ▲

14.12 Compare the hunting picture on the right with the similar picture from Europe on page 173. Make a list of the similarities and differences you can see. AT1C/L5

15 Science and Technology

▶ *WHAT technology was used in the Islamic world in the Middle Ages?* ATIC ■
▶ *WHAT did their scientists, doctors and mathematicians achieve?* ATIA ■

Muslim technology

The people of the Islamic world used a number of machines to save labour and make their work easier. They used waterwheels to grind corn. They even made paper models to plan engineering projects to make sure they would work.

They were also expert at using water to grow crops. They dug irrigation canals. Some of these were in underground tunnels, called *qanats.* This slowed down the rate at which the water evaporated. They used the *shaduf*—a pole with a bucket on one end and a heavy weight on the other—to raise water from a river. They also used the *saqiyha.* This was a chain of pots fixed to a wheel. It was turned by an animal walking round and round.

Arab engineers also built wells, dams and aqueducts to supply water to the cities. Their skill in using water was even used to tell the time. Ibn Jubayr saw this water clock in Damascus in about 1183.

Source 15.A

To the right is a gallery set with yellow arches in each of which opens a small door to the number of hours of the day. A device had been built so that at the end of each hour a couple of brass balls fall from the mouths of two brass birds set above two cups, one below each bird. When the balls fall into the cups, a noise is heard from them. The yellow door for that hour closes at once. At night the light from a lamp throws its ray upon the disc in front of it, making it appear to the eyes as a red circle.

This painting of a Muslim water clock comes from a book of knowledge written in 1206. A float, like the one in a lavatory cistern, let a very small amount of water flow into another tank at a steady rate. This was used to tell the time, as you can see in Source 15.A. ▶

15.1 How did the water clock work during the day?

15.2 How did the water clock work at night?

Muslim science

Muslim scientists were far ahead of others in Europe at this time. Something of what they knew came from China and India. Some came from Arabic translations of the writings of Greek and Roman scientists. This meant that Muslim scholars could build on what had been found out before. They did not have to find it out again for themselves. These ideas and methods were later translated from Arabic back into Latin for the benefit of people in Europe. This was one of the results of the Crusades.

Like their counterparts in Europe, Arab chemists tried to turn ordinary metals into gold. This science was called *alchemy.* Some of the methods used by the alchemists are still used today. They knew how to use filters, for instance, and had already discovered the properties of chemicals like sulphuric acid.

Jabir ibn Hayyan (or Geber) was one of the greatest of the Muslim scientists. He lived from about 721 to 815. He was so well-known that people later used his name as the author of books written long after his death. The influence of these Arab scientists can be seen in words we still

A vertical waterwheel in Syria ▶

use today, such as *al-kimya* (chemistry), *al-qalawi* (alkali) and *al-iksir* (elixir).

Ibn al-Haytham, a scientist from Basra, lived and worked in Egypt around the year 1000. He helped to find out more about how the eye sees and how a lens works. He even made a pinhole camera. The ideas in his *Book of Optics* were so advanced that scientists only took them further some six hundred years later.

Mathematics

The Arabs were also the leading mathematicians of the Middle Ages. Like the scientists, they too learned much from the work of the Greeks and Romans. Al-Khwarizmi, who lived from about 780 to 850, wrote a book on *al-jabr*. He also used numerals which came from India, instead of Roman numerals. He made use of another Hindu discovery as well. This was the idea of a number 0. This was called *sifra* in Arabic. Al-Khwarizmi showed zero with a dot. The Hindus used a small circle instead. People in Europe later used Arabic numerals as well. They found them much easier to use in sums than Roman numerals.

Omar Khayyam, who was born in Iran in about 1050, was another great Muslim mathematician. He was also an astronomer, but even better known as a poet. He wrote the poem *The Rubaiyat of Omar Khayyam*. His most important work as a scientist came in 1074 when he made a correction to the Muslim calendar. This made it even more accurate than the calendar we use today.

15.3 Add the Roman numerals XIV and XVIII together. Why is it much easier to use the Arabic numerals 14 and 18 instead?

15.4 What do we call *al-jabr*? What is our word for *sifra*? The name al-Khwarizmi eventually became *algorithm* in English. See if you can find out what it means.

Navigation

The astrolabe was an aid to navigation. It was used to calculate the height of the sun.

Muslim scientists may have invented the compass, although it is possible they could have learned this from the Chinese. They certainly used an astrolabe to help them navigate their ships at sea.

Medicine

The care and treatment of people who were ill was far more advanced in Islamic countries than it was in Christian Europe. Arab doctors were particularly skilled at treating the ailments which were very common in a hot and dusty land, such as diseases of the eye.

The Umayyad and Abbasid caliphs built splendid hospitals. They trained and employed doctors and nurses to staff them. The medicines used there included drugs and extracts taken from plants and animals. Experts wrote books so that other physicians could use the same methods to cure diseases. Ibn Jubayr saw two fine Ayyabid hospitals like these when he visited Cairo in about 1183 (Source 15.B).

The first Muslim physicians began by studying the ideas of the Greek physicians in Arabic translations. However, they made many new discoveries of their own. In turn, their methods were later passed on to doctors in Europe. The Moorish surgeon Al-Zahrawi, for instance, lived in Spain from about 940 to 1013. He wrote a manual of surgery which was later translated into Latin. It was still being used at Oxford at the end of the eighteenth century. Al-Zahrawi described how to use over 200 surgical instruments and how to set bones. He used antiseptics, knew how to stitch wounds, and how to extract teeth. He also trained midwives and nurses.

Al-Razi (or Rhazes) was one of the greatest of these doctors. He lived from 865 to 925 and used plaster of Paris to set broken bones. Ibn Sina (or Avicenna), who died in 1037, was another doctor who wrote books describing diseases such as measles and smallpox and their treatment.

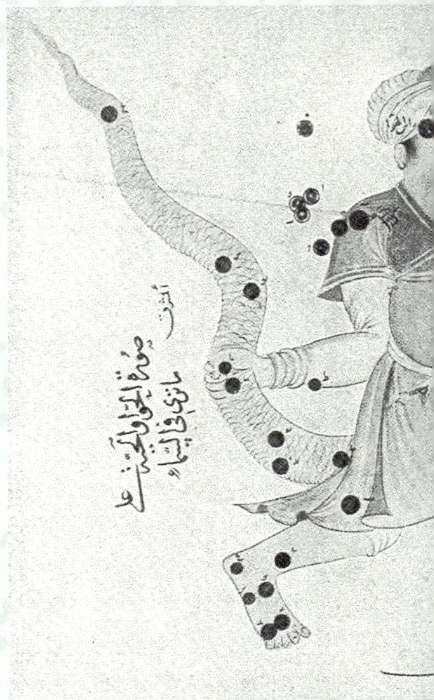

15.5 What does the picture above show? What are the black dots? Why do you think a merchant and a serpent are shown? What does a picture like this tell you about Muslim science? AT3/L5

Source 15.B

The Sultan [Salah-al-din] *can take great pride in the hospital in Cairo. It is large, handsome and almost like a palace. The director is a man of science and the hospital is stocked with a store of drugs and different types of medicine. The rooms are fully equipped with beds for the use of in-patients and attendants are on duty morning and evening to examine the sick and bring them food and medicine. Facing this hospital is another built for women and staffed with the people to attend them.*

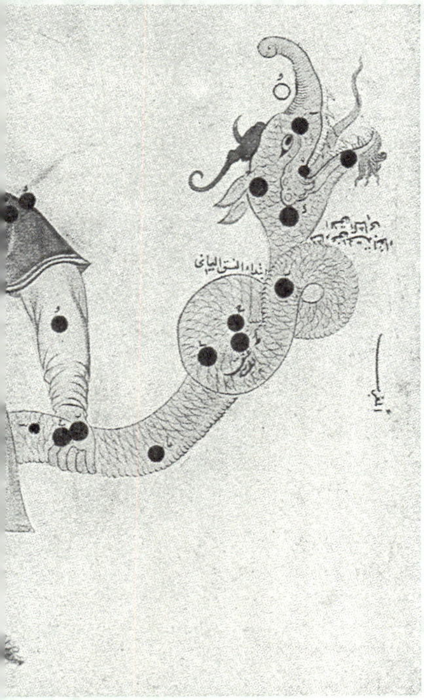

Many of these doctors and scientists living in Islamic countries were not actually Muslims themselves. Maimonides, for instance, was a Jewish doctor who lived between 1135 and 1204. He was born in Cordoba in Spain but went to work in Cairo as a physician at the court of Salah-al-din. Here he describes a typical working day.

Source 15.C

I live at Misr and the Sultan lives in Cairo about 2½ kilometres away. My duties to the Sultan are very heavy. I dare not leave Cairo but must stay during the greater part of the day in the palace. If one or two of the royal officers fall sick, I must attend to their healing. As a rule, I get to Cairo very early in the day. Even if nothing unusual happens, I do not return to Misr until the afternoon. I find my waiting rooms filled with people, both Jews and Gentiles, nobles and common people, judges and bailiffs, friends and foes.

I dismount from my animal, wash my hands, and attend to my patients. I write prescriptions and directions for their various ailments. Patients go in and out until nightfall.

Isaac Israeli, another Jewish doctor, who was born in Egypt in 832, wrote a number of medical works. In his *Guide for Physicians* he laid down a number of rules for doctors to follow.

Source 15.D

- *The chief task of the physician is to prevent disease. The majority of diseases are cured by nature. If you have the choice of bringing about a cure by nourishment or by drugs, choose the former.*
- *Never employ more than one drug at a time.*
- *Comfort and soothe the patient, even if you are in doubt, for by that means you support nature.*
- *If the patient does not follow your directions, give up the case.*
- *Do not visit the patient too often, nor remain long with him, unless the treatment demands it.*
- *Demand your fee from the patient when his illness is getting worse. The more he needs your treatment, the more highly you rate your cure, the higher will you stand in the eyes of the people.*

15.6 Which of Isaac Israeli's rules for doctors (Source 15.D) are still applicable today? In what ways was the daily routine of Maimonides (Source 15.C) similar to that of a doctor today? AT1A/L4

15.7 Write a paragraph describing the achievements of the medieval doctors and nurses of the Islamic world. AT1A/L5 AT1C ■

15.8 In what ways did Salah-al-din's hospital in Cairo (Source 15.B) resemble a modern hospital?

This picture shows a Muslim surgeon performing a Caesarian operation. He may have used opium as an anaesthetic. This method is still used today to deliver a baby when it is difficult for the baby to be born normally.

16 The Ottoman Empire

▶ *WHERE was the Ottoman Empire?* ATIC ■
▶ *HOW and WHY was it important?* ATIB ■
▶ *WHAT were the achievements of Mehmed the Conqueror and Suleiman the Magnificent?* ATIA ■

The Ottoman Empire

Towards the end of the Middle Ages, a new and powerful Muslim force took control of the eastern Mediterranean. This was the Ottoman Empire, based in Turkey. Its capital city of Istanbul (formerly Constantinople) became the centre of the Islamic world for the next 400 years.

Turkish horsemen

The Ottoman Empire began with the lands held by a warrior tribe in an area to the south of Constantinople. It was founded by a Turkish tribal prince called Osman, who captured a number of lands at the beginning of the fourteenth century. The empire continued to grow, largely at the expense of the Byzantines in Constantinople. In particular, they expanded into Europe through the Balkan countries such as Bulgaria.

On 25 September 1396 an Ottoman army led by the Sultan Bayazid won a convincing victory at Nicopolis on the Danube. They also defeated a large Hungarian army led by King Sigismund, even though it was strengthened by a large number of knights from other parts of Europe. Bayazid did not live long to enjoy his triumph. An even more ferocious Muslim army threatened from the east. This was the Asian leader Tamerlane. He defeated the Ottomans at Ankara in 1402 and Bayazid died in captivity the following year. This defeat was only a temporary setback, however. The next stage began with the accession of the Sultan Mehmed II ('the Conqueror') in 1451.

Mehmed the Conqueror

Mehmed II had been specially educated to become the next sultan. He attended a special school in the palace and was taught languages, warfare, government and science. On becoming sultan he made detailed plans to attack the Byzantine capital of Constantinople. Special guns were made. He even built a fort opposite the city to act as his base. On 29 May 1453 Ottoman soldiers swarmed across the city walls and took the city. The Byzantine Empire had lasted for a thousand years. Now an equally powerful empire took its place.

Mehmed II

16.1 An Ottoman writer described the Topkapi Palace in these words: 'Never before has a more delightful home been built by man'. What is there in the picture to justify this remark? AT3/L4

16.2 Write one or two sentences describing the Topkapi Palace from the picture.

16.3 Describe the weapons and armour of the Turkish horsemen (left). How do they differ from the Arab cavalry shown in the picture on pages 60–1? Suggest reasons for the differences. AT1A/L5

This picture of the Topkapi Palace in Istanbul was drawn by an Ottoman artist in the fifteenth century

Mehmed II made Istanbul his capital city. He encouraged people to live there. He even invited Christians, although this did not stop him turning some of the city's churches into mosques. This included the great cathedral, the Hagia Sophia. He also built new mosques, homes and buildings for his officials.

The picture map (above) shows the Topkapi Palace in Istanbul which Mehmed II built for himself on a headland overlooking the sea. It had sea walls and a heavily protected gatehouse. As you can see, the buildings were built around a series of courtyards.

The picture shows the Second Court where the sultan's ministers and advisers met. If you look closely, you can see the sultan himself in a private room. He is screened from his ministers by a curtain. Over 20 000 slaves worked there. The palace contained the throne room, council chambers for his ministers and the treasury where his money was stored. There was also a mosque, a swimming pool and barracks for the Janissaries (see page 81). He also built a school for slaves, a hospital, a bakery, kitchens and stables. A huge harem (private quarters for the women and children of the palace) was added at a later stage.

Suleiman at his court

Suleiman the Magnificent

Forty years after Mehmed's death in 1481, a new and even greater sultan succeeded to the throne. Suleiman I ('the Magnificent') succeeded to the throne in 1520 and reigned for nearly fifty years. This era is often called the Golden Age of the Ottomans. Not only did Suleiman have great wealth, he was also a great warrior and wise ruler. He employed efficient advisers as his ministers. He was also a man of culture who liked poetry and music.

In 1521 he seized Belgrade (now the capital of Yugoslavia) after a short siege. In 1526 he defeated the Hungarians at the Battle of Mohacs. Three years later he invaded Austria and besieged Vienna. This time his army was rebuffed. They suffered heavy losses through disease and famine and met stiff resistance when they attacked the city walls. After three weeks Suleiman decided to return home.

Suleiman celebrated his military success by making Istanbul a worthy capital for his great empire. He built the great Suleimaniye Mosque there and enlarged the Central Bazaar which had been built by Mehmed II in 1461. It is still said to be the largest shopping centre in the world under one roof. It had 67 streets lined with thousands of shops. Many of these streets, then as now, sold the same types of goods, such as carpets or rugs. Suleiman also rebuilt the magnificent Roman aqueduct which supplied Istanbul with fresh water.

The Siege of Belgrade in 1521

16.4 Compare the picture of Suleiman in his court with the painting of the Topkapi Palace on page 79. Make a list of the words you could use to describe the court of a Turkish sultan.

AT3/L4

16.5 What might have happened if Suleiman's army had conquered Vienna in 1529?

16.6 Compare the map of the Ottoman Empire in 1529 with the map of the Islamic world in 750 on page 60. Which parts of the Ottoman Empire in 1529 were not part of the Muslim world in 750?

AT1A ■ AT1C/L3

Suleiman riding with his army

16.7 Why do you think Mehmed II was called 'The Conqueror'? Why was Suleiman I called 'The Magnificent'? What did they achieve? AT1A ■ AT1B ■

16.8 What weapons, armour and methods of transport did Suleiman's forces use in battle? AT3/L4

16.9 Draw a Time Line like the one on page 67 to show the growth of the Ottoman Empire. AT1A/L3

Suleiman vastly increased the size of the Ottoman Empire. Now it included most of the Balkans, part of Russia, Turkey, Iraq, part of Iran, Egypt and much of North Africa. Throughout this empire, his soldiers and engineers built bridges, roads and caravanserais (see page 71) for travellers. Domes, minarets, bazaars and Turkish baths were built on similar lines to those in Istanbul itself. He also established the rule of law. The same system of justice was applied throughout the Ottoman Empire.

Map of the Ottoman Empire at its peak in 1529

An English observer called Anthony Jenkinson watched a procession in which Suleiman was preceded by 6000 cavalrymen dressed in scarlet. Then came 10 000 foot soldiers in yellow velvet. There were also 16 000 Janissaries in the procession. These were Christian slaves from the Balkans who were trained from childhood to fight for the sultan as an élite bodyguard. Then came 1000 pages all dressed in gold and 13 royal pages in gold or silver.

Source 16.A

Immediately after them came the Great Turk himself, with great pomp and magnificence, showing in his features and gestures a wonderful majesty. He was mounted upon a goodly white horse, wearing a robe of cloth of gold, embroidered most richly with the most precious stones.

After him followed six goodly young ladies, mounted upon fine white hackneys, clothed in cloth of silver, which were of the fashion of men's garments, embroidered very richly with pearl and precious stones.

This was not all. There were 50 more Janissaries and 3000 other men and a vast army of camels.

Suleiman died in 1566. He was succeeded by his son Selim II. Five years later, on 5 October 1571, the Turkish battle fleet of about 250 war galleys was heavily defeated at the Battle of Lepanto by a combined fleet of 225 galleys and galleasses (larger galleys) from Venice and Spain. The Turks lost most of their ships and suffered heavy casualties. Their naval force was destroyed. With it went their last chance of any further extension of the Ottoman Empire in the Mediterranean.

MEDIEVAL REALMS

FOCUS

▶ *WHY did Duke William of Normandy invade England in 1066?* ATIB ■

▶ *HOW did William and the Normans defeat Harold and the Saxons at the Battle of Hastings?* ATIC ■

17 The NORMAN CONQUEST

At 9.00 a.m. on Saturday 14 October 1066, 'the terrible sound of war trumpets' was heard in a valley north of Hastings in Sussex. Saxon and Norman soldiers were about to fight a terrible battle. They fought to decide who would be King of England: Duke William of Normandy or Harold, the Saxon Earl of Wessex. Harold had ruled much of England for nearly ten years but William had been promised the throne.

Why the battle was fought

The conflict began when Edward the Confessor died on 5 January 1066 without any children. It was not clear, therefore, who would succeed him as king. The dying Edward suggested it should be Harold, as you can see from the first of these extracts written by people who lived at that time.

Source 17.A

Harold, whom the king had named as his successor, was chosen king by the chief nobles of all England; and on the same day [6 January 1066] *was crowned with great ceremony. He immediately began to abolish unjust laws and to make good ones.*

Source 17.B

There came the annoying news that the land of England had lost its king, and that Harold had been crowned in his place. This cold-hearted Englishman did not wait for the people to choose, but breaking his oath, and with the support of a few evil-minded supporters, seized the throne of the best of kings on the very day of his funeral, and when all the people were in mourning.

17.1 Which source was written by a Norman? Which was written by a Saxon? Give reasons for your answer. AT2/L4

17.2 How do the two authors differ in what they write about Harold? What examples of bias can you find in what they say? AT2 ■

Site of the Battle of Hastings. In the distance you can see Telham Hill where the Norman soldiers assembled before attacking the Saxons across this valley. In those days it was open ground with wet marsh away to the right and thickly wooded ground to the left.

17.3 Which man is William in this picture? Which is Harold? How can you tell that Harold swore a sacred oath? AT3/L4

17.4 What was William's chief complaint against Harold in 1066?

Part of the Bayeux Tapestry (see page 84). Pictures like this tell us what happened at the Battle of Hastings in 1066.

Although William was Edward's distant cousin, he was not in line to the throne. When he became king it was by force—by the conquest of England. However, he had been promised the throne. Edward made the first of these promises in 1051 when Duke William visited England at a time when Harold was out of favour with the king. The second promise was made by Harold himself in 1064 after he had been taken prisoner by a French count. Duke William secured his freedom but made Harold swear a solemn oath before letting him return to England. A Norman writer tells us:

Source 17.C

Harold swore his loyalty to the Duke and took an oath of his own free will that he would use all his influence and wealth to ensure that after the death of King Edward the kingdom of England should pass to the Duke.

On the left you can see a Norman picture of Harold taking this oath. It comes from the Bayeux Tapestry. The Latin words read 'WHERE HAROLD MADE AN OATH TO DUKE WILLIAM'.

The invaders

As you saw in Source 17.B, the Normans were furious when they heard Harold had been crowned king. William decided to invade England, although some of his barons thought it too risky. He built a large invasion fleet and recruited a large army of soldiers from Brittany, Flanders and other parts of France, as well as from Normandy. He promised land in England and the spoils of victory as a reward. When everything was ready, he waited for a favourable wind.

The Saxons, meanwhile, prepared to repel the expected invasion. Then in September Harold heard bad news. The King of Norway, Harold Hardrada (who also had a claim to the English throne), had landed near York with an army of Norsemen. Harold marched north to face him. On 25 September he surprised and defeated Hardrada at the Battle of Stamford Bridge. However, by a stroke of bad luck, the wind in the Channel changed in William's favour while Harold was still in Yorkshire. William was thus able to make an unopposed landing at Pevensey in Sussex on 28 September. Without thinking, Harold rushed his exhausted soldiers south again. In his haste he left part of the army behind.

The Bayeux Tapestry

We know what happened next and about the events leading up to the battle from two types of evidence. First, there are the scenes from the Bayeux Tapestry. Second, there are the stories written by monks.

The Bayeux Tapestry is like a strip cartoon, 70 metres long but only 50 centimetres wide. Needlewomen, who may have been English, stitched it by threading coloured wools through the canvas to make 58 scenes. Latin captions tell us what is happening in each scene.

The tapestry tells the story of the conquest in pictures. The first part shows Harold in Normandy in 1064. Then comes the death of Edward the Confessor and Harold's coronation. After this we see the Normans preparing for the invasion. They cut down trees to build ships. They load the ships with horses, helmets, swords, lances and even barrels of wine. A sequence of scenes shows the ships sailing across the Channel and landing in England. There are even scenes showing the cruelty of the Norman soldiers, burning Saxon homes in Sussex and stealing cattle, sheep and pigs.

Experts think the tapestry was embroidered before 1077 when it may have been put on display in the new cathedral at Bayeux. It was probably paid for by Bishop Odo of Bayeux who is shown in several of the scenes. Odo was William's half-brother and had a reason, therefore, to glory in his brother's exploits. He even fought at Hastings himself, carrying a mace.

The story of the Norman Conquest

Most of the monks and priests who wrote about the Norman Conquest, such as William of Jumièges (Source 17.D), were Normans themselves. This is why we have to treat some of the things they say with caution. They may have been afraid to tell the truth or they may have wanted to win the favour of the king or of a rich and powerful bishop or abbot.

Source 17.D William of Jumièges

Duke William hastily built a fleet of three thousand ships. He filled it with mighty horses and most valiant men, with hauberks [coats of mail made from wire rings] *and helmets. Then when a favourable wind began to blow, he set sail, and crossing the sea landed at Pevensey where he built a castle at once. Then with others he hurried to Hastings where he built a similar castle.*

17.5 Is there any reason to think the Bayeux Tapestry may give us a one-sided version of the story of the Norman Conquest? AT2 ■

17.6 Write down the words in Sources 17.D and 17.E which describe things you can see in the pictures on these pages. Which picture tells you there was 'a favourable wind'? Why? AT3/L4

17.7 Which clue in Source 17.D tells us that William of Jumièges was a Norman writer?

17.8 Which of the Bayeux Tapestry scenes on this page shows: (a) Norman archers (b) Saxon house-carls (c) Norman knights? AT3/L4

17.9 Draw a picture of each type of soldier and label the weapons and armour you can identify. AT3/L4

Source 17.E
William of Poitiers

In the front he put foot soldiers armed with arrows and crossbows. In the second rank came the more heavily armed foot soldiers who wore hauberks. Lastly came the groups of knights. William rode among them himself, showing great courage. It gave him a good position from which to give orders by hand or by voice. The English took up their position on higher ground, on a hill next to the forest. They were on foot and stood close together.

William of Poitiers

The most detailed account of the battle was written in about 1071 by a priest called William of Poitiers. He was born in Normandy and had once served as a soldier there. He did not take part in the Battle of Hastings himself, but must have heard tales from the soldiers who did. In Source 17.E he describes how William positioned his soldiers to face the Saxons.

The Norman knights carried kite-shaped shields and wore hauberks and conical helmets with eye guards (visors). They fought with swords, maces (clubs) and lances.

Harold's best soldiers were his *house-carls*. They fought on foot with battle axes, wore hauberks and also carried long, kite-shaped shields which they placed close together to form a shield wall for protection. On either side were the peasant soldiers of the *fyrd*. They were armed with axes, javelins and slings with which they threw stones.

The Norman victory

The Bayeux Tapestry and the account written by William of Poitiers (Source 17.F) tell us about incidents which could have led to a Saxon victory.

Source 17.F William of Poitiers

The Norman foot-soldiers and knights from Brittany were frightened by the violence of the assault. They fled before the English. The whole army of the Duke was in danger of defeat. Some Normans even believed their duke and lord was dead.

But Duke William stopped them retreating further. He took off his helmet, and standing before them bareheaded cried, 'Look at me well, I am still alive and by the grace of God I shall yet prove victor.' The Normans were encouraged by these words. They surrounded thousands of pursuing Saxons and rapidly cut them down so that not one escaped.

Later that day the Normans pretended to retreat and then pounced on any Saxons who had been foolish enough to chase them. William of Poitiers claimed the Normans did this twice with great success.

Gradually the Normans, with their superior weapons and mounted knights, overwhelmed the Saxons. William of Poitiers describes the end of the battle in Source 17.G.

Draw a Time Line For 1066

Use information from this chapter to find the exact date for each of the events listed below. Arrange these events in chronological order. Draw a Time Line like the one on page 49.

- Death of King Harold
- Death of King Edward
- Harold crowned king
- William crowned king
- Battle of Hastings
- Battle of Stamford Bridge
- Norman landing at Pevensey

Source 17.G William of Poitiers

Evening was now falling, and the English saw that they could not hold out much longer. They knew also that their king and many of their greatest men had fallen. They began to fly as swiftly as they could. Many lay on the ground bathed in blood. Many fallen to the ground were trampled to death under the hooves of runaway horses.

17.10 Which parts of the story of the battle told in Source 17.F are shown in the scenes on this page? AT1C/L5

17.11 Look at the Bayeux Tapestry scenes and all the written sources in this chapter on the Norman Conquest. Make a list of pictures, words and phrases which tell you something about the terrors and horrors of warfare in the Middle Ages. AT1C/L6 AT2/L6

17.12 How and why did William let the Norman soldiers see his face in the middle of the battle?

Death of Harold

As you can see from the scene above, we do not know for certain how Harold died. The Bayeux Tapestry shows three soldiers under the Latin words *HIC HAROLD REX INTERFECTUS EST*. This means 'HERE KING HAROLD HAS BEEN KILLED'.

But which soldier is King Harold? The man closest to the word HAROLD seems to have an arrow in his eye. This is why many people think Harold was killed by a Norman archer. But look closely. Is the arrow in his eye? Has he 'BEEN KILLED'?

The man holding the battle axe has been badly wounded. He is falling backwards and may have been killed by a blow from the sword held by the knight on horseback. But why has the knight slumped forward?

17.13 Which of the three men in the Bayeux Tapestry picture do you think is Harold? How did he die? Write one or two sentences to explain your choice. AT2/L6

After the battle

William returned to Hastings and waited for the people of Britain to accept him as King. When they failed to do so, he destroyed land and property in the south and marched on London. When he was near the city, people went to meet him.

Source 17.H

The chief men of London and many others came to him, and giving hostages they surrendered and swore they would be loyal to him.

On Christmas Day, 1066, he was crowned William, King of England in Westminster Abbey. The Conqueror had won. But, as you will soon see, the Norman Conquest was not yet over.

18 BRITAIN UNDER THE NORMANS

FOCUS

▶ *WHAT effect did the Norman Conquest have on Britain?* ATIB ■

▶ *HOW did the Norman Conquest affect the English language?* ATIB ■

The knight on horseback was the key to winning a battle at the start of the Middle Ages. He was the medieval equivalent of a tank.

Source 18.A

*AD **1067**: This year the king marched to Devonshire and besieged the city of Exeter for eighteen days. Then the king was told the people in the North had gathered themselves together and would stand against him if he came. Whereupon he went to Nottingham, and built there a castle; and he advanced to York, and there built two castles; and the same at Lincoln.*

The rewards of victory

William gave generous rewards to the barons who fought with him at Hastings in 1066. They were given large estates as he advanced deeper into England. In return they swore to be loyal and faithful to him. They

York Castle

Lincoln Cathedral

18.1 Where did William build castles in 1067? What was their purpose? AT3/L3

18.2 Look at the Bayeux Tapestry scene on page 84. How do you think the Normans could build a castle so quickly? What do you think it was made of? AT3/L3

18.3 The castle in the photograph was built of stone at a later date. What does it have in common with the castle shown in the Bayeux Tapestry? AT1C/L3

18.4 Look at the picture of the medieval knight. Write two or three sentences describing the armour and weapons you can see. Was the knight sensibly dressed to face the enemy on a medieval battlefield? What big difference is there compared with the clothes worn by a modern soldier? Where would you see a shield like this today? AT1C/L5

also promised to send knights when the king needed them for a war. This was the *feudal system* which was common in Europe at that time. You can read more about it on pages 96–9.

Most of the land given away by William belonged to Saxon nobles called *thegns*. Many had been killed at Hastings. Since most had backed Harold, William had no qualms about giving their lands to the barons who went with him to England. As a result, land held by 4000 Saxon thegns was given to no more than 200 Norman barons and earls. Some of their estates were huge. They divided this land into smaller holdings and gave it to their supporters, the lesser nobles and knights. They held the land in return for services which they owed their lord, the baron.

Large estates were also held by the Church. William tried to make sure that those in the Church were loyal to him. He got rid of many Saxon abbots and bishops and appointed Normans. The problem was simple enough: how best to tighten the Norman grip on Britain. It proved hard to solve.

Quelling rebellion

William's problems began when he was crowned king in 1066. From now on, he and the Normans ran the government, collected its taxes and made its laws. He also had to conquer the rest of England to bring it into line. To do this he had to defeat the rival claimants to the throne, put down rebellions and clamp down hard on local acts of defiance. He had about 10 000 Norman soldiers to do this. But they were greatly outnumbered by the people of Britain: a million Saxons or more. Few of the Normans spoke English and only a few of the Saxons spoke French.

William was determined to show the Saxons he would not stand any opposition to his rule. We know how he did it from *The Anglo-Saxon Chronicle*. This was a diary of the years before and after the Norman Conquest. It was written by Saxon monks. They wrote down the main events year by year as in Source 18.A.

Rival claims to the throne

There were a number of rival claimants to the English throne:

1 As you saw on page 83, Harold Hardrada of Norway was killed by Harold and the Saxons at the battle of Stamford Bridge. Hardrada had claimed the throne because an earlier King of Norway, Cnut (Canute), had been King of England as well as King of Norway and Denmark.

2 Now that Hardrada was dead, Swein, King of Denmark, claimed the throne for much the same reason.

3 King Harold's sons, Godwine, Edmund and Magnus, also had good reason to think the throne should be theirs. Edward the Confessor had wanted their father to succeed him. This had been accepted by the Saxon Witan (the leading men who advised the king). In any case, they wanted to avenge their father. One of them came over from Ireland in 1067 with a naval force and 'would have stormed Bristol but the people bravely withstood them.'

4 Lastly, there was Edgar the Atheling. He was only a boy of 16 in 1066. *Atheling* was a word which meant a person with royal blood. Edgar was the great-grandson of Ethelred the Unready who reigned between 978 and 1016. Edgar had been chosen king by some of the Saxons immediately after Hastings. However, he later swore an oath of loyalty to William instead of pursuing his own claim to the throne.

Trouble in the north

You can see some of the problems faced by William and the Normans in these extracts from *The Anglo-Saxon Chronicle.*

Source 18.B

AD 1068: *This year King William gave Earl Robert the earldom over Northumberland; but the landsmen* [local people] *attacked him in Durham, and slew him. Soon afterwards Edgar Atheling came with all the Northumbrians to York but King William came from the South with a large army and put them to flight and plundered the town. The Atheling went back again to Scotland. After this came Harold's sons from Ireland, about midsummer, with sixty-four ships.* [They were defeated] *and Harold's sons went back to Ireland again.*

Source 18.C

AD 1069: *This year came from Denmark three of the sons of King Swein with two hundred and forty ships into the Humber. They were joined by*

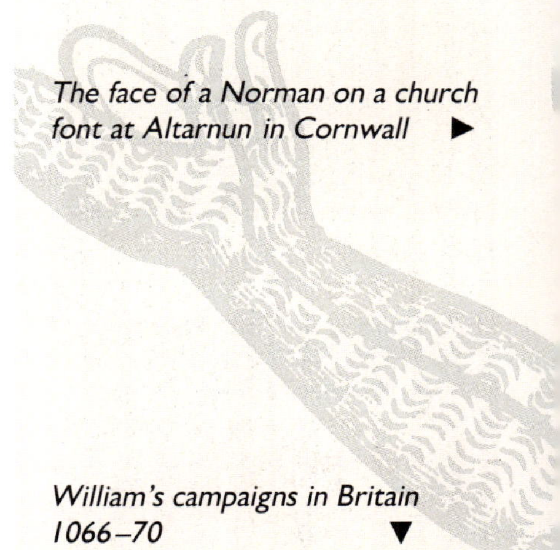

The face of a Norman on a church font at Altarnun in Cornwall ▶

William's campaigns in Britain 1066–70 ▼

18.5 Find the position of your town or village on the map. By which year did your area become part of Norman Britain? AT1A/L3

18.6 Give at least two reasons which might help to explain why Wales and Scotland were not conquered at this time. AT1B/L4

18.7 What two main types of opponent did William have to face in 1068 and 1069? How did he deal with them? AT1C/L4

18.8 Which 'shire' is referred to in Source 18.C? What happened to it?

18.9 Imagine William has just died. Use the information in Source 18.F to sum up his life in two or three sentences for a television news bulletin. AT1C ■

18.10 How would you have greeted this news if you had been (a) a poor Saxon peasant (b) a Norman knight (c) an English priest? In each case write a sentence to explain the reason for your attitude. AT1C/L6

18.11 What were William's good points? What were his bad points? Are these facts or opinions? AT2 ■

the Northumbrians and all the landsmen. Riding and marching full merrily with an immense army they advanced to York where they stormed and demolished the castle and slew many hundreds of Frenchmen. When the king heard this, he went northward despoiling and laying waste the shire.

William the Conqueror

By 1071 the Normans were firmly established in Britain. William had conquered England. In the next few years he also invaded Wales and Scotland, as you can see in Sources 18.D and 18.E from *The Anglo-Saxon Chronicle*.

Source 18.D

AD *1072:* *This year King William led a land and naval force to Scotland but found nothing there of value. King Malcolm* [of Scotland], *however, came and made peace with King William, and gave hostages, and became his man; whereupon the king returned home with all his force.*

AD *1079:* *This year came King Malcolm into England with a large army, which plundered Northumberland till it came to the Tyne, and slew many hundreds of men, and carried home much coin, and treasure, and men in captivity.*

Source 18.E

AD *1081:* *This year the king led an army into Wales and there freed many hundreds of men.*

Despite these offensives, William had more pressing problems to face back home in Normandy. King Philip of France and the Count of Anjou were threatening his French possessions. In 1087 he

went from Normandy into France with an army, and made war upon his own lord Philip, the king, and slew many of his men, and burned the town of Mantes.

But as William rode in triumph through the blazing ruins of Mantes, his horse stumbled and he was thrown to the ground. He died later at Rouen on 9 September 1087.

We know what William was like as a man from a summary of his career written by a Saxon monk some time after 1087.

Source 18.F

This King William was a very wise man and very rich. He was mild to the good men that loved God and very severe to those who opposed him. So very stern was he also and quick-tempered, that no man dared do anything against his will. He put earls in prison, even his own brother Odo, who was a very rich bishop in Normandy.

Amongst other things is not to be forgotten the peace he brought to this land. A man could travel across his kingdom weighed down with gold. No man dared slay another. He truly reigned over England. The land of the Britons [Wales] *was in his power and he built castles therein.*

It is true men had much distress at this time and very many sorrows. Castles he let men build, and miserably oppress the poor. He was greedy. He made many deer parks. Whosoever slew a hart or a hind was deprived of his eyesight. These things have we written concerning him, both good and evil.

Effects of the Norman Conquest

The effects of the Norman Conquest were seen in different ways by people in England. You can see this in the extracts below. Sources 18.G and 18.I are from *The Anglo-Saxon Chronicle* and were probably written by Saxon monks shortly after the events they describe. Source 18.H was written by a monk called William of Malmesbury who claimed to have Norman and English parents. He was born in about 1090 and died in 1143.

Source 18.G

In 1067 William laid very heavy tribute [taxes] *on men, and in Lent went over sea to Normandy, taking with him Archbishop Stigand, and Abbot Aylnoth of Glastonbury, and the child Edgar, and the Earls Edwin, Morkar, and Waltheof, and many other good men of England. Bishop Odo and Earl William lived here afterwards, and built castles widely through this country, and harassed the miserable people; and ever since has evil increased very much.*

Source 18.H

This [the Norman Conquest] *was a fatal day for England, a sad disruption of our dear country, through its change of masters.*

Drinking all night was a common practice among the Anglo-Saxons. They spent their wealth in this way while living in shabby and inferior houses. They were not like the Normans and French, who lived more sensible lives in noble and splendid mansions.

The arrival of the Normans revived religion, which everywhere had grown lifeless in England. Churches were founded in every village and monasteries in the towns and cities. They were built in a style which hadn't been seen before.

Source 18.I

AD 1075: *Earl Roger and Earl Waltheof, and bishops and abbots, resolved to drive the king out of the realm of England. But the traitors of King William were subdued.*

18.12 Do you think Sources 18.G and 18.I are likely to be reliable sources of information about the effects of the Norman Conquest? AT3 ■

18.13 How did the monks who wrote *The Anglo-Saxon Chronicle* change their minds between 1067 and 1075? What reasons may help to explain this? AT3/L4

18.14 How do the two photographs below and the photographs of church doorways on page 94 support what William of Malmesbury said in Source 18.H? AT3/L5

18.15 Why do you think William took Archbishop Stigand and 'other good men of England' back to Normandy in 1067? AT3/L3

18.16 Read about the effects of the Norman Conquest on the opposite page. Make a list of other French words or phrases we use in English today.

18.17 Draw a diagram like a spider with different pictures to show the effect the Norman Conquest had on Britain. AT1B ■

This hut was built at West Stow in Suffolk to show what the home of a Saxon thegn might have looked like 300 years before the Norman Conquest

The Norman castle at Castle Rising in Norfolk

Here are just a few of the ways in which the Norman Conquest of Britain changed the lives of the people and the appearance of the country.

1 **Castles** William and his barons built a large number of castles across Britain to make it easier to hold on to the lands they had taken. The first castles were built of timber. Later castles, like Dover (shown here), were built of stone. ▶

◀ 2 **Cathedrals and Churches** These were built by the Normans in a distinctive style. Some were even built using stone from Caen in Normandy. Great cathedrals were built in a number of cities, such as Winchester, Norwich, Peterborough and Durham (shown in the photograph).

3 **Abbeys** There were already a number of important abbeys in Britain before 1066. But after the conquest the Normans helped the great monastic orders such as the Cistercians to build fine monasteries, like Tintern Abbey in Gwent (in the photograph). ▶

The New Forest

4 **Towns** The Normans also built a number of new towns and made some existing towns bigger. They built a new town at Bury St Edmunds in Suffolk. It was laid out like a Roman town in front of the Abbey. It had a grid of straight streets crossing each other at right angles. These can still be seen today. Some towns had colonies of French settlers. We know about these from street names, like Petty France in London, French Row in St Albans and French Street in Southampton.

5 **Everyday Language** The Normans spoke French and made this the everyday language of the government and the law courts. This is why a number of the terms used by British lawyers today come from French, such as curfew (*couvre-feu*) felony (*félonie*) and jury (*jurer*).

6 **Forests** William the Conqueror and the other Norman kings who came after him, such as William II (William Rufus) and Henry I, were keen huntsmen. William Rufus was actually killed while hunting in the New Forest (shown above). These kings took over large areas of forest and made them royal property. Drastic punishments were handed out to poachers who killed the king's deer. The ordinary people hated the king's forest laws, which tried to stop them catching birds and animals to help make the food they produced go further.

7 **Europe** The Norman Conquest also meant that Britain was now firmly linked to France and western Europe. In the past her ties had been with Scandinavia, such as when Cnut (Canute) had been king of England, Denmark and Norway.

Britain and Normandy

You might think the Normans would have learned to speak English soon after the conquest: but you would be wrong. In practice, they treated England as a French colony. Normandy was their real home. For the next 138 years they ruled them both as if they were one country. For an even longer period, about three hundred years, England was ruled by kings who could not even speak English. Richard the Lionheart, often thought of as a great British hero, only lived in England for six months of his ten-year reign. It was King John who first made England his home. He had to. He lost Normandy, Anjou and other French possessions to the king of France in 1205.

The influence of the French was felt in many other ways. They changed the way in which churches, cathedrals and castles were built. Norman architects had a distinctive style. Saxon churches were simple in design with small doors and windows. Norman arches were massive. They were semi-circular in shape like those of the Romans (see page 29). This is why they are called *Romanesque* in Europe.

18.18 Look at the photographs on the left. Which is the Norman door and which is the Saxon door? AT1C ■

18.19 What type of decoration did the Normans use round their arches? AT1C/L4

18.20 How do you think you could recognise a door or window built by the Normans? AT1C/L4

The English language

The Normans made French the language which had to be used in courts of law and by the officials who worked for the king. French was the language spoken by the Normans and by educated Saxons. But English was the language of the common people. The English language was like a tree. It had many different roots. The Romans gave it Latin and Greek words. The Angles, Saxons, Jutes and Vikings also added to the mixture. In 1066 it was a language which was spoken rather than written.

English could have died out when the Normans made French (and Latin) the language of government in Britain. But English survived because it was the everyday language of hundreds of thousands of ordinary people. A medieval poet said 'Common men know no French. Among a hundred scarcely one.' Few people could read or write in those days. This meant they had no real reason to learn French. Only educated Saxons learned the language to give themselves prestige and the chance to work as a lawyer or for the king.

▲ *Delicate Norman carvings in stone round the arch of the South Door of the Norman church at Kilpeck in Herefordshire*

18.21 Read Source 18.J. Stratford is in the East End of London. What type of French did the prioress speak? How did it differ from that of one of the king's officials? AT1A/L5

18.22 Look at the picture on the right. Write one or two sentences describing this page from a medieval copy of a book by Chaucer. How does it differ from a book published today? AT1A ■ AT1C/L3

18.23 Use the dates given in this chapter to draw up a Time Line of Norman Britain. Make it like the Time Line shown on page 49. Show only the important events. AT1A/L3

For their part, many of the Norman barons, bishops, abbots and priests spoke only French and Latin. They made little or no effort to learn English. In 1191 a Norman bishop in disgrace tried to flee the country dressed as a woman. He was found out when an Englishwoman at Dover asked him a question. She could only speak English. He could only speak French.

But some Normans did learn enough of the language to make themselves understood. The lord and lady of the manor could not ignore the language spoken by their servants and by the people who worked on their estates. They soon picked up English words and phrases. Their children and their children's children picked up even more.

In time, after two or three hundred years, English began to replace French at all levels of society. It was first used in official documents in about 1250. These had previously been written in Latin rather than in French. By the end of the fourteenth century, many more documents were written in English. When Geoffrey Chaucer wrote *The Canterbury Tales* at the end of the fourteenth century, he wrote it in English. In this work, one of the finest written in the English language, he described one of the Canterbury pilgrims. She was a prioress—the head of a community of nuns in an abbey or priory.

Source 18.J

And French she spoke full fair and elegantly,
After the school of Stratford atte Bowe,
For French of Paris was to her unknown.

19 FEUDALISM

Coronation of a king in the early fourteenth century

The monarchy

At the time of the Norman Conquest almost everyone in Britain was a Christian. Together with the other Christian lands of Europe, Britain was part of Christendom. It was held together by monarchs, like the king of England, who got their power partly from the sword and partly from the Church.

William the Conqueror was the first of a long line of such monarchs in England. He took the crown by force and for a long time this was also how the monarchs after him held on to the throne. However, as you can see in Source 19.A (from *The Anglo-Saxon Chronicle*), he also took great care to make it clear that it was God's will he should be king.

Feudalism

If a Christian king got his authority to govern from God, likewise a baron got his power from the king. When William rewarded his barons with land, they did homage to him by swearing an oath of *fealty* (loyalty) to him (Source 19.B). They agreed to be his men in return for the gift of land (called a *fief*). People who owed a duty like this in return for a gift or fief were called *vassals*. This system was called *feudalism*.

FOCUS

► *WHAT was feudalism?* AT1C ■

► *HOW did feudalism affect the monarchy, barons and the people?* AT1B ■

Source 19.A

1066: *Then on midwinter's day Archbishop Aldred hallowed him to king at Westminster, and gave him possession with the books of Christ, and also made him swear, before he would set the crown on his head, that he* [William] *would govern this nation as well as any king before him did.*

19.1 What symbols of a king's power are shown in the picture of the coronation of a medieval king? Why do you think the people close to a monarch always made the coronation a big religious ceremony? How can you tell this from Source 19.A and the picture? AT1C ■

Source 19.B

1086: *This year the king wore his crown and held his court at Winchester at Easter. Afterwards he came to Salisbury; and all the landholders of substance in England went there as well and they all submitted to him, and became his men, and swore oaths of allegiance, that they would be faithful to him against all others.*

19.2 What did the writer mean when he said the landholders 'all submitted to him, and became his men'? AT3/L3

19.3 How does the seal on the next page reveal the way in which the early kings held on to power? AT3/L3

Labour services

The feudal system was like a ladder made up of different levels of society. At the top was the king on his own. At the bottom stood the great mass of ordinary peasants. Worst off were the serfs or slaves who did not hold land at all. Next in misery came the bordars and cottars who farmed small plots of about a hectare or so in return for labour services which they owed their lord. Above them came the villeins or villagers who had larger holdings of land. Some even employed other peasants to work for them.

These peasants were all vassals. They owed labour services to the lord of the manor who was above them, such as a knight, an abbot, bishop or noble. A labour service meant doing so much work each week or year for the lord of the manor. These services were recorded on documents as faithfully as if they were rents or money owing to the lord. You can see an extract from one of these documents below. It lists some of the jobs which a peasant woman had to perform on the Manor of Laughton in Sussex in 1292.

Source 19.C

Alice at Hamme holds 1 dwelling house and 14 acres [5.6 hectares] *of land and meadow. She shall make up a fifth part of a plough team for ploughing the lord's land or she shall pay 2d. And she must carry dung in her cart for 2 days or she shall pay 5d. She must harrow with her horse for 3 days or she shall pay 3d. And she shall carry the lord's corn in harvest for 2 days or pay 5d.*

This is the great seal of King Henry I. It was made by pressing the king's stamp into soft sealing wax to make the impression you can see here.

19.4 How is the king's name shown on this seal? Why was it written in Latin and not in English? Why isn't it shown as HENRY I so we can tell it apart from the seal used by HENRY II? AT1A/L5

19.5 Read Source 19.C. What farm animals and equipment did Alice appear to own? How do we know from this that medieval peasants often worked together as a team? How did her work for the lord vary during the year? How could she avoid doing this work? AT1C ■

This picture shows peasants working in the fields within sight of the great medieval castle owned by their lord. Many were glad of his protection at times when there were outbreaks of disorder. ▶

Grievances

Most peasants were not as lucky as Alice. Many hated having to work for the lord. They wanted to have the option (like Alice) of paying a rent instead. Above all they wanted their freedom. Freemen did not have to work at the lord's bidding.

The peasants had other grievances as well. The lord of the manor had many rights over the peasants who were his vassals. He (or she) could bring them before the manorial court (of law) and punish them. Peasants had to get permission from the lord before they could marry. They were not allowed to leave the village without his permission. If they escaped and were caught within twelve months, they were punished.

A Norman peasant

◀ *Domesday Book. The word* domesday *or* doomsday *means 'day of reckoning'.*

Domesday Book

We know a lot about feudalism and how it affected the peasants from an amazing document called the Domesday Book. This recorded facts about the villages and towns of Norman Britain in very great detail.

Source 19.D from *The Anglo-Saxon Chronicle*

AD 1085: *The king sent his men all over England into each shire telling them to find out what land the king himself had, and what land his archbishops, bishops, abbots and earls had. So very exactly, indeed, did he order them to carry it out, that there was not a yard of land, not even an ox, nor a cow, nor a swine was there left, that was not set down in this document. And all the records were afterwards brought to him* [at Winchester in 1086].

We know how the king's men worked from another document written at this time.

Source 19.E

They enquire by oath of the sheriff of each shire and of all the barons, priests, the reeve [a type of farm manager] *and six villeins from each town. They ask them the name of the manor. Who held it in the time of King Edward the Confessor* [before 1066] *and who holds it now* [1086]*?*

The king's men asked many other questions as well.

Source 19.F

How many hides [about 40 hectares] *are there in each manor? How many ploughs on the domain* [the land belonging to the manor]*? How many villeins are there? How many cottars? How many freemen? How much wood? How much meadow? How much pasture? What mills? What fish ponds? What was it worth in the time of King Edward the Confessor? How much is it worth now? Can more be got out of it than now?*

A Norman baron

19.6 Look at Sources 19.D to 19.F. How did the king's men get their information? Did they count everything themselves? Give reasons for wondering if the Domesday Book is really accurate. AT2 ■

19.7 Find the word SUFFOLK on the Domesday extract (right). On the next line see if you can find *car* standing for *carucates*. How many numbers like this—i, ii, iii—are shown against *car*? AT3/L3

19.8 Find similar abbreviations for *villeins* and *bordars* on the next line. How many of each are listed for the Abbot's manor at Risby? AT3/L3

19.9 What do you think it means when an entry says 'Then 2 ploughs, now 4'? When was 'then'? AT3/L3

19.10 Why do you think William ordered the Domesday survey to be carried out? AT1B ■

19.11 The next time you visit your public library, look at the local history section. You should be able to find a book there with a translation of the Domesday Book entries for your county. The entry for Risby on this page comes from the volume on Suffolk. Make a list of the animals, buildings and vehicles you might have seen in your town or village at that time. Why do you think people who study local history value the Domesday Book so highly? AT3/L5

A Domesday manor

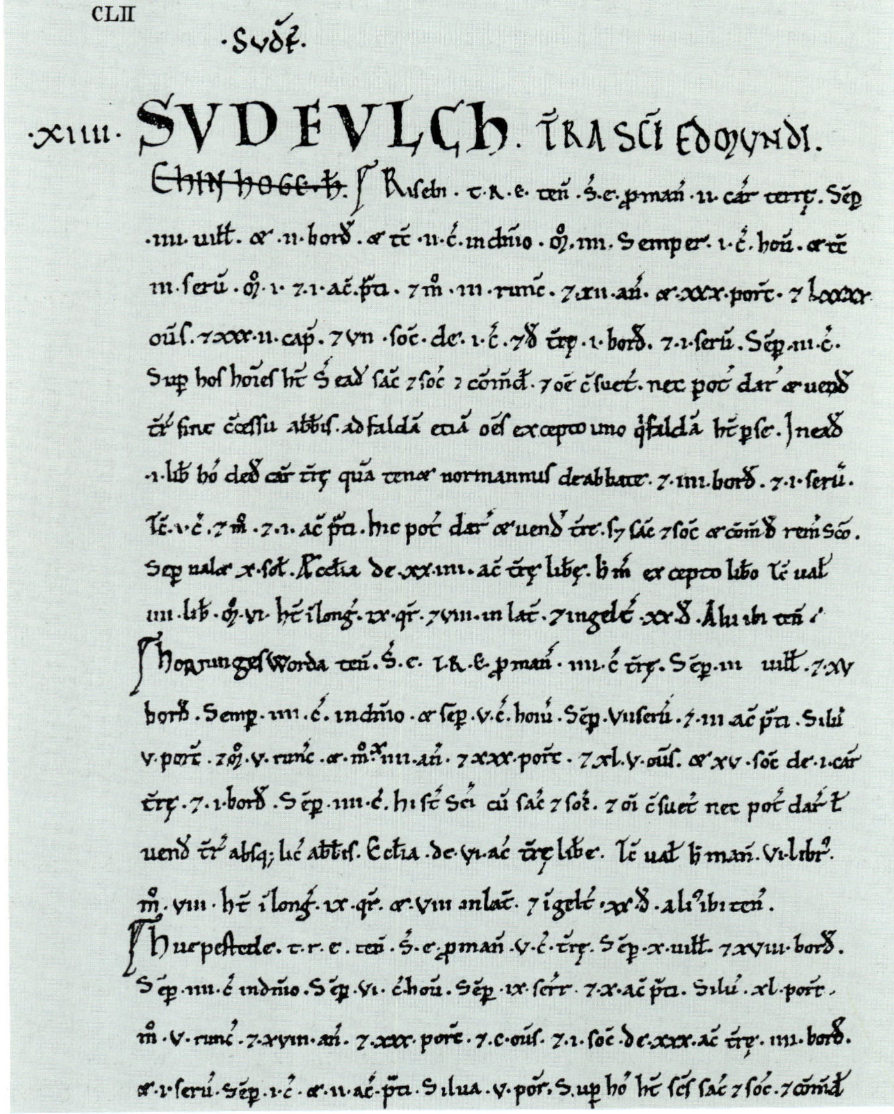

This illustration of part of a page from the Domesday Book shows the holdings of the Abbot of St Edmunds in the Suffolk village of Risby. Bishops and abbots were lords of the manor as well as barons and knights. The Abbot was head of the large abbey in nearby Bury St Edmunds.

This is a translation of the first few lines. See if you can recognise any of these numbers in the page from the Domesday Book. They are shown like this: i – ii – iii – iiii. Many words are abbreviated.

XIIII Suffolk Land of St Edmunds
Thingoe Hundred *St Edmunds held Risby as a manor before 1066; 2 carucates of land. Always 4 villeins; 2 bordars. Then 2 ploughs in lordship, now 4; always 1 men's plough. Then 3 serfs, now 1. Meadow, 1 acre. Now 3 horses, 12 cattle, 30 pigs, 90 sheep, 32 goats.*

[A carucate of land was about 50 hectares in extent. Lordship meant the rights of the lord over the land and over the people living on the manor. The hundred was part of a county—rather like a district council today]

The entry for Risby also tells us that a freeman called Norman held half a carucate of land there as well. The village priest had 24 acres of free land attached to his church. The value of the manor had been £4 before the conquest. Now it was worth £6 and paid 20d (8½p) in tax.

20 A MEDIEVAL VILLAGE

FOCUS

► *WHAT was it like to live as a peasant in a medieval village?* ATIC ■

► *HOW was the land divided between the farmers?* ATIC ■

► *WHAT farming methods were used in the Middle Ages?* ATIC ■

► *WHAT were the typical features of a medieval village and what do they look like today?* ATIA ■

◄ *This picture*—February—*was painted in about 1410 for the Duke of Berry, the richest man in France. It is one of the twelve paintings in his beautiful* Book of Hours. *You can see* June *on page 97.*

20.1 Apart from the snow, how do we know it was bitterly cold?

20.2 Most medieval cottages were very simple and let the smoke from a fire escape through a hole in the roof. How is this cottage different?

20.3 What was the reason for (a) the long fence (b) the barrels outside the door?

20.4 How can we use this picture to find out about medieval farming and everyday life, such as crops grown, animals, transport, and winter work outside? How do we know these peasants liked honey and kept pigeons for meat? AT3/L5

20.5 Compare the cottage in the painting with the medieval cottages in the photographs (opposite). What do you notice about (a) the roofs (b) the windows (c) the building materials used? How are they similar to, and how do they differ from, each other? Which cottage is most like the one in the painting? AT3/L6

20.6 Draw a sketch of a medieval cottage. Mark and label the features that make it different from a modern house today. AT1A ■

A peasant's life

In the Middle Ages most people in Britain lived on the land as peasants. Only a small number of people lived and worked in towns. For about five hundred years the way of life on the land changed slowly. We can learn something about this and about medieval farming from different types of clue.

These medieval cottages have been rebuilt at the open air museum at Singleton in Sussex

Paintings, like the picture from the *Book of Hours*, stained glass windows and wooden carvings in churches show what people looked like and how the land was farmed. Farm tools in museums, archaeological discoveries and old buildings tell us how people lived then.

Documents tell us who owned the land and what duties were owed by the peasants to their lord (as you saw on page 97). Wills list the furniture, tools and implements left by people when they died. Old receipts tell us what goods they bought and how much they paid for them.

Many documents only tell us about the people who were well-to-do and had something to leave in a will. They could read and write. Finding out how ordinary peasants lived—the vast majority of people in medieval Britain—is much more difficult.

We can learn something, however, from poems and stories written by the great writers of the Middle Ages. You can see two of these sources here. Geoffrey Chaucer wrote about the life of a poor widow in *The Canterbury Tales* (Source 20.A) at the end of the fourteenth century. William Langland lived at about the same time. He described the life of a poor peasant in his poem *Piers Plowman* (Source 20.B).

Source 20.A

Three large sows had she, and no more,
Three cows and also a sheep called Malle.
Her bower [inner room] *was covered in soot and also her hall* [main room]
In which she ate full many a slender meal.

Milk and brown bread, in which she found no lack,
Burnt bacon and sometimes an egg or two.

A yard she had, enclosed all about
With a fence and a dry ditch outside,
In which she had a cock, called Chanticleer.

Source 20.B

Says Piers Plowman: 'I have no penny to buy chickens. No, neither geese, nor pig. But only two green cheeses, a few curds, a little cream, a cake of oatmeal, and two loaves of beans and bran baked for my little ones. And, by my soul, I say I have no salt bacon. But I have parsley, cabbage, leeks and a cow and a calf and a cart mare to take manure to the fields. This is all we have to live on till the harvest season.'

20.7 Look at Sources 20.A and 20.B. What food did poor peasants eat in the fourteenth century according to these writers? AT3/L4

20.8 Chaucer wrote in a different type of English from that used today. We call it Middle English. This is why Source 20.A has been put into modern English. In the original he wrote:

Ful sooty was hir bour, and eek hir halle,
In which she eet ful many a sclendre meel.

What did 'eek' mean? How and why are some of the words he used different from those we use today? AT1A ■

20.9 Why can't we be certain that the lives of real peasants were like this in the Middle Ages? AT2 ■

20.10 Which part of Source 20.A is illustrated by the painting? AT3/L4

The open fields

The countryside in much of southern, eastern and central England was farmed by peasants working together in open fields. Instead of small fields separated by hedges, walls or fences, the farmland was divided into two or three huge open fields.

These had been shared out among the peasants in long strips. The number allocated to each farmer depended on the labour services owed to the lord of the manor. Some of the best land, however, was reserved for the lord's own use. This was called the *demesne*. It was here that the peasants had to work when called upon to do so by the lord or by his deputies, the bailiff and the reeve.

In time, some villeins were able to buy more land from their neighbours. As their holdings grew bigger, those of their less lucky neighbours got smaller. By 1500, many peasants had already earned the right to pay rent for their land instead of performing labour services for the lord of the manor. Many of these changes took place after the Peasants' Revolt in 1381. You can read about it on pages 154–7.

This map was drawn at a time when medieval strips were still farmed in this Essex village. As you can see, a number of the strips had been joined together (enclosed) to make larger square or oblong fields.

20.11 Draw an imaginary map of an open-field village. Mark and label the cottages and church in the village, the open fields, the common, a meadow by a river, and an oak forest. Name the crops in the open fields. AT1C/L5

20.12 Make a list of the advantages and disadvantages of the open field system. AT1B ■

20.13 Write a paragraph saying what differences you think you would notice if you could step back in time and see your home area as it was in the Middle Ages. AT1A ■

The strips were almost always scattered around the village, perhaps three strips in one field and four in the next. This had one advantage. It meant that most peasants got some good farmland as well as some bad. But they also wasted a lot of time going from one strip to another. Because of this, the villagers lived in huts or cottages in the village itself instead of in houses next to their fields.

Some areas of Britain, such as in the west, in much of the north, and in parts of the south-east had different systems of farming. Open fields were not to be found everywhere.

In a three-field system, Field A was sown with wheat, Field B with barley, and Field C left fallow (without any crops). The following year, Field A

The corrugated surface of this field is called ridge-and-furrow. It is a relic of open field farming. When medieval farmers ploughed the land, the heavy ox-plough turned the soil up to form ridges with long hollows (furrows) in between. They were preserved when these ploughlands were turned over to grass. There were many more fields like this in the past, but modern ploughs have flattened the fields once more.

The open field system is still partly in use at Laxton in Nottinghamshire. This is why some of the farmhouses are still in the centre of the village instead of in the fields.

grew barley, Field B was left fallow, and Field C was sown with wheat. This is called *crop rotation*. It helped to keep the soil fertile. During the fallow year, cattle and sheep grazed on the previous year's corn stubble and on the weeds. The manure helped to fertilise the land and their feet trod it well into the ground.

This type of farming was very wasteful, however. Weeds in a lazy peasant's strip soon spread to the strips of the farmers on either side. Paths between strips wasted good soil. Peasants always had to grow the same crops as the others each year. One peasant even admitted to cheating.

Source 20.C

When I went to plough, I ploughed so narrowly that I would steal a foot of land or a furrow from the half-acre of my neighbour. When I reaped, I would over-reap, or tell those who reaped with me to cut with their sickles that which I never sowed.

Villagers had other rights as well. They could take timber from the woods. They had grazing rights in the meadows by the river and on the common land. All the cattle in the village grazed in the meadow after the hay was cut in June. They were looked after by the village cow keeper or *hayward* armed with a horn. The hayward made sure the cattle did not stray into the meadows before the hay was cut.

Sheep were often grazed on land which was unfit for anything else. Relics of these common grazing areas can still be seen today—the village common. The shepherd guarded the sheep against sheep-stealers and wild animals. In the autumn the village pigs were taken by the swineherd to the oak forests to feed on the acorns. The number of animals each peasant could graze on these lands and in the meadows was strictly laid down according to their ancient rights.

Farming methods

Medieval writers, illuminated pictures in books, carvings in church, stained glass windows, tools and implements in museums, all tell us how the land was farmed in the Middle Ages.

The pictures you can see on these pages were probably drawn by monks. The carvings were made by skilled woodcarvers employed by the Church. Pictures like these, which were done by people living at the time of the scenes they portray, are called *contemporary* illustrations. Sources 20.D and 20.E below are contemporary accounts. They were written in the fourteenth century.

This picture of a plough team was drawn in about 1340

Source 20.D

I saw a poor man hanging on to a plough. He wore a coarse woollen coat and a hood so full of holes his hair stuck out. As he trudged over the land, following the plough, his toes protruded from his shabby shoes. His hose [stockings] *were spattered with mud. His fingers also stuck out of the holes in his worn-out gloves, which were coated with muck and filth. The poor man wallowed ankle-deep in thick mud and drove four heifers* [young cows] *which were so thin and weak you could count their ribs.*

His wife walked with him, carrying a long goad [a stick to prod the animals with]. *She was wearing a short coat and had wrapped herself in a thin sheet to keep out the cold. As she walked barefoot on the ice, the blood flowed. At the end of their strip of land, a small child covered with rags was lying in a small bread bowl. Two other children, about two years old, were on the other side crying so pitifully it was terrible to hear. The poor man sighed heavily and said, 'Children, be still'.*

Source 20.E

Can you make a haycock in the field or pitch the hay? Can you mow or stock or bind the sheaves? Can you reap or guide the reapers? Can you rise early? Can you blow the horn and keep the cattle together? Can you make shoes, or clothes, or herd sheep? Can you trim hedges, use the harrow, or drive the swine and geese?

20.14 Which pictures show harvest scenes? Why was corn an important crop in the Middle Ages?

20.15 How have these farming methods changed in the last 500 years or so? Which methods are still in use today on some small farms? AT1A ■

20.16 How did the writer of Source 20.D make his readers feel sorry for the poor man and his wife? Does this make any difference to the value of this extract as a source of information about the past?
AT2 ■ AT3/L5

This wood carving can be seen on the end of a bench (or pew) in the church at Altarnun in Cornwall ▲

20.17 Compare the information in Source 20.D with the picture of the plough team (opposite) drawn twenty or thirty years earlier. Write down the words or phrases in Source 20.D which describe or name features you can see in the picture. Compare these fourteenth century plough teams with the late-fifteenth century plough team shown in the painting on page 106. What changes had been made to the plough and the plough team in 150 years? AT1A ■

20.18 What other farming activities are shown in the picture on page 106? Compare it with the painting *February* on page 100. How many years separate these two paintings? What features are much the same in both pictures? AT1A ■

This carving can be seen on the underside of one of the wooden seats in Fairford Church in Gloucestershire ▶

This picture was painted at the end of the fifteenth century. It helps us to see how farming changed in the 400 years since the time of the Domesday Book.

A medieval village

You can get some idea of what a medieval village looked like if you visit the countryside today.

The most important building was the church. It was much more than a place of worship. People used it as we would treat a church hall. It was a place to meet people. In those days churches did not usually have pews. Instead, the nave of the church (see page 180) was covered with straw and the congregation stood throughout the service. Weddings took place in the porch and not inside the church as now. Sometimes miracle plays were performed in the churchyard.

20.19 Write two or three sentences to describe the Ightham Mote manor house. How was it defended? What building materials were used? AT1C/L5

20.20 What do the windmills all have in common? How are they different? Which two windmills are almost identical? What were they made of? How did they work? Use this information to write a short description of a typical medieval windmill. AT1C/L5

This is the village green at Cavendish in Suffolk. Many villages still have a green like this. The villagers met here. It was where the children played. On some village greens you can often find features which tell you about village life in the Middle Ages. Some still have the stocks which were used to punish offenders (see page 123). Others have a pond where travellers could let their horses take refreshment.

There are a number of windmills and water mills in Britain. They were the main sources of power before the coming of steam power. In the Middle Ages the windmill was used mainly for grinding the ears of corn to make flour. These photographs show a carved bench end in Bishop Lydeard church, Somerset (left), a drawing of a windmill in about 1340 (top left) and the windmill at Great Chishill near Cambridge (above).

The first manor houses, like those of the peasants, were probably made of wood, but were larger and more comfortable. Later manor houses were built of stone. This manor house is at Ightham Mote in Kent. Its largest room was the Great Hall. This was big enough to hold all the villagers at Christmas or at a harvest supper. The lord of the manor used the Great Hall as a courtroom to try cases when villagers had complaints against each other or had broken the law.

20.21 Why was timber often used to build houses in the Middle Ages? What were the drawbacks to using wood as a building material? What were the advantages? AT1B ■

20.22 Find out what evidence of medieval farming can be found in your home county. Can you see fields with ridge-and-furrow patterns? Are there any streets in your town with farming names, such as Haymarket or Windmill Lane? Is there a common or a green in your town? AT1A/L5

The priest in charge of a village usually had a number of strips in the open fields which he farmed for his own use. All villagers had to give a part of their crops to the Church. This was called a tithe. *It was usually a tenth of the harvest. The priest kept this corn in a large barn, called the* tithe barn, *close to the church. The huge tithe barn you can see here is at Great Coxwell in Oxfordshire.*

21 The Church and the King

FOCUS

► *WHY was the Church so powerful in the Middle Ages?* AT1B ■

► *HOW and WHY did the Church clash with the king?* AT1B ■

Gargoyles like these can often be seen on medieval churches and cathedrals

The Church

Bishops and abbots were used to power in the Middle Ages. By 1150 the Church in Britain was a huge and very rich organisation. It owed its power and wealth to the fact that almost everyone in Britain was a Christian and there was only one Church—the Roman Catholic Church. The Archbishop of Canterbury was the leading priest in the Church in England. He looked for spiritual guidance to the Pope in Rome—the head of western Christendom.

21.1 What was the main reason for erecting these gargoyles? (Clue: The weather)

21.2 What do you think the expressions on the faces show? What does this tell you about how people looked on life and death? AT1C/L6

21.3 What do you notice about the clothes of the pilgrims in the picture opposite? Write one or two sentences comparing these people with the Canterbury pilgrims on page 180. AT3/L4

21.4 Where in Britain today are bishops still treated as if they were lords? AT1A/L3

◄ *Towering cathedrals, like Ely, and many country churches stood out as landmarks in the countryside. They could be seen for miles around. They were superbly built compared with the simple huts and cottages where most people lived. To the peasants this was proof of the power of the Church. Religion played a much bigger part in their everyday life then than it does for most people today. Many went to a place of worship two or three times a week. They hoped the next life would be easier than life on earth. They believed in Heaven and the torment of Hell.*

The medieval Church approved of warfare if it was in a good cause. Many knights fought in the Crusades (see page 64). Bishop Odo of Bayeux fought with William at Hastings. Bishops and abbots who held land from the Conqueror provided knights and soldiers when he needed them. Church towers often had battlements and abbeys had thick walls. This huge gatehouse protected the abbey at Bury St Edmunds.

You can get some idea of the power of the Church if you visit a great cathedral like Ely. A building like this would be a magnificent achievement if built today with the aid of modern machines. But medieval cathedrals were built by hand. The cost was enormous.

The Church was immensely rich. Its wealth came from different sources. As you have seen, the peasants paid a tenth of their produce to the Church as a tithe. Rich people gave money and sometimes property when they died. These funds paid for new cathedrals and met the cost of running the Church. Great wealth gave the abbots and bishops great power. They were treated as if they were earls and barons.

The King

The medieval kings of England were Christians. But they did not want the Pope interfering in the way they ruled the country. In particular, they insisted that it was their right to appoint the Archbishop of Canterbury and other leaders of the Church, such as abbots and bishops. To the king, they were the same as the barons. They had been granted huge estates. In return he expected them to do homage as vassals. This meant the king must have the right to appoint and dismiss them.

The Church didn't like this at all. Some churchmen thought that kings should be vassals of the Pope since, in their eyes, the authority of a king to rule a country was granted by God at the coronation ceremony, and the Pope was God's representative on earth. They wanted the Church to be distinct from the State. The Church had its own laws—called canon law—to control priests and other clergy. Canon law was often more lenient with offenders than the king's law. This didn't seem fair to the king or to other lay people (people who are not priests).

The Pope and the Archbishop of Canterbury had a number of powers they could use to force a king or baron to do as they wanted. In particular, they could *excommunicate*. This was a terrible punishment for a devout Christian. It meant excluding them from holy communion.

This picture shows pilgrims taking refreshment at an abbey. Many medieval people went on pilgrimages to the Holy Land or to a holy place, such as the tomb of St Thomas Becket at Canterbury. They believed that if they prayed at a shrine such as this, their sins would be forgiven and they would go to Heaven. People who were ill hoped to be cured. The Church affected the everyday life of ordinary people in many other ways. The poor and needy looked to the local abbeys to supply many of the social services which we expect the State to provide today. Bishops built almshouses where old people who were poor and needy could live. The almoner in an abbey or priory gave alms—money, food or clothing—to the poor and unemployed. The Church also built hospitals for the poor and sick (see page 151) while the first schools were run by monasteries.

Henry II and Thomas Becket

Relations between the Church and the king reached a crisis when King Henry II appointed his leading minister, Thomas Becket, as Archbishop of Canterbury in 1162. Becket was Chancellor of England and one of Henry's closest friends. A writer at the time said

Never have there been two men more harmonious and friendly in Christian times.

Stained glass window in Canterbury Cathedral showing Henry II (left) with Thomas Becket (right)

King Henry II

Henry II was a Frenchman, born at Le Mans in France on 5 March 1133. He became King of England in 1154. He was already Duke of Normandy and Count of Anjou. Since he had earlier married Eleanor of Aquitaine, he now ruled an empire stretching from the Scottish border to the Pyrenees.

Henry's first job was to make everyone respect the monarchy after a period when the barons had had too much power. One way to do this was to improve the system of law. He wanted to see fair play for everyone. Special courts of law, called the *assizes*, were held. He also tried to get rid of the system which helped priests to escape punishment under the law. In short, Henry II reformed the system of government.

In appearance he was square-built and thickset, with a bullet-shaped head and freckled face. He spoke Latin fluently as well as French and was a highly educated man. He was also very energetic and restless by nature. His main fault was his violent temper. In the end he quarrelled with his own sons and died in 1189 at Chinon in France.

Becket's seal

Thomas Becket with Herbert Bosham (right)

Thomas Becket

Thomas Becket was born in London in 1118. He was the son of wealthy Norman parents. He worked as a lawyer, then as a merchant and lastly as an assistant to the Archbishop of Canterbury. In appearance he was tall, dark and handsome with a great amount of charm. He was also very, very ambitious.

He was appointed Chancellor of England in 1155 when he was 37 and the king only 22. He did the job well for seven years and soon gained the respect and friendship of the king. At this time Becket dressed in splendid clothes, hunted in the forests and enjoyed a life of ease and luxury. He dined with the king and revelled in his company.

When Henry II made him Archbishop of Canterbury in 1162 he was not even a priest. He had to convince the Church he was his own man and not the king's puppet. He did this by defending the rights of the clergy against the king. But he fell out with Henry and had to leave the country.

After his murder in 1170, the monks of Canterbury were astonished to find he wore prickly sackcloth under his fine robes. His personal attendants claimed he had slept on the floor with a stone for a pillow, taken only bread and water at mealtimes and woken every day before dawn to pray.

21.5 What was Becket's reaction to the idea of becoming Archbishop? Where and what was the 'sacred seat'? What did Becket mean when he said 'What a religious man, what a holy man'? How did he change? Why did he wear sackcloth?

AT1C/L6

21.6 Why do you think Henry wanted Becket to be Archbishop?

Herbert Bosham, one of Becket's friends, described Becket's reaction when the king asked him to be the next Archbishop of Canterbury.

Source 21.A

The Chancellor, pointing to the bright clothes he was wearing, said with a smile, 'What a religious man, what a holy man you want to put in the sacred seat and in charge of that famous and sacred group of monks! Know surely that if by the will of God this should happen, you would quickly turn away from me. Our friendship which is now so great would be changed into bitter hatred. I am sure you would want to interfere in Church affairs. You would demand some things which I could not accept'.

The quarrel

As Becket had forecast, the two men soon quarrelled over who should control the Church. Henry II wanted the clergy to be subject to the same laws as other people. Up to then, they had had the right (called *benefit of clergy*) to be tried by a Church court instead. In 1163 Henry demanded that offending priests be handed over for punishment. Becket refused. In 1164 he opposed Henry once again and was forced into exile. While there he excommunicated some of the king's advisers.

He returned in 1170 after the Pope arranged a truce for him with the king. But Becket was stubborn. He still believed he was right. He made clear his opposition to the king's proposals and suspended three of the bishops who had taken the king's side.

Henry was furious when he heard the news. 'Will no-one rid me of this turbulent priest?', he cried. Four knights—Reginald FitzUrse, William de Tracy, Hugh de Morville and Richard le Breton—took him at his word. Without waiting to see if the king really meant what he said, they set off for Canterbury. Edward Grim and William Fitz-Stephen were both in the cathedral on 29 December 1170 when the four knights burst in. You can read what they saw in the sources which follow.

The martyrdom

This picture was painted to illustrate a manuscript written in about 1180. If you look closely, you can see that it is two pictures in one: the murder scene on the left, and the murderers doing penance on the right.

Stained glass window at Canterbury showing Henry doing penance

Edward Grim takes up the story (Sources 21.B to 21.D).

Source 21.B

The four knights followed behind with rapid strides. With them was an evil priest, called Mauclerk. They entered the church with drawn swords, horrifying onlookers by their looks and the clanging of their arms.

Angrily, the knights called out, 'Where is Thomas Becket, traitor to the King and realm?' As he answered not they cried out the more furiously. 'Where is the Archbishop?' In a clear voice he answered, 'I am here, no traitor to the King, but a priest. Why do you seek me?'

'Pardon and restore to communion those whom you have excommunicated, and restore their powers to those whom you have suspended,' they cried.

This picture of the martyrdom of Thomas Becket was painted in about 1190 to illustrate a prayer book. If you look up the meaning of the French word ours *in a dictionary, you should be able to identify the leader of the knights, Reginald FitzUrse.*

21.7 *Mauclerk* comes from the French words *Mal* and *Clerc*. Why was this an appropriate name? What did the knights want Becket to do? Use the sources to work out the name of the fourth knight who 'prevented any from interfering.' Who was the monk next to Becket in the pictures? Quote two bits of evidence which confirm this. AT3/L4

21.8 How do the two pictures of the martyrdom differ? Work out carefully which part of which source (21.B, 21.C, 21.D or 21.E) is illustrated by these pictures. AT3 ■

21.9 Which source tells us that the knights knew it was a very great sin to commit murder inside a cathedral? AT3 ■

21.10 How does William Fitz-Stephen's account of the murder (Source 21.E) differ from Edward Grim's (Sources 21.C and 21.D)? Write down two or three reasons which may explain why they differ. Do these differences matter when we study history? Would they matter more to a modern policeman? AT2 ■ AT3 ■

21.11 What evidence in this chapter shows that medieval Christians thought suffering and pain could help them get to Heaven? AT1C/L6

Source 21.C

They laid unholy hands on him, pulling and dragging him that they might kill him outside the church, or carry him away a prisoner. He pushed them off, saying, 'Touch me not Reginald; you owe me fealty and obedience; you and your accomplices act like madmen.'

The knight angered at this, waved his sword over the sacred head. 'No faith,' he cried, 'nor obedience do I owe you against my fealty to my lord the King.' Scarce had he said the words than the wicked knight leapt upon him suddenly and wounded him on the head and by the same blow wounded the arm of him who tells this story.

Source 21.D

He received a second blow on the head but still stood firm. At the third blow he fell on his knees and elbows. Then the third knight inflicted a terrible wound as he lay, by which the sword was broken on the pavement and his blood stained the surface of the church with the life and death of the martyr. The fourth knight prevented any from interfering. As to the clerk who had entered with the knights, he put his foot on the neck of the martyr, calling out to the others, 'Let us away, knights, he will rise no more.'

William Fitz-Stephen was also there. This is what he wrote afterwards.

Source 21.E

With them also was Master Edward Grim, and he, putting up his arm received the first stroke of the sword aimed by William de Tracy at the archbishop's head. By this same stroke the archbishop was wounded in the head as he bent forward and Grim in the arm severely.

As the archbishop knelt down, a second stroke was dealt him on the head, at which he fell flat on his face. While he lay there stricken, Richard le Breton smote him with such force that the sword was broken against his head and the floor of the church.

St Thomas

The Pope was horrified, as were most people in Christendom. Becket was canonised in 1173 and became St Thomas. The day of the murder, 29 December, became St Thomas's Day and his tomb in Canterbury Cathedral became a shrine.

Henry II was filled with remorse and came back to England to do penance at the tomb of his former friend. On Saturday 12 July 1174, he walked barefoot into Canterbury wearing a woollen smock. All day he lay at the shrine and was flogged by all the bishops, abbots and monks in the cathedral. An eyewitness said he prayed all day and night:

He neither took food nor went out to relieve nature and would not permit a rug to be provided for him.

But although Henry II did penance for his crime, he still kept control of the English Church.

Time Line

1118 Thomas Becket born
1133 Henry II born
1154 Henry II becomes king
1155 Becket made Chancellor of England
1162 Becket made Archbishop of Canterbury
1164 Becket forced into exile
1170 Becket murdered
1173 Becket made a saint
1174 Henry II does penance

22 MAGNA CARTA

FOCUS

▶ *WHAT was Magna Carta?* AT3 ■

▶ *WHY was it important?* AT1B ■

▶ *HOW did the barons force the king to agree to its terms?* AT1C ■

The Great Charter

Magna Carta, the 'Great Charter', is one of the most famous documents in the world. It lists the rights of people in Britain in 1215. This recognition of people's rights has had a great influence on people in many other countries as well.

Although Magna Carta is indeed a great charter of liberties, it was not written to guarantee the freedom of the peasant. Its purpose was to force King John to restore the privileges of the barons and the Church. But it did lay down an important principle. In future, the king had to obey the law like everyone else.

Seal of Stephen Langton

The quarrel with the Pope

The events which led up to Magna Carta in 1215 began about ten years earlier when King John's armies were defeated by the King of France. Normandy was lost in 1204 and Anjou in 1205. Out of Henry II's huge empire, only Britain and a small part of France was left. In 1205 King John refused to accept Stephen Langton as Archbishop of Canterbury. Langton had been chosen by the Pope, but John insisted that the king had the right to choose the head of the English Church.

The Pope intended to have his own way. He put England under a Papal Interdict. This meant that all the churches were closed. John retaliated by seizing Church lands. Many people were upset but John paid no heed. He even forced a number of monks and bishops into exile. The Pope went further. He excommunicated John in 1209 and later said the oath of fealty to the king was no longer valid. When the French king began to prepare for war, John submitted at last to the Pope in 1213. Cardinal Langton became Archbishop of Canterbury and the Papal ban on church services was lifted.

King John

King John was born on Christmas Eve, 1167. He was nicknamed John Lackland because, as Henry II's youngest son, he was unlikely to inherit the throne. When he was ten, however, he became Lord of Ireland and in 1199 succeeded his brother Richard I to the throne.

As a person, he was noted for his fine clothes and luxurious way of life. In fact, his love of food proved too much and he died at Newark Castle in 1216 after dining too well on peaches and beer.

John's main problem as king was that he never had anything to show for all the years of warfare and all the money he spent. One or two great victories might have made the cost easier for the barons to bear. In a way he was no worse than any other medieval king, since they, too, were often vicious, ruthless, untrustworthy, cruel and violent. His main mistake was to quarrel with both the Church and the barons at the same time.

Most of the tales later told about John were written by monks. He came to be known as a peculiarly evil and wicked king. But some modern writers have been kinder to

Effigy of King John in Worcester Cathe

him. They see John as an able ruler who helped local government by giving charters to the towns. Even so, he could not control the barons and he did lose much of his inheritance as well as his argument with the Pope.

Civil war

During the years of dispute with the Church, John demanded large sums of money from the barons to pay for the upkeep of his army. The barons resented having to send soldiers to help recover his lost territories. They were also afraid John was taking away many of their rights. They feared he was concentrating too much power in his own hands.

In 1214 they met secretly with Cardinal Langton at Bury St Edmunds to draw up a charter to make the king give back these rights. You can see what happened next in the sources which follow. They were written by a monk called Roger of Wendover who died in 1236.

Plaque in the abbey at Bury St Edmunds ▶

Source 22.A

About this time [20 November 1214] *the earls and barons of England met in secret at Bury St Edmunds Abbey. They all swore on the great altar that, if the king refused to grant these liberties and laws, they themselves would withdraw from their allegiance to him, and make war on him until he did so.*

At Christmas, King John held court at Winchester for one day, after which he hurried to London. The nobles came to him there in military array, and demanded that he confirm the liberties and laws laid down in the charter and laws of Henry I. The king, hearing the bold tone of the barons, much feared an attack and asked for a truce until Easter.

22.1 Who chose Thomas Becket as Archbishop of Canterbury in 1162? Was John right to insist the choice was his and not the Pope's in 1205?

22.2 Why do you think people were upset when the Pope put England under an Interdict? What difference do you think it made to their lives?

AT1B ■ AT1C/L6

22.3 Why did the barons have to send knights and soldiers to fight in the king's army?

22.4 What is meant in Source 22.A by (a) 'allegiance' (b) 'military array' (c) 'truce'?

22.5 How likely is it that Source 22.A was written by someone who may have known about these events at first hand?

AT3/L5

King John in Westminster Abbey

Runnymede

Before the Easter meeting John took a number of precautions against the barons. He tried to reduce their support by making many nobles 'swear fealty to him alone against all men, and to renew their homage to him'.

Source 22.B

In Easter week, the nobles assembled a very large army and said they would force him to give them satisfaction. The king replied with the greatest indignation, 'Why, amongst these unjust demands, do not the barons ask for my kingdom also?' At length he angrily declared with an oath, that he would never grant them such liberties as would render him their slave.

The barons then moved their army to London.

Source 22.C

The rich citizens were favourable to the barons, and the poor ones were afraid to murmur against them. The barons then sent letters throughout England to those earls, barons, and knights still faithful to the king. They told them to abandon the king. If not, the barons would make war against them and destroy their castles. The majority, on receiving this message, set out to London and joined them, abandoning the king entirely.

Source 22.D

King John, when he saw that he was deserted, pretended to make peace and told the barons he would willingly grant them the laws and liberties they wanted. They in their great joy appointed the fifteenth of June for the king to meet them, at a field lying between Staines and Windsor. Accordingly, at the time and place agreed on, the king and nobles came to the appointed conference, and when each party had stationed themselves apart from the other, they began a long discussion. At length, King John, seeing that he was inferior in strength to the barons, granted the laws and liberties, and confirmed them by his charter.

22.6 What was the name of the meadow where the Charter was sealed? AT3/L3

22.7 How did John try to take away the support of the barons? How did the barons try to increase it? Were they successful? Write a paragraph explaining why John eventually agreed to the Charter. AT1B ■

22.8 The first paragraph in Source 22.E is called a *preamble*. Was it strictly true?

22.9 Do you think Roger of Wendover was biased in any way, either for or against John? Or was he neutral? Give a reason. AT2 ■ AT3/L5

22.10 Write down the clauses in the Charter which tell us that (a)the barons resented sending soldiers to fight for the king (b)the king had acted illegally in the past. AT3/L4

22.11 What was the importance of Clause 39? To which class of people did it apply? Which people appear to be excluded? Was this fair? Is it right to think of Magna Carta as a great Charter of Liberties? AT2/L5

22.12 Write one or two sentences saying why Clause 12 and Clause 40 were both of very great importance to the people of Britain. What would happen today if the government tried to go against these principles? AT1C/L6

Magna Carta

In Source 22.E you can read just a few of the 63 clauses laid down in Magna Carta. As you go down the list, make a note of any clauses you think still apply today.

Source 22.E

John, by the grace of God, king of England, lord of Ireland, duke of Normandy and of Aquitaine, count of Anjou, to his archbishops, bishops, abbots, earls, barons, justiciars, foresters, sheriffs, reeves, ministers, and all his bailiffs and faithful people, greeting.

1 In the first place we have granted that the English Church shall be free and shall keep its own privileges intact.

12 No scutage [money paid by a baron instead of sending men to join the king's army] *or aid* [tax] *shall be demanded in our kingdom except by the common consent of our realm.*

16 No one shall be forced to do a greater military service than they owe.

30 No sheriff or bailiff of ours, nor any one else, shall take the horses or carts of any free man for carrying purposes except by permission of that free man.

35 There shall be one uniform measure of wine, beer, corn and cloth throughout our whole kingdom. Furthermore, it shall be the same with weights as with measures.

39 No free man shall be taken or imprisoned, outlawed or exiled, or harmed in any other way, except by the lawful judgement of his equals or by the laws of the land.

40 To no one will we sell, to no one will we refuse, to no one will we delay right or justice.

52 If any one shall have been dispossessed or removed by us without legal judgement of his peers, from his lands, castles, or his rights, we will restore them to him immediately.

Given by our hand in the meadow that is called Runnymede, between Windsor and Staines, on the fifteenth day of June, in the seventeenth year of our reign.

Time Line

1167 King John born
1199 John becomes king
1204 Loss of Normandy
1205 Loss of Anjou; King John refuses to accept Stephen Langton as Archbishop
1208 Papal Interdict
1209 King John excommunicated
1213 John submits to the Pope
1214 Barons meet at Bury St Edmunds
1215 Magna Carta
1216 Death of King John

23 GOVERNMENT AND PARLIAMENT

The king's officials

It was hard for a medieval king to know what was happening in the rest of his kingdom. It was not easy to send or receive a message. The roads were poor and even short journeys could take several days. Despite this, medieval kings did a lot of travelling. They had to make their presence felt in the country. Wherever they went, relatives, servants, barons, knights, soldiers (the household cavalry) and other members of the royal household went too. You can get some idea of the size of a royal progress from this description of the journey which Thomas Becket made to Paris in 1158 on behalf of the king.

Source 23.A

He had above two hundred on horseback, knights, clerks, butlers, serving

FOCUS

- *HOW did Parliament begin?* AT1B ■
- *HOW was the country governed in the Middle Ages?* AT1C ■
- *HOW was the law upheld in the Middle Ages?* AT1C ■

◀ *Medieval kings were often on the move. They led expeditions against their enemies. They hunted. They made frequent journeys through the kingdom to show their power. A journey like this was called a* royal progress.

23.1 Look at Source 23.A. What were Becket's main duties in 1158? How many people were there in his retinue? AT1C/L3

23.2 How did Becket entertain himself during the long journey to Paris in 1158? AT3/L3

23.3 Why do you think the barons made John promise to hold the Court of Common Pleas 'in a fixed place' in future? AT1B ■

23.4 What use do you think historians make of the Chancery rolls and the Exchequer pipe rolls? AT3/L5

23.5 Make a tally stick. Fold a narrow strip of paper (or thin card) lengthways. Cut notches in the edge to show a sum of money. Give one half to friends as a receipt and ask them to say what sum of money it represents.

▲ *Ladies hunting in a forest. Women played an important part in medieval life but not in government. In 1135 the English barons refused to accept Henry II's daughter Matilda as Queen when he died.*

men and esquires. He also had eight carriages each drawn by five horses. When they entered a French village, first came about two hundred and fifty footboys—six or ten abreast—singing in French. Then came the hounds with the huntsmen and keepers. Then the iron-bound wagons and the packhorses. Next came the squires, butlers, servants, knights and clerks. Last came the Chancellor and some of his nearest friends.

Because the monarch was at the very centre of government, leading royal officials were also to be seen in the large retinue accompanying the king. Even judges went too, until King John promised in Magna Carta that

The court of common pleas shall not follow our court, but shall be held in a fixed place.

As the business of government grew, so did the number of royal officials. They had documents to write. There were taxes to collect. They couldn't do this on horseback following the king. Sooner or later, part of the government, at least, had to have a permanent home. This is why the main offices of State such as the office of the Chancellor and that of the Treasurer were in Westminster by the end of the thirteenth century.

The Chancellor was the king's secretary. He kept the Great Seal which proved a document came from the king. The Chancellor had a number of clerks working for him. They wrote the king's letters, recorded grants of land and drew up official documents. They wrote on sheets of parchment. These documents, called Chancery Rolls, were stored in the Chancery. The king also had a seal which he could use on his travels. This was in the hands of the Keeper of the Privy ('Private') Seal.

The revenue (annual income from taxes) which was needed to pay the soldiers and run the royal household had to be counted, checked and recorded. This job was done at the Exchequer. It got its name from the table, with a pattern like a chess-board, where the royal tax collectors sat to do business. The records of the Treasury were stored on pipe rolls. They were called this because they were written on sheets of parchment which were tied end to end to form a long roll or pipe.

◀ *At Easter and again at Michaelmas (29 September) the king's officials took half the money they had collected in taxes to the Exchequer. To show they had paid, they were given an unusual receipt. A piece of wood about 20 cm long was marked with notches of different sizes to show the sum of money handed over. The bigger the notch, the bigger the sum of money involved. When the clerks had finished their calculations, the sticks were split in two. The Exchequer kept one half, the sheriff kept the other. These sticks were called tallies or tally sticks.*

Parliament

The Chancellor, Treasurer and other leading officials, together with a small group of trusted nobles, met regularly as the King's Council. They were the king's right-hand men. They gave him advice, drafted his laws and issued important documents called *writs.*

The members of the King's Council also met together as part of a much bigger group called the Great Council. Eventually this became the House of Lords. It was presided over by the monarch and consisted of all the lords of the land who held land directly from the king: the tenants in chief. This meeting of earls, barons, bishops and abbots was not a parliament (since there were no common people present) although it did help to make laws and levy taxes.

As you saw on page 117, Magna Carta said:

No scutage or tax shall be demanded in our kingdom except by the common consent of our realm.

This meant that the king could not raise taxes without the consent of the people. So when the kings who reigned after John wanted extra money to pay for the cost of a war, they had to get the approval of the people who would pay it.

The first parliament, in which commoners represented the shires (counties) and citizens and burgesses represented the cities and towns, was summoned by the rebel leader Simon de Montfort in 1265. Ten years later King Edward I summoned the first of his series of important parliaments. This was a big step forward but it was not a democratic system as we know it. The representatives of the Commons (as they were called) were not elected by the common people at all. They did not represent the peasants. Instead, they were the leading citizens and men of wealth from the towns and some of the foremost knights from the shires.

Source 23.B Writ of Summons to the Parliament of 1295

We intend to seek advice at a meeting with the earls, barons and other principal men of our kingdom. The aim will be to provide remedies against the dangers now threatening the kingdom. We have commanded them to be with us on the Lord's day next after the feast of St Martin [11 November], *at Westminster. We strictly require you to cause two knights from your county, two citizens from each city, and two burgesses from each borough, to be elected without delay. Cause them to come to us at the time and place already mentioned.*

Identical summonses were sent to the sheriffs of every county. A similar summons, but with different wording, was sent to the two archbishops, eighteen bishops, seventy abbots, seven earls and forty-one barons who formed the Great Council.

In the next two centuries, Parliament grew in importance. In 1309 it would not approve the king's demand for taxes until he heard a number of grievances. This was one way of making sure Parliament had a say in how the country was governed. Parliament soon began to make laws as well, in addition to approving the laws proposed by the king and his council. In 1377 the Commons elected a Speaker to tell the king what they had decided. By 1400 they were meeting separately from the House of Lords and had played a part in forcing Richard II to give up the throne. By 1500 Parliament was well able to stand up to the king.

23.6 Look at the painting. On which side (to Edward's left or to his right) did most of the abbots and bishops sit? Where did the Lords sit? AT3/L3

23.7 Two important churchmen are seated on the extreme left and right holding their croziers (crosses). What position did they hold in the Church? AT3/L3

23.8 The painting shows Edward I on the throne in the centre. If you look closely, you can see that the artist has labelled the picture to show the names of the two men wearing crowns on either side of Edward. Alexander III, King of Scotland, is on his right. Llywelyn ap Gruffydd, Prince of Wales, is on his left. Use the information in the Time Line below to estimate the date when this Parliament met. AT1C/L5

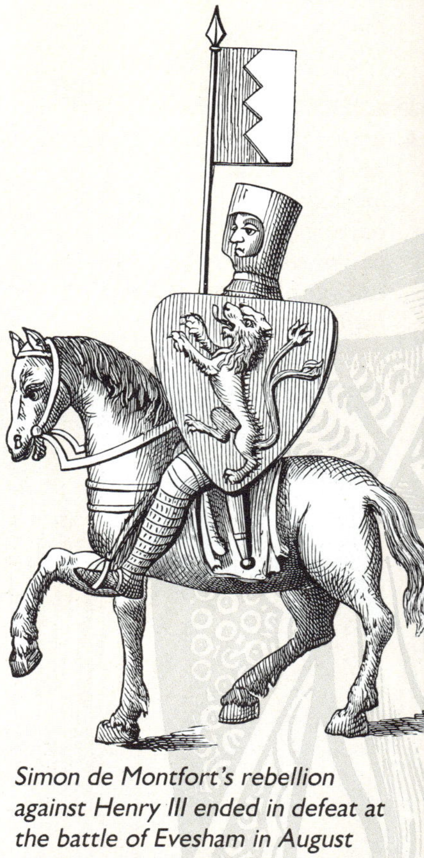

Simon de Montfort's rebellion against Henry III ended in defeat at the battle of Evesham in August 1265. His parliament, earlier the same year, paved the way for our present House of Commons.

This painting shows Edward I presiding over Parliament. As you can see, the king's ministers sit in the centre of the hall on sacks filled with wool. Wool was chosen because it brought wealth to the country as Britain's chief export at that time. If you look closely, you can see clerks, equipped with quill pens, making a written record of the proceedings.

Time Line

1249 to 1286	Alexander III	King of Scotland
1254 to 1282	Llewelyn ap Gruffydd	Prince of Wales
1272 to 1307	Edward I	King of England

Law and order

For some years after the Norman Conquest different laws were in force in different parts of the country. But the changes made by Henry II to the legal system helped to bring together a system of law that was common to all parts of the land. This became known as the *common* law.

Until 1215 the question of whether a person accused of a crime was innocent or guilty was sometimes decided by a *trial by ordeal*, exposing them to fire or ducking them in water. In 1166 Henry II introduced the idea of trial by jury. 'Twelve free and law-abiding men' from the offender's own district might know the offender and could say whether they thought he had committed the crime or not.

Henry also sent judges around the country to ensure a common system of justice throughout the land. These courts were called the *assizes*. In this way he tried to make everyone equal in the eyes of the law.

In London there were different courts to hear different types of case. Criminals were tried at the Court of King's Bench. People who had complaints against each other settled their disputes in the Court of Common Pleas. The Court of the Exchequer dealt with cases where people were in debt to the government. The Court of Chancery heard cases where people could complain about an injustice or something they thought was unfair.

Source 23.C

1447 *The jurors say that Simon Jackson is a foul-mouthed rascal and Alice Highley a common stealer and carries away cocks, hens, sheaves of corn, and other things.*

1457 *The jurors say William Hinchliffe of Woolley and Robert Wright of Hemsworth are common players at forbidden games.*

This picture is like a strip cartoon. Can you pick out the crime, the arrest, witnesses in court and the judges? ▼

Court of King's Bench in about 1450

Sanctuary door-knockers, like this one on the door of Durham Cathedral, were a welcome sight for criminals fleeing from justice. Once inside a church they were safe from capture. They could leave unpunished if they confessed and promised to leave England for good. This was called 'abjuring the realm'. People who did so had to wear a long gown made from sackcloth and carry a cross as they walked towards the port from which they were to leave Britain.

23.9 How can you tell from Source 23.C that the role of a medieval jury was not the same as that of a modern jury? AT1C/L3

23.10 Look at the painting of the Court of King's Bench. How many judges are shown in court? Did they wear wigs in 1450? How did the guards control the prisoners? AT3/L3

Medieval street name in York. Other towns have names which recall medieval punishments, such as the Gallowgate in Newcastle upon Tyne and Gallowtree Gate in Leicester.

23.11 Look at the painting showing the story of a crime. Draw a flow chart or diagram, telling the story of the crime in the order in which you think it happened. AT1C ■

23.12 Look at Source 23.D. What crime had been committed? Was it murder? Which piece of evidence seems to suggest that one of the fatal blows was not struck in self defence? AT1B/L4

23.13 Why did William go to the Chapel of St Mary? Why was the port of Dover assigned to him?

23.14 If William failed to leave Dover within three days, he was said to be on the outside of the law, and could be killed on sight. What were such people called? AT3/L3

23.15 The photographs on this page show some of the relics of medieval punishments which can still be seen today. What relics like these can be seen near your home town or village? AT1C ■

Time Line

1166 Trial by jury introduced
1215 Magna Carta; the Pope bans trial by ordeal
1265 Simon de Montfort's Parliament
1275 Edward I's first Parliament
1350 Every town ordered to erect a set of stocks
1377 House of Commons elects a Speaker

The ducking cage or ducking stool was a terrifying punishment for anyone afraid of drowning. The victim was lowered into the water and submerged against their will.

Source 23.D
A crime committed in London in 1276

Last Sunday at the hour of 4 o'clock in the afternoon, there arose a dispute between Gervase le Noreys and William de Lindeseye. William illegally assaulted Gervase with a knife, giving him a wound in the left side of the back and another under the right breast, from which wounds he immediately died. After which the said William fled to the Chapel of St Mary Barkingchurch. On the following Wednesday, the said William, acknowledging that he had committed the crime, abjured the realm. And the port of Dover was assigned to him, to set sail within three days therefrom.

Wooden stocks like these can still be seen in many towns and villages. In 1350 every town was ordered to erect such a set of stocks.

◀ *This is a gibbet or gallows by the side of the road on a lonely moorland near Elsdon in Northumberland. The body was left hanging in chains as a warning to others.*

24 ENGLAND, IRELAND WALES AND SCOTLAND

FOCUS

▶ *WHAT were England's relations with Scotland and Ireland in the Middle Ages?* ATIC ■

▶ *HOW did Wales become part of the kingdom of England and Wales?* ATIB ■

Strongbow in Ireland

The Normans ignored Ireland until 1166. In that year most of the different kings of Ireland agreed to accept Rory O'Connor as High King in Dublin. But Dermot of Leinster refused and was driven out of his lands. He appealed to Henry II for help. This gave the English an excuse to intervene. Richard de Clare, Earl of Pembroke ('Strongbow'), agreed to help him recover his kingdom. In return, Dermot promised Strongbow he could marry his daughter and that he would succeed him as King of Leinster when he (Dermot) died.

In 1169–70 Strongbow led a small army of 200 Anglo-Norman knights and 1000 foot soldiers to Ireland. They captured Dublin and other major towns in the south east. When Dermot died in 1170, Strongbow took the title of King of Leinster. King Rory laid siege to Dublin but his army was defeated.

Having one of his barons as King of Leinster made Henry II wary. Some said he was jealous. This is why he went to Ireland in 1171 to assert his authority. He made Strongbow and most of the other Irish kings acknowledge him as their overlord. In return, he promised to protect them as their feudal overlord. The Pope approved this and gave Henry the title Lord of Ireland.

In fact, the Normans behaved badly in Ireland, as you can see from Source 24.A. This was written by Gerald of Wales in about 1185.

Richard de Clare, Earl of Pembroke. He was called 'Strongbow' after his father Gilbert Strongbow

The Pale

By 1280 the Gaelic chieftains had fought back and the English influence was confined to the Pale around Dublin. In the rest of Ireland the local kings and chieftains ruled as before.

In 1314 some of the Irish chieftains were very impressed by the Scottish victory over the English at Bannockburn (see page 130). They invited Robert the Bruce's brother, Edward Bruce, to be their king. He landed in Ulster with 6000 Scottish soldiers and was crowned King of Ireland near Dundalk in 1316. Two years later, English soldiers from Dublin defeated and killed him at the Battle of Dundalk.

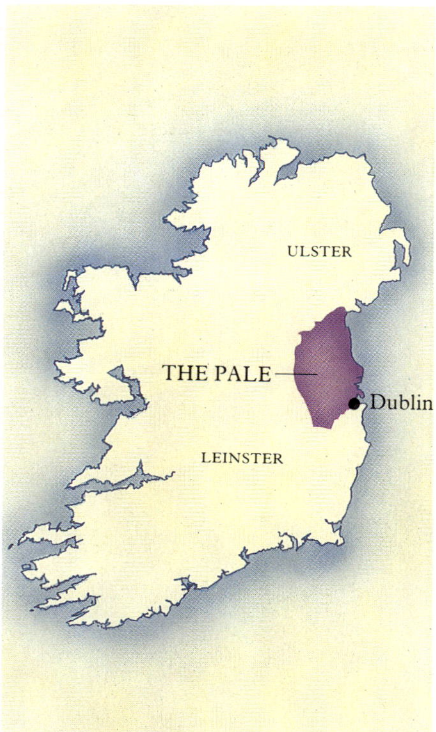

Map of medieval Ireland

Source 24.A

I speak from my own knowledge. We took away the lands of the friendly Irish and gave them to newcomers from England. Command of the government and the army fell into the clutches of men who had more of the thief in them than the soldier. They were rascals intent less on attacking the enemy than on looting the good citizens.

Nothing has been done to establish a settled state of things in the island, either by subduing hostile districts, building castles, or opening up forest roads by felling the trees on either side.

24.1 How do we know Gerald of Wales had been in Ireland not long after Strongbow's expedition?

24.2 What mistakes did the English make in Ireland?

24.3 How could you use the painting of Strongbow to pick him out from other knights at a tournament? AT3/L5

24.4 Look at the armour worn by knights and soldiers in the pictures on pages 87 (eleventh century), 112 (twelfth century), 171 (thirteenth century), and 157 (fourteenth century). When do you think the picture of Strongbow was painted? Use the same evidence to say roughly when you think the effigy of the Irish knight (in the photograph below) was made. AT3/L6

24.5 The area around Dublin controlled by the English was called the *Pale*. What would you mean today if you said someone was 'beyond the pale'? How and why do you think this phrase began?

This effigy of a knight is from Kilfane in County Kilkenny

Despite this success, the English made little real attempt to make Ireland part of their kingdom. The chieftains continued to control much of Ireland outside the Pale. Many wanted Ireland to be free of outside influence. From time to time they opposed the English in Ireland. This was why Richard II led an expedition in 1394. He forced the chieftains to acknowledge his rule. However, by the end of the Middle Ages the links with England had been greatly weakened. Ireland could only loosely be called British by then.

The Marcher Lords in Wales

Wales, like Ireland, was a land of many kingdoms at the time of the Norman Conquest. Like the Irish, the chieftains often fought each other. As a result, there were no clear-cut boundaries between the territories controlled by each chieftain. Much of the land seemed mountainous and uninviting to the Norman barons after the conquest.

This is why they settled mainly in the fertile lowlands. The Earls of Shrewsbury, Chester and Hereford and other marcher lords, as they were called (after the word *march*—meaning a border) took land from Welsh landowners. They built castles and manor houses, and treated their Welsh estates as if they were private kingdoms instead of lands held by them as vassals of the king.

Map of medieval Wales

Criccieth Castle was built in about 1230 by Llywelyn the Great

Llywelyn the Great

Many of the Welsh chieftains accepted the English king as their overlord: but some did not. As a result, it was never clear which areas of Wales were part of Norman Britain and which were not. From time to time some marcher lords and chieftains grew more powerful than their neighbours. From 1155 to 1197 Rhys ap Gruffydd, the Lord of Rhys, ruled the powerful kingdom of Deheubarth in the south. Despite this, he took care to acknowledge Henry II as his overlord.

In the thirteenth century, two Welsh princes founded a great kingdom in Gwynedd in the north west. They expanded it to include much of the rest of Wales as well. This meant that, for the first time, most of Wales was one country, under one leader.

Llywelyn the Great was Prince of Gwynedd from 1195 to 1240. He could have been seen as a threat to the king of England, but Llywelyn took care to do homage to the king. He even married King John's daughter Joan, although this didn't stop him taking advantage of the chaos in England to extend his Welsh empire even further.

When Llywelyn died in 1240, however, it was far from clear who would succeed him. In fact, it took ten years for his grandson, Llywelyn the Last, to establish his claim.

Llywelyn the Last

When Edward I came to the throne in 1272, Llywelyn made the error of not doing homage to him as overlord. Henry III had been a weak king. Edward, by contrast, was a formidable soldier. He led an expedition to Wales in 1276 and forced Llywelyn to surrender. He allowed him to keep the title Prince of Wales but restricted his princedom to Snowdonia.

Five years later Llywelyn made his final mistake. A medieval chronicler takes up the story.

Source 24.B

AD 1282: *At the dead hour of night, on Palm Sunday, Llywelyn, prince of Wales, and David, his brother, surrounded the castles of Rhuddlan and Flint with a large army. Afterwards, they devastated with plunder and fire the greater part of the marches. The king, hearing of this, but scarcely believing it, assembled an army.*

Llywelyn ap Gruffydd

Llywelyn ap Gruffydd was not strictly the heir to Gwynedd, since he had an older brother, Owain. But Llywelyn was a ruthless man, and very ambitious. He fought his brothers—Owain, Rhodri and David—to become undisputed leader of Gwynedd in 1254. He later expanded his territory by leading raids on the marcher lords and was accepted as overlord by most of the Welsh barons.

With Henry III's agreement he took the title of Prince of Wales in 1267. But he badly mishandled his relations with the new king Edward I when he came to the throne in 1272. As a result, the Welsh people lost their independence.

This is why he was later known as Llywelyn the Last.

Caernarfon Castle ▶

Conwy Castle

He reduced all Wales towards the mountains of Snowdonia under his authority, and gave large portions of the territory which he acquired to his earls and barons.

Llewelyn, taking with him a numerous army, descended into the lowlands, leaving the mountainous district to his brother David.

The marcher lords attacked him and slew a great number of the Welsh. In this battle the head of prince Llewelyn was cut off and carried to London, where it was placed on a stake on the top of the Tower of London.

David was captured and executed the following year. Edward I took over Llywelyn's lands and made them part of his kingdom. He passed a law, the Statute of Wales, which helped to join Wales to England. In future Wales was to obey English laws, and the land would be divided into shires as in England, to make it easier to govern.

To make sure the Welsh would not rise up again, Edward built a series of magnificent castles. They included Harlech, Caernarfon, Conwy and Beaumaris. Each castle was extremely expensive to build, as you can see on page 166, but they were immensely strong, with powerful towers forming part of the double ring of walls. They were also economical to run, since they could be defended by only a small garrison of soldiers.

24.6 What was the news that so surprised King Edward at Easter 1282? What did he do about it?

24.7 Why do you think Llywelyn left Snowdonia instead of waiting to face Edward's army? AT1B ■

24.8 Look at the map on page 125. In which part of Wales did Edward build most of his castles? Why? Write down two or three reasons which could explain why Edward built most of his castles along the coast. AT1B ■

Medieval Scotland

Scotland was not a tempting target for the Norman kings. As you saw on page 91, William the Conqueror led an army into Scotland in 1072, 'but found nothing there of value.' Like Wales, it was mountainous and, like Ireland, it was a long way from London. However, unlike Wales or Ireland, it had a single monarch. There were times when the King of the Scots did homage to the English king, as you can see from Source 18.D on page 91. As a result, the English monarchs assumed they were Scotland's overlords.

Despite this, there were many occasions when Scottish or English soldiers crossed the border and raided the land on the other side. These border skirmishes lasted, off and on, for hundreds of years.

Edward I

In general, relations with the English monarchy ran smoothly enough. The two royal houses were often linked by marriage. Alexander II (1214–49) married the sister of Henry III. His son, Alexander III (1249–86), married Henry III's daughter Margaret.

Alexander III was childless. When he died, his grand-daughter Margaret, aged three, succeeded to the throne. In July 1290, Edward I agreed with the great lords of Scotland that she should marry his son Edward (then aged 6). But the Maid of Norway, as she was called, died two months later and left Scotland with a problem. Who should be the next king or queen of the Scots?

As overlord, Edward claimed the right to decide this for himself. The Scottish lords agreed and, in 1292, Edward picked John Balliol from a number of other claimants to the throne. Balliol was crowned King John at Scone Abbey the same year. You can see what happened next in Sources 24.C to 24.E (opposite). They were written by a monk from Westminster Abbey.

English soldiers fight off a Scottish raiding party in the border country

▼ *Map of medieval Scotland*

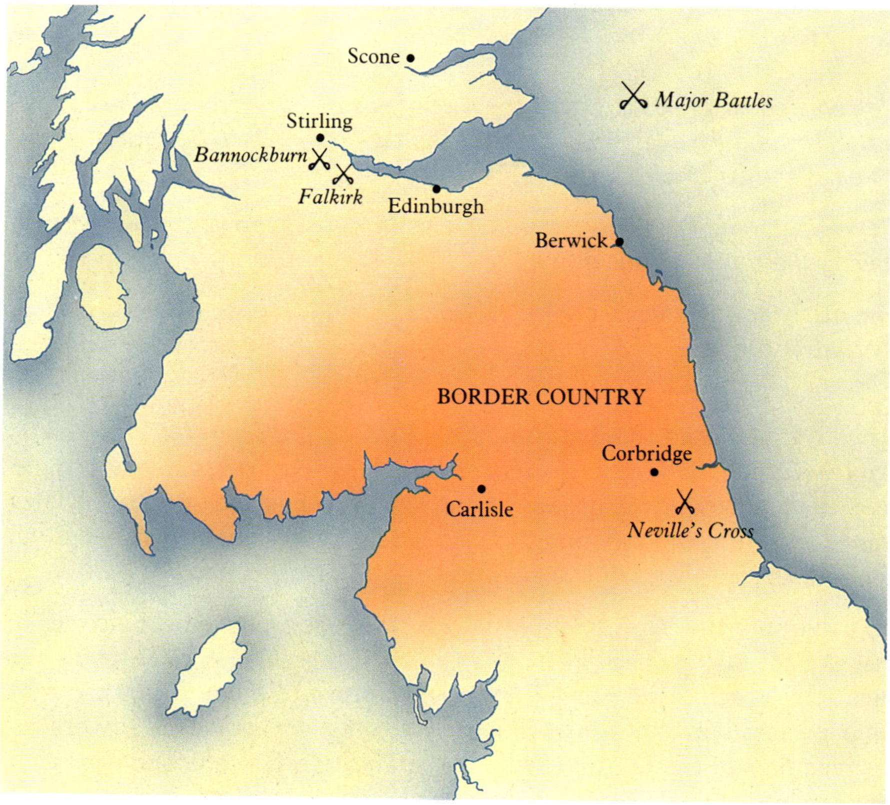

24.9 Write one or two sentences describing the picture above. What type of place was under attack? What defences did it have? AT1C/L5

24.10 Look at the map on the left. Suggest a possible location for the picture above. AT3/L4

24.11 Write down reasons why we might wonder if everything written in Sources 24.C, 24.D and 24.E is accurate or not. AT2 ■ AT3 ■

24.12 Which Source, 24.C, 24.D, or 24.E is illustrated by the photograph underneath? What does it show? What was its significance in the dispute between England and Scotland? AT1C/L5

24.13 Write two or three sentences giving reasons why Edward invaded Scotland. Why do you think he wanted three castles? Would you have agreed to this request, if you had been King of the Scots? Or was it just an excuse to invade Scotland? AT1B ■

Edward I

Edward I was born in 1239 and died in 1307. When he succeeded to the throne in 1272 the reputation of the English crown was at a very low ebb. The mistakes made by his grandfather, King John, had been continued by his father, Henry III.

Edward I's greatest success was to restore the fame and power of the English monarchy once more. He did this mainly through his skill as a soldier and also through the reforms he made to the law and to the founding of Parliament.

He was very tall and striking in appearance, but also bad-tempered and often cruel. He suffered serious setbacks towards the end of his reign and his popularity fell when he continued to raise taxes to pay for his wars. When he died, in 1307, he was still a long way from making Scotland part of his kingdom.

Source 24.C

***AD 1295:** John Balliol, King of Scotland, forgetful of his homage and vow of fealty* [to King Edward], *sent ambassadors to France. There he secretly made an alliance against the King of England. Edward (being ignorant of it) was greatly deceived. When he asked for help in his war* [against France], *and received a doubtful answer, he demanded that three Scottish castles be put in his hands as security till the end of the war. But as the Scots refused to do this, the king, being now more certain of their treachery, marched with his army towards Scotland.*

Source 24.D

***AD 1296:** Advancing into Scotland, he came to the Maiden's Castle* [Edinburgh]. *As the garrison refused to surrender, he employed engines of war. These shot forth large stones and beat down many houses and the tops of the towers. Alarmed at this, the garrison immediately surrendered the castle. And in that place, the royal insignia of the kingdom of Scotland were discovered and taken to Westminster.*

Source 24.E

Edward went on to Stirling and found the castle there empty with no one to resist him. The garrison had fled in fear. Afterwards King John gave up the kingdom of Scotland. Edward I returned to Berwick upon Tweed by way of Scone. He gave orders that the stone on which the kings of Scotland used to be crowned should be taken to London. It was a sign that the kingdom had been conquered.

Robert the Bruce

In 1297 a young Scotsman called William Wallace took advantage of the fact that Edward was preparing to fight the French. He led a rebellion against the English and defeated a small English army at Stirling. The Scots were delighted and flocked to Wallace's support. They drove the English back across the border. But Edward led a large army into Scotland once more and put Wallace to flight at the battle of Falkirk in 1298. Wallace continued to harass the English forces until betrayed in 1305.

The execution of Wallace (see Source 24.F), a hero and a patriot in Scottish eyes, was a mistake. The following year Robert the Bruce, who had a legitimate claim to the Scottish throne, led yet another rebellion. At first he fought using guerrilla tactics and harassed the English enemy, but by 1314 he had assembled a substantial army as well.

On 23–4 June 1314, Robert the Bruce and the Scottish army fought a great battle against the English at Bannockburn. A monk from Cumbria tells us what happened.

Source 24.G

The great horses of the English charged the pikes of the Scots, as if entering a dense forest. There arose a great and terrible crash of broken spears and of war horses wounded to the death. The English in the rear could not reach the Scots because the front rank of soldiers was in the way. There was nothing for it but to take flight. In the confusion of their retreat many nobles and other soldiers fell with their horses into a great ditch called the Bannock Burn.

Robert the Bruce's crushing victory firmly established him as King of Scotland. The great nobles and bishops of Scotland issued the declaration at Arbroath in 1320, which made their position clear.

Source 24.H

If he [Robert the Bruce] *were to give up what he has already begun and willingly subject this kingdom to the King of England or to the English, we would treat him at once as our enemy and make someone else our king. Even if only a hundred of us survive, we will never, under any circumstance, accept English rule.*

In 1323 Robert the Bruce's claim to the throne was recognised by the Pope and then by the English king as well in 1328.

In fact, the English did not keep their part of the bargain and in 1330 border warfare broke out once again, as it often did in the Middle Ages. Nonetheless, Robert the Bruce's great victory at Bannockburn secured Scottish independence from England for hundreds of years.

Source 24.F

***AD 1305:** A certain Scot, by name William Wallace, an outcast, a robber, a sacrilegious man, a fire-raiser, and a murderer, a man more cruel than Herod, and more insane than Nero, who fled from the battle of Falkirk, leaving his people to be slain by the sword, was at last taken prisoner by the king's servants and brought to London. He was condemned to a most cruel but amply deserved death.*

Robert I of Scotland

Robert the Bruce was born in 1274 and became Earl of Carrick in 1292. He claimed the Scottish throne through his great-great-great-grandfather, Malcolm III.

At first Robert supported Edward I, even though his grandfather, Robert de Bruce, had been one of the claimants to the Scottish throne in 1290. Later he changed sides for a time to join William Wallace, but returned in 1302 to acknowledge Edward as his lord. He seized his chance when Wallace was executed in 1305. He murdered his rival, John Comyn, in 1306 and then seized the throne of Scotland. This was treason, of course, and Robert was hunted as a fugitive from justice.

When Edward I died the following year, however, Robert's fortunes recovered. The new English king, Edward II, was weak and incompetent. For the next few years Robert slowly built up his support. One by one he attacked the Scottish nobles who backed the English. Then, in 1314, he won a stunning victory over Edward II at Bannockburn. He died in 1329 at Cardross Castle near Glasgow.

24.14 Whose support do you think Robert the Bruce valued most: the Pope, the English king, or the Scottish nobles? What was important about the Declaration of Arbroath? AT1C/L6

24.15 Why were the English defeated at the battle of Bannockburn? AT1B ■

24.16 List the statements in Source 24.F which tell you that the writer was biased against Wallace. AT3/L5

24.17 What type of warfare is illustrated in the picture opposite? What effect do you think the border wars had on the people living in the border counties of England and Scotland? AT1B ■

The Battle of Neville's Cross on 17 October 1346 was one of a series of battles between England and Scotland in the fourteenth and fifteenth centuries. Despite this, relations between the two countries hardly changed.

Time Line

Year	England	Ireland	Wales	Scotland
1154–89	Henry II			
1155–97			Lord Rhys of Deheubarth	
1166		Rory O'Connor named as High King of Ireland		
1170	Murder of Becket	Strongbow victorious		
1171		Irish chieftains submit to Henry II		
1189–99	Richard I			
1195–1240			Llywelyn ap Gruffydd	
1199–1216	John			
1215	Magna Carta			
1216–72	Henry III			
1246–82			Llywelyn the Last	
1249–86				Alexander III
1267			Llywelyn Prince of Wales	
1272–1307	Edward I			
1283			Edward conquers Wales	
1286–90				Margaret, Maid of Norway
1292–96				John Balliol
1296				Edward I invades Scotland
1298				Battle of Falkirk
1305				William Wallace executed
1306–29				Robert I
1307–27	Edward II			
1314				Battle of Bannockburn
1316		Edward Bruce crowned King of Ireland		
1327–77	Edward III			
1346	Battle of Crecy			Battle of Neville's Cross
1377–99	Richard II			
1394		Richard II in Ireland		
1399–1413	Henry IV			
1400–1410			Owain Glyndwr's rebellion	

25 A MEDIEVAL TOWN

FOCUS

▶ *HOW and WHY did towns grow in the Middle Ages?* AT1B ■
▶ *HOW were they built and defended?* AT1C ■
▶ *WHAT was it like to live in a medieval town?* AT1C ■
▶ *HOW were the towns governed and what problems did the townspeople have to face?* AT1C ■
▶ *WHAT can we learn about medieval town life from towns today?* AT1A ■

Why towns grew

At the time of the Norman Conquest, Mamecestre (Manchester) and Snotingehame (Nottingham) were small villages. Large towns in those days had only two or three thousand people. Norwich had a population of at least 5000 and was one of the largest towns in England.

We know about these towns from the Domesday Book compiled in 1086. It recorded the names of the boroughs (towns) and the number of burgesses (citizens) in each town. Many of these boroughs were little more than groups of wooden houses with thatched roofs, a few shops and workshops, a cattle market and one or two churches. After the Norman Conquest, they became more important for a number of reasons.

Some towns grew in size because of their position, such as a town at the mouth of a river, which became a port. Many towns grew up where a river could be crossed by a ford (Oxford) or by a bridge (Cambridge). Merchants were always passing through these towns. Local shops and markets did a lot of business with the traders. The large market towns had a main square where horses, cattle, sheep, pigs, poultry, fish, corn, wool, butter, vegetables, salt, cloth and many other products were on sale.

Some towns, such as Newcastle, grew up around a castle, which protected the local people. Some, like Bury St Edmunds, became important because of the work done by a great abbey or a cathedral. Shire (or county) towns were especially important. This was where the sheriff did his work on behalf of the king. The Normans usually built castles in these towns, such as those at Norwich and York.

25.1 Write one or two sentences to say how the Norman house (left) differs from the fifteenth century house (right). AT1C ■

25.2 Why do you think that, despite the greater fire risk, most medieval houses were built of wood and thatch instead of with brick or stone and tiles? AT1B ■

Norman house in Lincoln

25.3 What would happen to a street if all the houses had jetties like *Bayleaf*? Why do you think jettying was used? Was it safer? Did it provide more space upstairs? Was it more attractive? AT1B ■

25.4 How can you tell the house in Lincoln is a Norman house (see page 94)? Which parts of this building do you think were built at a later stage? AT1A ■

25.5 Look at the painting. What does it tell you about a medieval town? What buildings can you see? What building materials were used? Write a paragraph describing this town. AT1C ■

25.6 In what ways do the streets in the painting differ from modern streets? AT1A/L4

This picture of a medieval town shows a doctor picking herbs in his walled garden. He used them to make medicines for his richer patients.

Some towns were new and many had new suburbs, such as the *New Land* in King's Lynn. French, Jewish and Flemish settlers came to live in many of these towns. Norwich already had 43 French burgesses by the time of the Domesday Book.

Even at the end of the Middle Ages, however, medieval towns were still green to look at. They were small by our standards, so no one lived far from the country. Inside the town walls there were gardens and meadows as well as farmland. In some towns, people even had strips of land on which to keep a cow and a few pigs.

How a town was built

Over the years, houses and streets changed. Many new houses and streets were built like those you can see on pages 122, 138, 139 and 141. More people used coal as a fuel. New ways of letting light into a house were introduced, although it was not until the sixteenth century that glass windows and tall chimneys became common.

Bayleaf, *a fifteenth-century house in Sussex*

Bayleaf has been rebuilt at the Weald and Downland Museum in Sussex so that people can see what a medieval home really looked like. Notice how the upper floor of this house juts out. Overhanging wooden beams supported the floor above. This type of building is called *jettying*. In contrast, the Norman house in Lincoln was built of stone. The owners of these houses would have been rich. Poor people's homes were much smaller. They had wooden frames with thin plaster walls (like *Bayleaf*) but were often thatched with straw. This is why most of them fell down long ago and why only a few can be seen today.

How a town was defended

Many medieval towns were surrounded by walls. Some of these walls and the gateways through them can be seen today, although often in ruins. The cost of building the wall was met by the citizens. We know about this from records which tell us how much was paid to the masons, carpenters and ditchers employed by the town.

Source 25.A Annual cost of repairs to the King's Lynn town wall in the fifteenth century

Ironworkers and smiths	*£14*
Carpenters and sawyers	*£17*
Masons and tilers	*£15*
Ditchers	*£43*
Timber	*£21*
Stone and tiles	*£9*
Sand and cement	*£5*
Other expenses	*£19*
Total	*£143*

Average wages

Ditcher	*2s*	[10p]	*a week*
Carpenter	*2s 6d*	[12½p]	*a week*
Mason	*3s*	[15p]	*a week*

25.7 Why is there a continuous path on top of the wall at Rothenburg? Why was it roofed? How was it built? What workers would have been needed to build this wall? AT1C/L5

25.8 Use the information from Source 25.A and the photographs to explain why the town wall at King's Lynn may have looked like the one at Rothenburg in the Middle Ages. AT3/L5

25.9 What is the average weekly wage today? How many times greater is it than the average wage of a worker on the King's Lynn town wall? Work out roughly how much it would cost to do a similar amount of work today. AT1A/L5

The tops of almost all town walls today are open to the skies. But this town wall at Rothenburg in Germany shows us what many of them may have looked like in the Middle Ages. ▶

Ruins of the town wall in King's Lynn, Norfolk

Clues to the position of an old town wall can often be found in street names, such as Kirkgate, Westgate, Northgate and Newgate. Barbican Road in York and the Barbican area of London are both named after a *barbican*. This was a tower in front of a gatehouse. The word *fosse* (or *foss*) as part of a street name may indicate the position of the ditch dug outside the wall.

The main danger for most towns in the later Middle Ages came from criminals and outlaws. Nonetheless, there were enough civil wars, skirmishes and revolts to make most people grateful for the walls surrounding their town. On 15 August 1311, at a time of unrest in England, Sir Richer de Refham and the aldermen of London issued a set of orders from the London guildhall (Source 25.B).

25.10 How many men defended the Bisshopesgate Gate? Who locked the gates at night? Are these facts or opinions? AT2/L3

25.11 Place tracing paper on top of the map. Use the information in Source 25.B to mark in roughly where you think the medieval town wall of London was situated. Shade or colour in the approximate position of the Bishopesgate Ward. AT3/L4

25.12 Look at the three town gates from England, Wales and Scotland in the photographs below. How do they differ from each other? What do they all have in common? Use this information to write two or three sentences describing the features you would expect to see in a medieval town gate. AT3 ■

Source 25.B

For the safe-keeping of the City, it is ordered that the Gates shall be watched day and night. At the Gate of Bisshopesgate, every night there are to be six men from Bisshopesgate Ward, six from the Ward of Bradestrete, six from the Ward of Cornhille and two men from the Ward of Lymestrete, all well armed. And Robert Cook and John le Little are chosen to keep the keys of the gate.

The great Gates of the City are to be closed each night at the beginning of curfew being rung at St Martin's le Grand, and not opened afterwards that night. A chain is to be drawn across at Castle Baynard and fastened at the same hour. To keep the Postern [another gate] *near the Tower, there are to be twelve men of Tower Ward, well armed.*

The other Gates listed were: Ludegate, Newgate, Aldresgate, Crepelgate, Alegate, Bridge Gate.

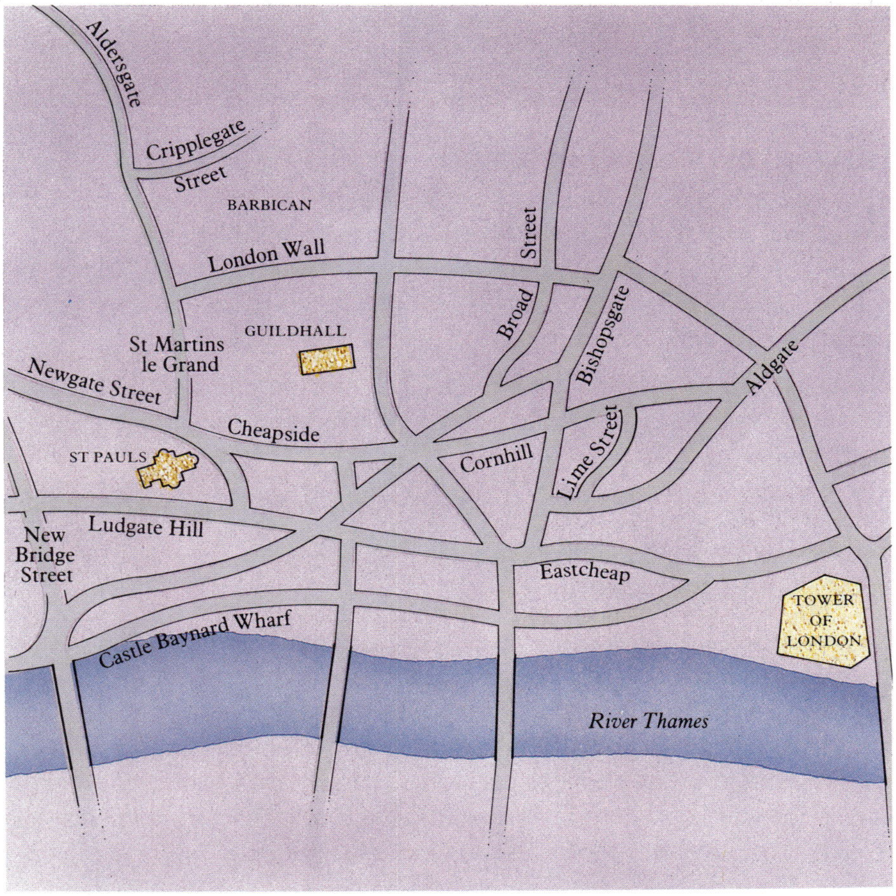

Map of London showing some of the streets and buildings named in the 1311 order

Town gates—King's Lynn, England

Town gates—Monmouth, Wales

Town gates—St Andrews,

◀ *Medieval buildings in Exeter*

How a town was governed

Three distinct classes of people lived in a medieval town. The people of wealth and power were at the top. They were the ruling class from whom the mayor and aldermen were chosen. They made regulations to control the town. In King's Lynn in Norfolk, for instance, they banned trading on Sundays except for the keepers of taverns and cooks.

The burgesses or freemen came next. They elected the town's officials. As freemen they had many privileges. At King's Lynn, for instance, a freeman had

a right to have all his sons taught free of charge at the Free School in Lyn.

People in the lowest class had few rights. They did most of the hard work and got few of the benefits.

Most townspeople wanted to govern themselves. They didn't like paying taxes to the king's officials. They wanted to elect their own officials and run their own affairs. This is why they asked the king to grant them a charter which would give their town the right to hold a fair or a market and grant them other privileges as well. In return, they had to pay a lump sum to the king each year. They could then use tolls from traders entering the town to pave the streets and pay for other services.

Source 25.C Charter granted by King Henry III to the Prior and Convent of Pontefract

Know that we have granted to the Prior and Convent of Pontefract, that they and their successors may have for ever one market every seven days on Wednesday in their town of Barnsley. They may have there one fair every year lasting for four days starting with the eve of St Michael's Day and two days following that day.

In 1205 King John granted a charter to King's Lynn in Norfolk. It gave them some very strange-sounding rights. These included

Soke and Sack, Toll and Theme, Infang Theft and Outfang Theft.

This meant that the town had the right to seize, try and punish a criminal caught inside and outside the town's limits.

The free schools in medieval towns were usually only for boys

25.13 Look at Source 25.D. Draw a graph to show these figures. What were the total tolls collected in Hereford in (a) the first week of March 1207 (b) the first week of July 1207? Give a reason which may explain the difference. Is your reason a fact or an opinion? AT2/L3

25.14 Look at Source 25.E. Why did the tolls in London vary in amount? Are there any modern tolls like this? What was this toll? Was it Lastage, Passage, Pavage, Pontage or Stallage? AT3/L4

Norwich was granted a charter in 1404 permitting the city to elect a mayor and two sheriffs to run the city's affairs. This fine guildhall was built to house the officials who controlled the city. ▶

The charter also gave the freemen other rights which meant that in every port except London, the merchants of Lynn did not have to pay tolls, such as *Lastage*. This was a duty paid on goods sold by the *last*—a unit of weight (about 2 tonnes). *Passage* was a toll paid to a ferryman to cross a river. *Pavage* paid for the upkeep of roads and streets and *Pontage* for the repair of bridges. Traders paid *Stallage* for the right to sell their goods in the market. The right of 'Assize of Bread and Beer' gave town officials the power to control the price of many foods as well as bread and beer.

Many of these tolls were collected at a tolbooth. A document records the tolls paid by carts, horses and wagons passing through the five town gates at Hereford in 1207.

Source 25.D

	1st week of March	*1st week of July*
Waye Gate	*0d*	*32d*
Igene Gate	*5d*	*20d*
Wythmersh Gate	*2d*	*15d*
Bishop Gate	*7d*	*20d*
St Owen's Gate	*2d*	*6d*

Another document tells us about the state of the roads leading into the city of London.

Source 25.E

1356: *The people who bring food and goods by carts or horses to the City complain that they are often in peril of losing what they bring. They say the roads outside the Gates are torn up and the surface broken. We have agreed, therefore, that every cart entering the City, that brings food or wares for sale, shall pay one penny and every horse one farthing. Carts that bring sand, gravel, and clay, shall pay 3d a week. Carts that bring wheat and flour from Stratford to the City, shall pay 3d a week. Carts that bring firewood for sale, one farthing. Carts that bring charcoal for sale, one penny.* [6d = six pennies = sixpence = 24 farthings = 2½p]

25.15 Look at Source 25.C. Find out if Barnsley still holds its market day on a Wednesday. On which days of the year did Barnsley hold its annual fair?

25.16 When was your town granted a charter? Is there a guildhall in the town? Did it have a free school in the Middle Ages? Is there any sign today of the tolls which traders had to pay in the past, such as a sign listing toll charges, a tolbooth, or a street name like Tollgate Road? AT1C/L5

25.17 Compare the two medieval shopping streets in the paintings. Which shop sign indicated a barber's shop where a man could get a shave? How does it differ from the similar sign for a barber's shop in the other painting? AT3 ■

25.18 How were these streets surfaced? What do you notice about the roofs and windows? How do they differ? AT3 ■

25.19 What did most medieval shops have in common? Write a paragraph describing a typical medieval shop using the information you can get from the pictures and sources on these pages. AT3 ■ AT1C ■

25.20 How did the tailor's shop (opposite) differ from the shops in these paintings? AT3/L4

25.21 What features in the photographs (below) can you identify from the paintings? AT3/L4

25.22 Is there a market cross or market hall in a town or village near your home? Are there any streets with medieval trade names? What changes have taken place since the Middle Ages? AT1A ■

At the shops

We know a lot about the shops and markets of medieval towns from pictures like these which were painted by artists living in the Middle Ages. They painted the things they could see every day.

As you can see from the photographs, we can also get some idea of what medieval shops and markets looked like from buildings which have survived more or less intact since the Middle Ages.

◀*Medieval shops, like this modern glassware shop in Salzburg, Austria, had signs instead of name plates to tell shoppers what they sold. Some towns still have shops with signs like these, such as a striped barber's pole or a bull's head outside a butcher's shop.*

Medieval shops in Lavenham in Suffolk

Lavenham market cross (left) and toll house (right). The cross had steps so market traders could display their wares on the ledges.

Street sign in Canterbury. Butchers often sold their meat in one particular street, like this one. In many towns it was called the Shambles—as you can see in Source I on page 140. Many other medieval traders, such as bakers and fish merchants, also had shops next to each other in the same street. This is why the streets of many towns were given trade names like those in Source 25.F.

25.23 Read the poem. How did medieval traders advertise their wares? How is this done today? Has there been any improvement? AT1A ■

Source 25.F Street Names in York

Baker Street
Colliergate
Coppergate
Fishergate
Lead Mill Lane
Coney Street
Market Street
Mill Lane
Pottery Lane
The Shambles
Swinegate
Tanner Row

Writers, like Chaucer, often give us a vivid picture of what people said and what they thought in the Middle Ages. This is something you cannot find out from a museum, building or painting. In a poem called the *London Lyckpeny*, a man called John Lydgate described the sounds you might have heard when shopping in London in about 1400.

Source 25.G

'Hot peas!' one begins to cry
'Strawberries ripe!' and 'Cherries in the rise!'
One bade me come near and buy some spice.

Then to Cheapside I was drawn,
One offered me velvet, silk and lawn,
Another he taketh me by the hand:
'Here is Paris thread, the finest in the land.'

Drapers much cloth me offered anon.
Then met I one, cried 'Hot sheep's feet!'
One cried 'Mackerel!' 'Rushes green!' another greeted me.
One wanted me to buy a hood to cover my head.

Then I hied me into East-cheap;
One cries 'Ribs of beef and many a pie!'

Medieval shop in Dol de Bretagne in France ▶

Town problems

We can get a very good idea of what it was like to live in a medieval town if we look at the cases heard in law courts.

Source 25.H London 4 June 1327

John Brid made a hole in a moulding board in his bakehouse. It was like a mouse-trap, there being a gate provided for closing and opening the hole. When his neighbours came to bake their bread in his oven, he put their dough on this board to make loaves. One of his servants sitting in secret beneath the table opened the gate and craftily withdrew some of the dough a little bit at a time.

William atte Sele, John atte Barnette, Robert de Bertone, John de Polberowe, Robert de Brokesbourne, Roger de Miltone, and Richard de Honesdone, bakers, and Alice de Brightenoch and Lucy de Pykeringe, bakeresses, were also charged with the same offence. It was agreed that all the bakers should be put in the pillory, with their dough hung from their necks.

Source 25.I London 1 November 1319

The wardens for inspecting meat sold in the shambles brought two beef carcasses taken from William Sperlyng of West Ham before the Mayor and Aldermen. He says the flesh is good and clean and fit for human food. But the jury say the carcasses are putrid and poisonous, and come from animals that have died of disease. It was judged that William Sperlyng should be put in the pillory and his carcasses burnt beneath him.

Source 25.J London 11 November 1364

John Penrose in the tavern of Walter Doget, sold red wine to all who came there, unsound and unwholesome for man, to deceive the common people. The judgement is that John Penrose shall drink a glass of the same wine which he sold the common people. The rest of the wine shall then be poured on his head and he shall give up the calling of a vintner in the City of London for ever.

Source 25.K London 19 November 1378

It is ordered that all butchers who sell meat within the City, shall close their shops before the time for candles being lighted. They shall sell no meat by light of candle, but by clear daylight only.

◀ *This picture from 1293 shows a London baker being pulled through muddy streets to the pillory. His underweight loaf is tied to his neck. Offenders stood on the pillory with their neck and arms sticking out of three holes in a wooden frame. Some were badly injured by the objects thrown by a jeering crowd.*

Medieval bakery

25.24 Was John Penrose's punishment more or less severe than John Brid's?

25.25 How do we know the 'bakeresses' in the picture were not guilty of John Brid's crime?
AT3/L3

25.26 What effect do you think the punishment of the pillory had on a trader?

25.27 Which evidence tells us that William Sperlyng was not alone in trying to defraud the public by selling rotten meat?
AT3/L5

25.28 Which king thought the Thames stank (see page 131)?

25.29 How can these sources be used to find out about everyday life in London in the Middle Ages? Which clues tell you about the cooking, lighting and toilet arrangements in people's homes? How did people relax? Why were the streets dirty?
AT3 ■

By-laws and court cases also show some of the problems which plagued the towns at a time when there was no mains gas, electricity, water, drainage or refuse collection.

Source 25.L
London 13 January 1302

Thomas Bat agreed to repay the City of London if any fire should arise from his houses covered with thatch. He agreed that he would have these houses covered with tiles by the end of May.

Source 25.M
London 1189

Let all the aldermen have a hook and cord [to pull down burning thatch]. *Before every house there should be a tub full of water, either of wood or stone.*

Source 25.N
London in the thirteenth century

1281: *No swine shall from henceforth be found in the streets. Any so found let them be killed.*
1297: *Pig-sties that are in the street shall be speedily removed.*

Source 25.O
London 23 April 1309

The people in the town put ordure that has been collected in their houses in the streets of the city, whereas they should have carried it to the Thames or out of the town. We do forbid this practice. Also no person shall have any dung raked or removed to the front of the houses of others.

Source 25.P Letter from the king, 29 August 1357

When passing along the water of the Thames, we have seen dung and other filth upon the bank of the river. We have also noticed the fumes and other abominable stenches arising therefrom. If tolerated, this may cause great peril to the people living in the city as well as to nobles and others passing along the river. Therefore, we do command you cause as well the banks of the river, as the streets and lanes of the city and its suburbs, to be cleansed of dung and other filth without delay.

25.30 How do these sources help us to know that people in the Middle Ages were worried about (a) the risk of fire (b) pollution and health? Write one or two sentences to say what solutions were proposed in each case. AT3 ■

25.31 Describe the street in the photograph. Why do you think many medieval streets were so narrow? What do you think it was like to live and work in a street like this in the Middle Ages? AT1C ■

25.32 How and why was the decision of the mayor and aldermen of London in 1309 overturned by the king in 1357? AT1A/L3

Medieval street in the small town on St Michael's Mount in France

26 TRADE AND INDUSTRY

FOCUS

▶ *HOW did merchants trade in the Middle Ages?* AT1C ■
▶ *WHAT industries and crafts were important in the Middle Ages?* AT1C ■
▶ *HOW were they organised?* AT1C ■

26.1 Who were the travellers in this carriage? Roughly how many people do you think it held?

26.2 What type of illustration is this? Who do you think drew it? Is it a realistic drawing?
AT2/L5 AT3/L5

26.3 What do you think it was like to travel in a vehicle like

26.4 Look at the pictures on the next page. Draw a picture of a medieval merchant ship and label it to show the features you can identify. Write one or two sentences saying what the ship looked like and how it moved through the water. How was it steered? What happened when it put into harbour?
AT1C ■

26.5 What goods are shown on the quayside at Danzig (right)? How were they lifted? How did this machine work? Write a paragraph to describe what you would have seen on the quayside in Danzig when this picture was painted. AT1C/L5

Overland travel in the Middle Ages

Travelling overland in the Middle Ages was a hardship for most people. For one thing it was very slow. When Queen Eleanor died near Lincoln in 1290, it took nearly two weeks for her body to be brought the 150 miles (240 km) back to London. This was largely because the roads were so poor. They were made of earth without proper foundations, drains or a hard surface on top. They were often little more than dirt tracks—muddy when wet and cracked and dusty when dry.

Many travellers preferred to go across country on horseback. They could ride through the woods, skirt the open fields and stop the night at a tavern in a town or in an abbey in the country. They had to take care, of course, to avoid places where outlaws were known to hide. This is why a law was passed in 1285 making landowners clear the forest for 60 metres on either side of a road approaching a market town.

There were other hazards as well. Large lumbering carts and wagons, pulled by oxen or by horses, took corn, vegetables and firewood to the towns. Occasionally there were processions of nobles, knights and their ladies, or even a royal progress (as you saw on page 118). Merchants would also be seen. They often carried the goods they had to sell in large baskets, one on either side of a pack animal. Teams of packhorses took wool to the great fairs and to the ports for export overseas.

An alternative form of travel was by river. Barges and open boats sailed up many of Britain's rivers, carrying corn, coal and even passengers to inland towns.

26.6 Write a sentence describing the medieval merchant in Nuremberg (below). What type of activity does the picture show?

Panel depicting a wool merchant in Nuremberg in Germany

Woolpack and merchant ship depicted in a stone carving at Tiverton parish church in Devon

Medieval trade

Merchants who traded overseas sent their goods by merchant ship like the one shown in this carving in Bishop Lydeard Church in Somerset

After the Norman Conquest, Britain's trade with other countries in Europe grew rapidly. Fine leather from Cordoba in Spain, for instance, was used by leather workers. This is why they were called *cordwainers*. Silks were imported from Italy, wine came from France and top quality woollen cloth from Flanders. Pitch, tar, timber, furs and fish were some of the products supplied by Scandinavia and northern Europe.

In return for these products from Europe, British merchants exported the finest wool. Hides, skins and corn were other leading exports. In the later Middle Ages, woollen cloth was sold abroad as well. Cloth from Stamford in Lincolnshire was already being sold in Venice by 1265.

Merchants did much of their business at the great annual fairs as well as at the weekly markets. For instance, St Ives in Cambridgeshire had an annual fair in August. It was granted this right by King John in 1202. For a week, all the town's business was done at the fair.

Many merchants made great fortunes from trade. Woollen merchants in East Anglia and the Cotswolds used their money to help build magnificent churches, such as those at Fairford in Gloucestershire and at Lavenham in Suffolk. They also built splendid new homes there as well. Many of these can still be seen today.

◀ *Some towns in England, such as London, Ipswich, King's Lynn and Hull, traded with the powerful European ports which belonged to the Hanseatic League. These included Hamburg, Lubeck and Danzig (or Gdansk) which you can see in this medieval painting. Goods to and from Britain were loaded and unloaded at ports like this.*

Heavy industry

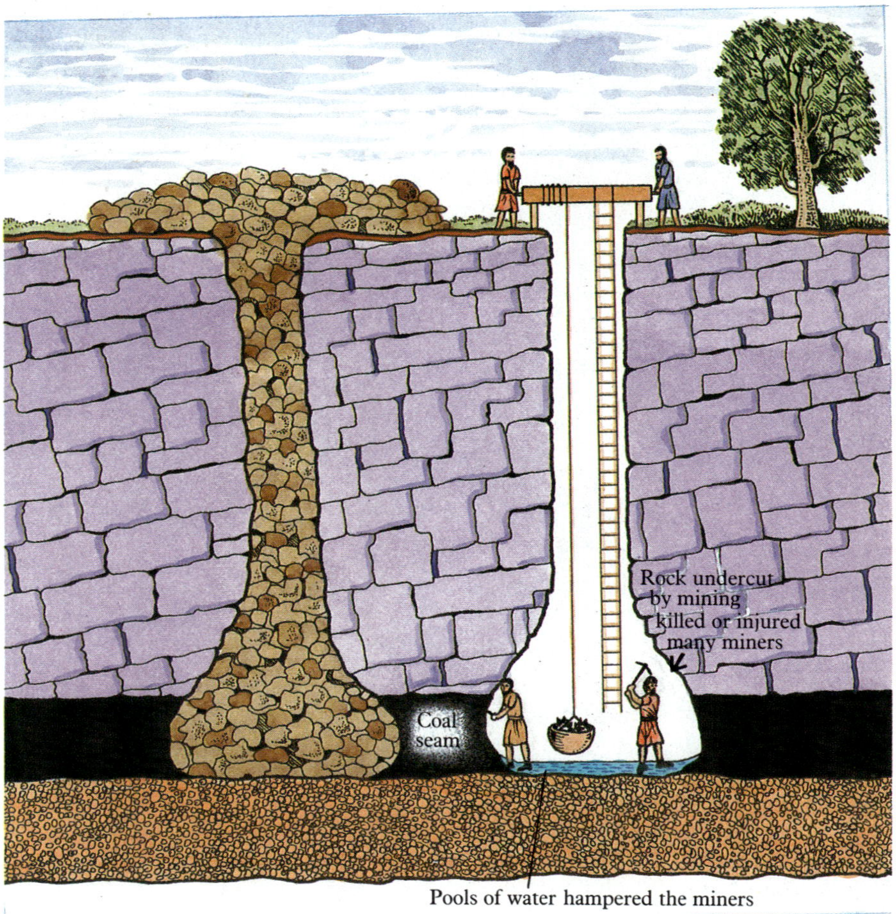

A medieval bell pit

Most medieval goods were hand-made by craftsmen. These craft workers lived in the towns but depended on people in the country for many of the raw materials they used, such as stone, wood, iron, leather, wool and glass (made from sand).

They used wood for fuel—either as firewood or as charcoal. Coal was also mined from small bell pits sunk in the ground. Much of it was sent to London by ship from Newcastle upon Tyne and used in people's homes. A few workers used it for heating, such as boiling the huge vats of dye used to stain cloth.

Source 26.A

***11 July 1369:** John Wirhale, Roger Cooke, Henry Cornewaille and Geoffrey Prudhomme, were chosen to hold the office of Meters* [inspectors] *of sea-coal coming into the City of London; and sworn that they would well and trustily make measures of coals so coming thither.*

◀*This picture was printed by William Caxton in one of the first books printed in Britain, at the end of the fifteenth century*

26.7 How can we prove that Londoners used coal in the Middle Ages? Why was it called sea-coal? AT3/L3

26.8 Look at the picture of the coal mine. Why was it called a bell pit? What did the miners do with the earth they dug out of the ground when they sank a new bell pit? AT1B/L3

26.9 What type of worker is shown in the medieval picture (below)? What tools did he use? Draw or trace this picture and label the tools you can identify. AT1C/L5

26.10 Look at Source 26.B. What was the writer's complaint against the smiths? Which words describe their appearance? What working clothes did they wear? What tools did they use? AT1C/L6

26.11 What do you think the smiths wanted when they cried out 'Coal! Coal!'?

26.12 Look at Sources 26.B and 26.C. If the poem describes London blacksmiths, is it likely to have been written before or after 1394? Give a reason. AT1A/L4

26.13 Two of the tools used by a medieval craft worker are shown in disguise in the carving at Lavenham (right). What are these tools? How were they depicted? What type of worker used them? What is the value of this carving as a source of information? AT3/L5

26.14 Look at the medieval glass works (below). How many different jobs are shown here? Did the workers wear special clothes? Draw a strip cartoon to show how glass was made in the Middle Ages. Your first picture might show people digging sand. The last picture will probably show glassware being carried away to be sold. AT1C/L5

The metal workers

Iron ore was usually smelted near the place where it was mined. It was mixed with charcoal and heated until white hot. This was done using bellows. The charcoal was made by slowly baking wood in a pit covered with turf to stop the heat getting out. However, the furnace could not be made hot enough to melt the iron completely. As a result, it was brittle and easily broken. Hammering the hot iron in a forge, however, made it more workable so that it could be bent and shaped.

Towards the end of the Middle Ages, many cutlers (knife-makers) began to use water wheels to turn grindstones to sharpen their blades. Water power was also used to lift the huge hammers which forged (beat) the hot metal.

Source 26.B Medieval poem

Swarthy, smoky smiths, smattered with smut,
Drive me to death with the din of their clanging.
Such noise at night ne'er heard man never.
The hunch-backed creatures cry 'Coal! Coal!'
And blow their bellows till their brains do burst:
Their bodies shielded by a bull's hide apron.
Their legs protected against flying cinders;
With heavy hammers that are hard to handle
They strike strident strokes on a stock of steel;
'Luss! Buss! Lass! Dass!' they roar together.
Their din would drive the devil mad!
'Tick! Tack! Luss! Buss! Lass! Dass!'
May no man sleep for all this racket?

Woodcarving under a seat in Lavenham Church in Suffolk

◀ *Medieval glass workers used sand as their main raw material. If you look carefully, you can see workers digging and carrying sand, heating it to a high temperature in a furnace, using a long tube to blow a ball of glass into shape, inspecting the finished glassware, and taking it away to be sold.*

Source 26.C Rule of the London Blacksmiths in 1394

By reason of the great nuisance, noise and alarm experienced by the neighbours around their dwellings; it is ordained from henceforth that no one of the said trade shall work by night, but only from the beginning of daylight to 9 of the clock at night.

Source 26.E Regulations of the Craft Guild of Berwick on Tweed in 1283

- *Whoever shall fall into old age or poverty, or into hopeless sickness, and has no means of his own, shall have such help as the Aldermen, Dean, and Brethren of the guild think right, and such as the means of the guild enable to be given.*
- *No woman shall sell ale from Easter to Michaelmas, at dearer than two pence a gallon; nor, from Michaelmas till Easter, at dearer than a penny. And the names of the ale wives shall be registered.*

Medieval crafts and guilds

We can get some idea of the crafts and trades of the Middle Ages simply by looking at surnames today. People then were often known by the name of their trade. In a fourteenth-century poem, for instance,

Cissie the Shoemaker, Wat the Warner [gamekeeper], *Hugh the Needleseller, Davy the Diker and Rose the Dishseller*

sat together in a tavern in London. In time, names like these stuck. Jack the Fuller became Jack Fuller and Lucy the Brewster (a female brewer) became Lucy Brewster.

Source 26.D Trade surnames

Cloth Industry		Merchants/Shopkeepers		Crafts	
Dyer	*Webb*	*Brewer*	*Cook*	*Mason*	*Smith*
Fuller	*Spinner*	*Brewster*	*Mercer*	*Carpenter*	*Miller*
Weaver	*Taylor*	*Butcher*	*Merchant*	*Tiler*	*Cooper*
Webster	*Sherman*	*Baker*	*Draper*	*Slater*	*Potter*
Webber	*Walker*	*Spicer*	*Chandler*	*Thatcher*	*Barber*

26.15 Look at the table of surnames. What craft names like these are represented in your school? What work did a miller, slater, tiler, cooper, mercer and sherman do? What goods did a draper, spicer and chandler sell? AT1A/L4

26.16 What other surname on this list means the same as Webster, Webber and Webb? (Clue: What is a web?)

26.17 Which job on this list was the same as that of (a) a brewster (b) a merchant (c) a fuller?

Each craft or trade was organised into guilds. These were not trade unions. They were run by the employers, not the workers. Each guild had its own strict rules which had to be obeyed. Master craftsmen trained youths, called apprentices, in the skills of their trade. Apprentice mercers (merchants), for instance, were even taught French because they were expected to trade in France. They were bound to their master for a long period of training by a written document, called a contract. They qualified as master craftsmen when they successfully produced a 'master piece' in front of a leading member of the guild.

The other employees in a workshop were called journeymen. This came from the French word *journée* meaning day. In other words, they were workers who were paid by the day.

The guilds were very powerful. You can see this from the rules of the Cutlers' Guild in Source 26.F. London had (and still has) twelve great livery companies—the City Guilds. The 'livery' was the uniform worn by the members of the guild. Not only did they control the way their craft or trade was organised, they even provided their members with some of the benefits which we expect the State to provide today (Source 26.E).

Source 26.F Rules of the London Cutlers' Guild in 1344

- *No cutler shall make any sale on a Sunday.*
- *No-one shall take an apprentice for a term less than seven years.*
- *Every work shall be made by day and not at night; under penalty of fine of 16 shillings* [80p].
- *No one in the trade shall receive the apprentice or journeyman of another until his period of service has been fully accomplished; under penalty of a fine of 16 shillings.*
- *No cutler shall keep a shop, or receive an apprentice, if he be not a freeman of the City of London.*

26.18 Look at Sources 26.E and 26.F. Could anyone set up in business as a cutler in London in the fourteenth century? For how many years did a trainee cutler have to serve as an apprentice? AT3/L4

26.19 Look at the medieval painting (left). What important event in the life of an apprentice is shown here? To which guild do you think these workers belonged? Which rule of the Cutlers' Guild was much the same as the one controlling London's butchers in Source 25.K on page 140? How did the Craft Guild of Berwick on Tweed help its old or needy members? AT3/L4

This was the hall of the guild of Corpus Christi. It was one of the three guilds which controlled the woollen industry in Lavenham in Suffolk.

Source 26.G
The poor at work—from a fourteenth-century poem

The poor in the cottages are overwhelmed by their children and the rent they have to pay the landlord. What they earn from spinning, they spend on porridge to quieten the babies crying out for food, and on the rent of their homes. They themselves go hungry. There is extra misery in winter—rising at night in the narrow room to rock the cradle, carding and combing wool, washing and rubbing cloth, winding woollen thread. The misery of these women who dwell in hovels is too sad to speak of.

The woollen industry

Much of Britain's wool was exported in the early Middle Ages. Its importance was so great, the King's ministers even sat on woolsacks in Parliament (page 121). By 1300 the wool from over 10 million sheep was being exported each year—most of it to Flanders. Much of the wool came from sheep reared by monks on the estates of the great Cistercian monasteries.

Gradually, more and more woollen cloth was made in Britain. At first it was made in the large towns, such as London. But from the thirteenth century onwards, much of it was made in the West Country, the Cotswolds and the West Riding of Yorkshire. This was because it was easier to build fulling mills in those areas. Fullers used waterwheels to drive hammers which beat the cloth and helped to get the grease out of the wool.

Woolmark used by the cloth merchants of Lavenham in Suffolk as their trade mark

Dyeing cloth was important at a time when people enjoyed wearing gaily coloured clothes

26.20 Which processes in the manufacture of woollen cloth are shown in the pictures on these pages? Who did this work? AT3/L4

26.21 Can you think of a reason why fulling mills were situated in areas like the Cotswolds and the West Riding of Yorkshire? AT1B/L4

26.22 What information about a cloth finisher can you obtain from the photograph? What tools were used? How was the woollen cloth sold? Was it folded like a blanket or made into a long roll? What evidence is there in this picture that the woollen cloth on the table had been stretched on a tenter? AT3/L5

26.23 What tools and implements did a dyer use? How was the vat of dye in the picture heated? Did the dyers wear special working clothes? What is the value of a picture like this? AT3/L5

26.24 Look at Source 26.H. From which industries do these well-known phrases come? What do they mean today? AT1A/L4

26.25 What evidence in this chapter proves that many women went out to work in the Middle Ages? Name some of the jobs they did. Was it rewarding work? AT3/L4

The raw wool was carded (brushed) with a tool which looked like a thick comb. It was wound on to a rod called the distaff. Carding straightened the fibres in the wool to make them parallel to each other.

The woollen fibres were then twisted and spun into a continuous length of fine yarn. This was wound on to another rod, called a spindle, using a spinning wheel.

The yarn was woven into cloth by a weaver using a loom. One set of threads—the *warp* threads—was fixed to the loom at right angles to the shuttle which the weaver used to weave the *weft* threads under and over to make the cloth.

The cloth was later processed by a cloth finisher using large shears to trim the rough edges of wool to make it smooth and ready for use. The cloth finisher, the fuller, washed and scoured the cloth with fuller's earth to take out the grease. The wet cloth was dried outside by stretching the cloth on a special rack called a *tenter*. Hooks fixed the cloth to this tenter.

The yarn was sometimes dyed in a vat of coloured dye by the dyer or, as you can see in the picture, after it had been woven into cloth.

The cloth was produced by families working in their own homes. Often they used a room upstairs with a long window to get as much light as possible. These houses are called weavers' cottages today. Carders and spinners spun the yarn provided by the cloth merchant. It was then passed on to weavers to make into cloth and later sent to the dyer and fuller.

In some areas, a family bought a pack of wool themselves and carried out every process to turn it into a piece of cloth. A writer said:

They carry the wool to their houses on their heads and backs and so make the wool into yarn or cloth and sell it the following week when they journey back to Halifax.

Source 26.H

'hammer and tongs'
'spinster'
'on tenterhooks'
'dyed in the wool'
'masterpiece'
'too many irons in the fire'
'spin a yarn'
'the distaff side'
'carrying coals to Newcastle'
'spindle legs'

Woodcarving in Spaxton Church, Somerset, showing a cloth finisher with the tools of his trade ▶

27 HEALTH AND DISEASE

FOCUS

- *WHAT did people know about health and disease in the Middle Ages?* ATIC
- *WHAT was the Black Death and how did it affect people in medieval Britain?* ATIA

Health and disease

Unlike the people of the Islamic world (page 76), the people of medieval Britain knew little about health and disease. Doctors were few and far between. Those who had been trained had only a simple understanding of the human body. Since they did not know what caused an illness, they were unable to cure or prevent it.

Medieval doctor treating patients in his surgery

Some doctors even thought eating fresh fruit caused fever. Most thought diseases were caused when the body got out of balance. If patients shivered, they gave them hot drugs made from herbs. If patients sweated, then cooling drugs were used. Many fell back on an old remedy: they deliberately drew blood from the patient. They thought that if a patient lost blood, the fever would go away.

Even the best-known doctors of the day used remedies which strike us as ludicrous. John Arderne, a leading doctor who treated the king, wrote a book in 1370. It was called *De Arte Medicinae*. His cure for a stone in the kidney was a hot plaster smeared with honey and pigeon dung.

27.1 Why did Margaret Paston distrust the London doctors? AT3/L3

27.2 What does the painting on pages 132–3 tell us about the treatment of diseases in the Middle Ages? AT3/L5

27.3 What do the sources on pages 140–1 tell us about the way in which Londoners tried to prevent the spread of diseases? AT3/L6

27.4 Write one or two sentences to describe the doctor treating his patients in the medieval painting opposite. Can we use this picture to say all medieval doctors were like this? AT2 ■

27.5 What would a lazarhouse be called today? Was this an effective way of dealing with an infectious or contagious disease? Why was it called a 'lazarhouse'? (Clue: Who was Lazarus?)

27.6 What trade sign do some barbers' shops still use today? How does this recall the time when barbers were also surgeons? AT1A/L4

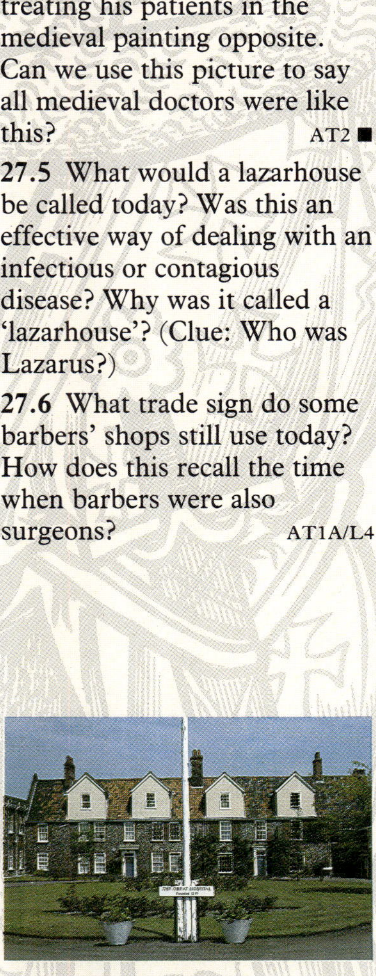

This is the Great Hospital in Norwich. It was founded in 1249 by the Bishop of Norwich to look after poor people who were sick. Many other hospitals, such as St Thomas' in London, were founded in the Middle Ages. There were over 250 of them by the end of the fourteenth century. People who suffered from leprosy were kept in special hospitals called lazarhouses. This was one of the reasons why leprosy as a disease died out in Britain, although we know today that leprosy is not easily passed on to others.

As you can imagine, when bubonic plague reached Britain and Europe in 1348, doctors could do nothing to stop it spreading or to provide a cure. This picture, painted at the time of the Black Death, is thought to represent the anguish of people at that time.

In many towns, the only medical help came from barber-surgeons. The Company of Barber-Surgeons was founded in London in 1461. They used surgical instruments, such as scalpels, saws, splints and probes. Since they had little knowledge of human anatomy, they usually did more harm than good, although some doctors (such as Gilbert Anglicus) knew that cancers should be removed.

The skills of these barber-surgeons can be judged from the fact that they also drew blood and extracted teeth as well as shaving their customers. The best that could be said of them was that all these tasks needed a steady hand and a good eye. A Norfolk lady called Margaret Paston probably had the right idea about medieval doctors when she wrote to her husband in 1464:

Source 27.A

***8 June 1464:** Also for God's sake beware what medicines you take from any physicians in London. I shall never trust them because of your father and my uncle.*

Most people in Britain lived in the countryside, a long way from a doctor or barber-surgeon. This is why women played a big part in the treatment of illnesses in these areas. The country housewife and the lady of the manor used old household remedies, magic potions and herbs as medicines. The best thing they did was to nurse their patients back to health. It was amazing what rest in bed and nourishing food could do.

Diseases like the plague were often blamed on bad air. If the air stank, a place was unhealthy. This is why towns like London tried to clean their streets of dung and filth. They had the right answer but the wrong reason. It was only hundreds of years later that scientists identified the germs which actually caused these diseases. In the meantime, insanitary conditions in medieval towns, villages and cottages meant that sores and cuts frequently went septic. People badly afflicted with skin diseases were often treated as lepers.

Burial of plague victims

The Black Death

The Black Death began in China in 1333. It reached the Middle East by 1347 and Europe in 1348. It was spread by fleas in the fur of black rats.

Source 27.B tells us about the symptoms of the plague. It was written by a man called Boccaccio who was 35 when the plague reached Florence in 1348.

Source 27.B

The first signs of the plague were lumps in the groin or armpits. After this livid black spots appeared on the arms and thighs and other parts of the body. Few recovered. Almost all died within three days, usually without any fever.

Source 27.C was written by a monk called Robert of Avesbury who died in about 1356.

Source 27.C

The plague started in Dorset about 1 August 1348 and spread quickly. It attacked a very large number of people in perfect health. Not one lived more than three or four days at the most. About 1 November 1348, the plague came to London, and killed off many people every day. Until after Easter, more than two hundred bodies were buried daily in the new cemetery near Smithfield.

Source 27.D was written by Henry Knighton. In his chronicle he wrote that he was present when King Edward III visited Leicester Abbey in 1363.

Source 27.D

Then the grievous plague entered the country from Southampton, and came to Bristol. Almost everyone in the town died, struck as it were by sudden death. There were few who kept their beds more than three days. After this the plague broke forth on every side.

27.7 Are Sources 27.B, 27.C and 27.D eyewitness accounts of the plague? AT3/L5

27.8 What were the symptoms of the plague? How did it spread? How long did it take to reach London from Dorset? AT1B/L4

27.9 The plague reached Norwich in January 1349. Use the scale on a road map to work out roughly the speed at which it spread. Since China is about 8000 miles (13 000 km) away, would you have expected the plague to reach London by 1348? AT1A/L7

27.10 On which point of fact did Robert of Avesbury and Henry Knighton disagree? AT2 ■

27.11 If Robert of Avesbury was correct, roughly how many people died in London from the plague? AT2/L6

27.12 Why was it called the Black Death?

Many of the plague victims were buried in mass graves, called plague pits. This churchyard at Sandwich in Kent is believed to be one such site.

The effects of the Black Death

The Black Death cut Britain's population from about 4 million in 1348 to 2.5 million less than two years later. Whole villages were wiped out, hundreds of thousands of peasants and over half the population of many towns died. In Sources 27.E, 27.F and 27.G, Henry Knighton describes its effect on everyday life.

Source 27.E

Few cared about riches or anything else. Sheep and cattle went wandering over fields and through crops. There was no one to go and drive or gather them. There was such a lack of workers that no one knew what he ought to do. In the following autumn no one could get a reaper for less than 8d [3p a day] *with his food. Many crops perished in the fields for want of some one to gather them.*

Source 27.F

The king made an order that labourers should not be paid more than they had been used to [before 1348]. *But the labourers would not listen. If anyone wished to have them he had to give them what they wanted, and either lose his fruit and crops, or give in to their greedy demands. And when it was known to the king that many abbots and knights had given higher wages, he imposed heavy fines on them. Many labourers were sent to prison and made to swear they would not take higher daily wages. The same was done with the other craftsmen in the boroughs and villages.*

Source 27.G

Many buildings fell into ruins for lack of inhabitants. Many villages and hamlets became desolate, not a house being left in them, all having died who lived there.

In the following winter, there was a great shortage of labour. All essentials became dearer. What in times past had been worth 1d was now worth 4d or 5d [about 2p].

Lords who had tenants lowered the rent so that their tenants should not go away. Those owed daywork by their villeins, had to free them, or offer them a smaller rent, so that their homes should not be ruined and the land remain uncultivated.

27.13 Which source tells us the Black Death caused wages to rise in the towns as well as on the land? AT3/L6

27.14 Write a paragraph describing the effects of the Black Death on everyday life in the countryside. AT1B ■

27.15 Why were abbots and knights punished as well as the labourers? What was the king trying to do? AT1C ■

27.16 What effect did the Black Death have on the feudal system? AT1B ■

This ruined church lies abandoned in the fields of West Norfolk. There is a farmhouse nearby but not the village you would expect to see. Historians call this type of settlement a deserted village. *Some were abandoned because of the Black Death. Others disappeared because landlords turned their estates into sheep walks to profit from the demand for wool.*

28 The End of the Middle Ages

FOCUS

▶ *WHAT was the Peasants' Revolt. WHY did it occur and WHAT effects did it have on Britain?* AT1A ■

▶ *WHY were the Wars of the Roses fought?* AT1B ■

▶ *WHAT do we owe to the Middle Ages?* AT1A ■

The start of the Peasants' Revolt

The Black Death made many country people discontented. This unrest came to a head when peasants in the east and south east led a rebellion in 1381. It began with a tax. In 1377 the government imposed a poll tax of

four pence [2p] *of each person of the realm, as well males as females, above the age of fourteen years.*

Poor people thought this was unfair, since they had to pay the same as a rich person. In 1379, however, a new tax was introduced in which each earl of England paid £4 and all the mayors of the large towns paid £2. Since most families with children under the age of sixteen only paid a total of 4d (2p), they thought this was much fairer.

John Ball preaching to the peasants

But in 1381 the government went back to the method used earlier in 1377. Only this time they wanted more money. Every person had to give

three groats [12d–5p] *as well by the males as by the females, who have passed the age of fifteen years.*

The outcry was enormous. People refused to pay the tax—as you can deduce from Source 28.A. Refusal soon led to rebellion. It began in earnest on 30 May 1381 when the king's tax collectors in Essex were told by the peasants of Brentwood, 'they would have no dealings with them nor pay them a penny'. Violence erupted and spread to neighbouring villages and across the Thames into Kent. The rebels seized towns and marched on London.

They had a captain called Walter Tyler and with him in company was Jack Straw and John Ball.

Source 28.A Population of counties according to the poll tax returns

	1377	1381
Norfolk	*88 797*	*66 719*
Suffolk	*58 610*	*44 635*
Kent	*56 557*	*43 838*
Essex	*47 962*	*30 748*

Source 28.B

In England the noblemen exercise great control over the common people. They keep them in serfdom. Their tenants have to work on the lord's lands, harvest their corn, make their hay and cut their wood. These unhappy people began to stir saying why should they be kept like beasts. If they laboured or did anything for their lords, they should receive wages.

A foolish priest from Kent called John Ball agreed. He told them: 'Why should we be kept in serfdom? We be all come from one father and one mother, Adam and Eve. They are clothed in velvet and we in poor cloth. They have their wines and we drink water. Our labours keep and maintain their estates.'

28.1 Look at the painting showing the king's barge at Rotherhithe. How many in the king's party appear to be armed? How many of the peasants are armed? Do you think this is likely? Was the artist biased for or against the king? AT2/L5 AT3/L5

28.2 Why do you think the population of each of the counties in Source 28.A appeared to fall by at least 25% between 1377 and 1381? Draw a graph to show these figures.

28.3 What message did John Ball preach to the peasants? Do you think he was 'foolish'? AT1C ■

In Source 28.B you can see how Sir John Froissart, a French writer living at that time, explained the reasons for the Peasants' Revolt.

Rotherhithe

On 12 June 1381 a huge crowd of peasants from Kent assembled at Blackheath on the south bank of the Thames. A similar crowd from Essex had gathered on the north bank as well. On the following day, 13 June 1381, King Richard II (then aged 14 years) and his leading advisers rowed down the Thames on a barge to Rotherhithe intending to speak to the rebels. But the peasants

saw the king's barge coming, they began to shout, and made such a cry, as though all the devils of hell had been among them.

Much to the anger of the crowd, the barge pulled away again without landing.

And when these people saw that, they cried all with one voice, 'Let us go to London' and so they took their way thither.

Richard II tries to land at Rotherhithe

Wat Tyler

The official records of the City of London tell us what happened when the peasants reached the city.

Source 28.C Thursday, 13 June 1381

On that day a huge crowd of common people from Kent and Essex approached the City. By the aid of treacherous commoners within the City, who rose in countless numbers there, they entered the City together. Passing straight through it, they went to the mansion of the Duke of Lancaster, called 'The Savoy', and burnt and levelled it to the ground.

Sir John Froissart described what happened the next day when Richard met the peasants.

Source 28.D Friday, 14 June 1381

The king asked them pleasantly: 'I am your king. What do you want?' Those who heard him said: 'We want you to make us free for ever.' 'Sirs,' said the king. 'I agree. Go home to your homes and villages and I shall cause charters to be made fixed with my seal containing everything you demand.' Then the king ordered more than thirty clerks the same Friday to write them with all speed.

The City of London account tells us what happened later that same day.

Source 28.E Friday, 14 June 1381

The infuriated rabble made its way to the Tower of London. Entering it by force, they dragged forth the Archbishop of Canterbury [and four others]. *All of whom they beheaded in the place called Tower Hill. Then carrying their heads through the City upon lances, they set them up on London Bridge, fixing them there on stakes. Many others were beheaded in Cheapside. In the Vintry, there was a very great massacre of Flemish workers. Hardly was there a street in the City in which there were not bodies lying of those who had been slain.*

On the following day, the City of London chronicler praised the actions of the Lord Mayor.

Source 28.F Saturday, 15 June 1381

This nightmare lasted to Saturday, 15 June. At Smithfield, in the presence of the king and the lords and knights on the one side, and the infuriated rabble on the other, Sir William Walworthe, the then Mayor, most manfully, by himself, rushed upon Walter Tylere. He first wounded him in the neck with his sword and then hurled him from his horse, mortally pierced in the breast.

However, other people living at that time told a different story. Sir John Froissart described the death of Wat Tyler in these words:

Source 28.G Saturday, 15 June 1381

The mayor of London came up with twelve well-armed horsemen, and said: 'Thou knave, how art thou so hardy in the king's presence to speak such words?' Then the king said to the mayor: 'Set hands on him.' The mayor drew out his sword and struck Tyler so great a stroke on the head, that he fell down at the feet of his horse. Then a squire of the king's

28.4 Imagine you are a peasant in 1381. Write a diary describing what you see and do during the Peasants' Revolt. AT1C ■

28.5 Look at the painting showing the moment when William Walworth struck Wat Tyler. What is unusual about this picture? How is the 14-year old king portrayed? AT3/L5

28.6 How do Sources 28.F, 28.G and 28.H disagree about the killing of Wat Tyler? Write down possible reasons which might explain this. Make a list of the differences between these sources. AT2 ■ AT3 ■

28.7 Look at each source in turn. Write down any words and phrases which suggest the writer may have been biased against the common people. AT2 ■

Wat Tyler is killed by William Walworth

28.8 What part did Richard II play in the Peasants' Revolt? Was it to his credit or not? Why do you think he agreed to the demands in Source 28.D?

AT1C ■

28.9 Write two or three sentences to say if you agree or disagree with the writer of Source 28.F that it was a 'nightmare'. AT1C/L6

28.10 Look at Sources 28.B and 28.D. Make a list of the causes of the Peasants' Revolt.

AT1B ■

28.11 Which causes (called long-term causes) had been making the common people angry for many years? AT1B/L5

28.12 What do you think short-term causes are? Name a short-term cause of the Peasants' Revolt in 1381.

AT1B/L5

alighted, called John Standish, and he drew out his sword and put it into Wat Tyler's belly, and so he died.

Then the people, seeing their captain slain, arranged themselves in manner of battle and their bows before them. Thus the king began a great act of courage. He departed from all his company and all alone he rode to these people and said to them: 'Sirs, what aileth you? Ye shall have no captain but me. I am your king. Be all in rest and peace'.

Another chronicler gave this version of the same encounter.

Source 28.H Saturday, 15 June 1381

Wat Tighler came to the king with great confidence, holding in his hand a dagger. He took the king by the hand and shook his arm roughly, saying, 'Brother, be of good comfort, for you shall have praise from the commons and we shall be good companions.'

One of the king's attendants said aloud he knew him to be the greatest thief and robber in all Kent. Wat tried to strike him with his dagger and would have slain him, but the mayor of London, William Walworth, arrested him. And because he arrested him, Wat stabbed the mayor with his dagger. Luckily the mayor was wearing armour and struck back at Wat and gave him a deep cut on the neck, and then a great cut on the head. And during this scuffle one of the king's household drew his sword and ran Wat two or three times through the body, mortally wounding him.

And when the common people saw him fall, and knew not how for certain it was, they began to bend their bows and to shoot, wherefore the king himself spurred his horse, and rode out to them, commanding them that they should all come to Clerkenwell Fields.

In fact, the king was playing for time. The mayor had gone back to London for reinforcements. When they arrived, the revolt in London collapsed. The peasants went home but the rebellion in the country continued for several weeks. In the end, however, many of the ringleaders were caught and either executed or imprisoned. In Cambridge, John Shirle of Nottingham was even hanged for saying

in a tavern in Bridge Street, Cambridge, that John Ball was condemned falsely and that his death shall not go unpunished.

As for the king, he went back on his word. An Act of Parliament in May 1382 decreed

that all obligations made by compulsion and menace in the time of this riot shall be wholly quashed.

Medieval painting of the Battle of Barnet, 14 April 1471

Source 28.I

[**1449**] *Right worshipful husband, I recommend me to you and pray you to get some crossbows. Your houses here be so low that no one can shoot out with a long bow, though we never before had so much need.*

Partrich [a servant] *and his fellows have made bars to bar the doors crossways and they have made holes on every side of the house to shoot out at, both with bows and hand guns; but the holes made for hand guns be hardly knee-high from the floor, so no one can shoot out of them with hand bows.*

The Wars of the Roses

You saw earlier (on page 120), that medieval kings ruled with the aid of a Council. The barons and earls who advised the king and ran the great offices of State had immense power and great wealth. This was a cause of rivalry, especially when a royal favourite quarrelled with the king or queen.

In the fifteenth century, a long drawn-out conflict was fought for the throne between the great families of York (white rose) and Lancaster (red rose). They were backed by private armies of supporters who fought the battles of this, the first English Civil War.

It was called the Wars of the Roses. But although the fighting lasted, off and on, from 1455 to 1485, there were long periods of relative quiet in-between. Nonetheless, many great nobles were killed and warring armies disturbed country life—as you can see in Source 28.I. This is part of a letter written by Margaret Paston from her home in Norfolk to her husband in London.

There were three major wars during the Wars of the Roses. The first, between 1459 and 1461, ended with the Battle of Towton when Edward, the son of Richard, Duke of York, deposed Henry VI. As Edward IV, he was supported at first by the powerful Earl of Warwick, but Warwick soon changed sides when Edward resisted his attempts to acquire greater power. Instead, he supported Queen Margaret and her son, Prince Edward, in their attempt to restore the House of Lancaster to the throne.

This was the start of the second War of the Roses (1469–71). Edward IV fled to France but raised a new army and returned to Britain. He defeated Warwick at Barnet, and Margaret and Edward at Tewkesbury in 1471.

Source 28.J The Battle of Barnet in 1471

On Easter Day in the morning, the fourteenth day of April, right early each of them came upon the other. But there was such a great mist that neither of them could see the other properly. There they fought from four o'clock in the morning until ten o'clock.

As it happened, the Earl of Oxford's men had upon them their lord's livery which was much like King Edward's livery; and the mist was so thick. As a result the Earl of Warwick's men shot and fought against the Earl of Oxford's men, thinking and supposing they were King Edward's. The Earl of Oxford and his men cried 'Treason! Treason!' and flew away from the battlefield with eight hundred men.

28.13 Give one reason for the defeat of Warwick at Barnet. AT1B/L3

28.14 How does the medieval painting of the Battle of Barnet contradict Source 28.J? Which do you believe? Why? AT3/L6

28.15 Which of the Wars of the Roses affected Margaret Paston? What precautions did she take? What was her problem? AT1C/L5

28.16 How did life in the Middle Ages differ from life today? AT1C ■

Memorial to the Battle of Towton fought near York in 1461

Time Line

1337 Hundred Years War begins
1348 Black Death in England
1377 Richard II becomes king
1381 Peasants' Revolt
1399 Henry IV becomes king
1413 Henry V becomes king
1422 Henry VI becomes king
1453 Hundred Years War ends
1461 Battle of Towton; Edward IV becomes king
1471 Battle of Barnet
1483 Edward V becomes king
1483 Richard III seizes power
1485 Battle of Bosworth Field; Henry VII becomes king

The third war began soon after Edward IV died on 9 April 1483. His 12 year-old son Edward V was deposed by his uncle, Richard, Duke of Gloucester, on 26 June 1483. He was put in the Tower of London together with his brother. The two young Princes in the Tower were never heard of again.

The new king, Richard III, was challenged by Henry Tudor, a distant Lancastrian claimant to the throne. In 1485 he landed in Wales and defeated and killed Richard III at the Battle of Bosworth Field. As Henry VII he began the long reign of the Tudors.

What we owe to the Middle Ages

For most people who study history, 1485 is a convenient place to make a break between the Middle Ages and the modern world. By this time Britain had changed. Only a few peasants still owed labour services to their lord. Merchants were making great fortunes from foreign trade. The feudal system had faded away. It was out of place at a time when the freemen in the towns ran their own affairs and sent burgesses to Parliament. Britain had also changed in relation to Europe. The Hundred Years War (1337–1453) ended British hopes of hanging on to any substantial territory in France. Now only Calais remained.

The people of the Middle Ages left us a legacy, however, which can still be seen and felt today. We owe the survival of our language and the birth of many of our great institutions to this period. They include Parliament, the law courts, the oldest universities, the first great books written in the English language, and many, if not all, of our customs and traditions.

They also left us the remains of many fine castles, cathedrals, abbeys and churches—as you can see in the remaining chapters of this book.

Morris dancing is one medieval tradition which can still be seen ▲

Castles & Cathedrals

29 How and why castles were built

FOCUS

▶ WHY were castles built in the Middle Ages? AT1B ■
▶ HOW and WHY did they change? AT1A ■
▶ HOW were they built? AT1C ■

Why castles were built

This picture shows the Tower of London in about 1450. This was the first large stone castle to be built in Britain. It was started by William the Conqueror in about 1078. Later monarchs added other buildings to it. It was used in different ways during the Middle Ages: as a stronghold in times of unrest, as a royal palace, as a prison and as the home of the Royal Mint (where coins were minted).

Medieval castles were built for many different reasons. First and foremost, they were built as secure strongholds where a great lord or lady, a knight and his family, or the king and the royal household could live. The king owned many such castles and used them when making a royal progress (see page 118). He appointed a custodian or constable to look after them while he was away.

Castles were also built to impress people, to show off the immense wealth, power and authority of the king or a great baron. Imposing fortresses were built to subdue rebellious people, like the castles built by Edward I in Wales (pages 126–7).

Some castles were built as administrative centres. They were used as a base, to rule an area the size of a county or run a large estate. They had to be in a central position to do this. This is why many castles were built in county towns like Lancaster, York, Norwich and Warwick.

There were many different types of castle, but almost all had certain things in common:

- They usually controlled a routeway, such as a bridge or ford across a river, a gap between two hills, a narrow valley, an estuary used by ships and boats, or a strip of lowland between the hills and the sea.
- They had a strongpoint, such as a keep or tower, to which everyone could retreat if the enemy broke through the walls.
- It was hard for the enemy to get close to the castle walls because of a moat, river, the sea, or a steep hill.
- They commanded a wide view of the surrounding countryside.
- They made the most of any natural defences, such as a cliff jutting out into the sea, an island, a site inside the bend of a river, or on a hill.
- They were usually built of local building stone and timber.
- They had a safe supply of water. This was essential in case of siege.

29.1 Why do you think William the Conqueror built a huge castle in London? AT1B ■

29.2 Look at the map on page 135. Where was the Tower in relation to the rest of medieval London? Why was it built by the Thames? AT1B ■

29.3 What part did the Tower of London play during (a) the Wars of the Roses (pages 158–9) (b) the conquest of Wales (page 127) (c) the Peasants' Revolt (page 156)? AT3/L4

29.4 What types of site were chosen for the castles at Criccieth and Caernarfon on pages 126–7? Write a sentence in each case saying what advantages the site had. AT1B ■

29.5 Write down the statements in the list (left) which apply to the motte and bailey castle in the picture opposite. AT1B ■

29.6 Find out about the nearest castle to your home. Why was it built? What type of site does it have? Write down the statements in the list which apply to this castle as well. AT1B ■

Source 29.A

They make a mound of earth as high as they can and then encircle it with a ditch as wide and as deep as possible. They enclose the space on top of the mound with a palisade [fence] *of very strong hewn logs firmly fixed together. Within the enclosure* [the inner bailey] *is a keep which overlooks the entire wall.*

Source 29.B

Arnold, lord of Ardres, built on the motte a wooden house. The first storey was on the ground where there were cellars and granaries, casks, and domestic utensils. In the storey above were the dwelling and living rooms of the residents and the great chamber in which the lord and his wife slept.

In the upper storey of the house were attic rooms, in which on the one side the sons slept, on the other side the daughters. High up on the east side was the chapel. There were stairs and passages from storey to storey, from the house into the kitchen, from room to room.

The first castles

The idea of building castles was first brought to Britain by the Normans. As you saw on page 84, they built a wooden fort on top of an artificial hill, called a *motte*, at Pevensey in 1066. These *motte and bailey* castles were built like sandcastles—as you can see from the description by a medieval writer in Source 29.A.

As you can see from the picture below, another fence extended down the hill to form the outer bailey. Farm buildings, stables and workshops were built there. A medieval writer described a wooden keep like this in 1117 (Source 29.B).

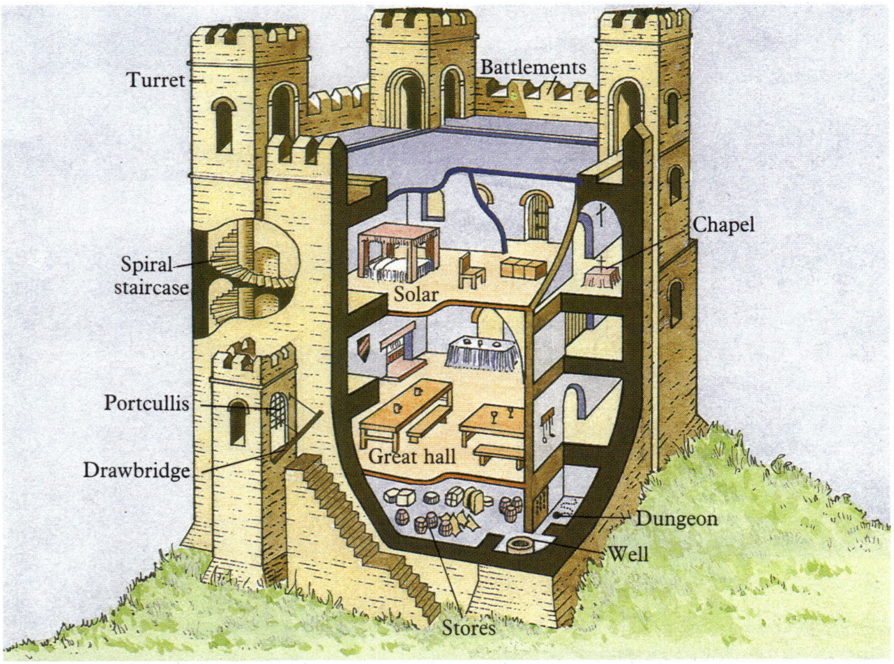

Stone keeps

The main disadvantage of the motte and bailey castle was that it could be easily set on fire, either by flaming arrows or by blazing torches. We know that many wooden castles were burned to the ground in this way. That is why permanent castles were built of stone.

The first stone castles, such as the Tower of London, were begun in the reign of William the Conqueror. They followed the same basic design as the motte and bailey castle, but because of the weight of a stone keep, they were not always built on top of a motte. The square or rectangular keep (sometimes called a *donjon*) was built inside a large courtyard, or bailey, surrounded by a wall. The walls of the keep were immensely thick. Battlements at the top gave protection to the archers and crossbow men who stood guard there. Many Norman keeps like this were built in the twelfth century, such as those at Dover and Castle Rising shown in the photographs on pages 92–3.

If the enemy managed to break through the walls, the defenders retreated into the keep. As you can see from the picture on the previous page, the entrance was on the first floor and could only be reached by a flight of stairs in the forebuilding.

The wall of a stone keep was often angled outwards at the base to give it extra strength. This was called the batter.

Battlements, or crenellations, *as they are often called, consisted of gaps in the wall—* embrasures*—through which an archer could fire at the enemy. They were often fitted with hinged wooden shutters to give added protection. The upright walls in-between the embrasures were called* merlons.

Siege warfare

Later castle builders had to change the design of the castle because besieging armies were beginning to use huge catapults to knock down walls. Many new ideas about siege warfare were brought back to Europe by the Crusaders. In Source 29.C, an Arab writer, Usamah Ibn-Munqidh, describes the siege of Shayzar in 1138.

Source 29.C

The Byzantines [Crusaders from Constantinople] *set up against it frightful mangonels which they had brought with them for hurling weights. These mangonels could throw a stone further than an arrow. One time they hurled a large millstone against the house of a friend of mine. This one stone destroyed the whole building from top to bottom.*

On another occasion he watched Muslim engineers at work digging a *sap* or tunnel under a castle held by Crusaders.

Source 29.D

I went down in the trench, while the arrows and stones were falling on us like rain, and entered the tunnel. On the sides were pillars, across which stretched a plank to prevent the earth above falling down. It extended as far as the foundation of the barbican [a gatehouse]. *They stuffed the tunnel with dry wood. Early the next morning they set it on fire. The layers of mortar between the stones of the wall began to fall. Then a crack was made. It became wider and wider and the tower fell.*

This picture from an illuminated manuscript shows a trebuchet hurling a stone during a siege

29.7 How did a Norman castle built in 1066 (page 84) differ from a castle built at the end of the Norman period?
AT1A ■ AT1C ■

29.8 How would you identify a square keep (a) from inside the castle (b) from the outside? What features would you look for? AT3/L4

29.9 Would Arnold, Lord of Ardres, have recognised the square keep in the picture on the previous page? Rewrite Source 29.B to describe a stone keep. AT3/L5

29.10 How can you tell that the defenders of this keep were able to survive without fresh supplies of food and water? AT1C/L5

29.11 Read Sources 29.D and 29.E. Are these facts or opinions? AT2/L3

29.12 Write one or two sentences describing a trebuchet from the picture (left). How do you think it worked?

29.13 What can Sources 29.C, 29.D and 29.E tell you about siege warfare? AT3 ■

29.14 Which of these three sources is an actual eyewitness account? How can you tell? AT3/L5

29.15 How was a battering ram used? How did the men of Tyre deal with it? AT1C/L5

29.16 Write two or three sentences to describe a medieval sap or tunnel. How did it work? AT3/L4

Fifteenth century picture of the siege of a French castle

New buildings were often built on the site of a motte and bailey castle. A round wall, like the one you can see here at Restormel Castle in Cornwall, sometimes followed the line of the old wooden palisade. Castles like this are called shell keeps. *Wooden and stone buildings inside the wall housed the residents of the castle.* ▶

'Murder holes' or machicolations *above the barbican at Lewes Castle in Sussex*

Another Syrian, Ibn al-Qalanisi, described the wooden siege towers built by Crusaders to attack the Muslim city of Tyre in 1112. These towers were pushed against the wall and covered with branches, mats and wet leather to protect the soldiers inside as they tried to batter down the walls with a long pole called a *battering ram.*

Source 29.E

On 1st Ramadan [2 March 1112] *the men of Tyre hurled fire* [flaming pitch and firewood] *close to the smaller tower. The wind fanned the flames and completely burned it out.*

They made grappling irons to seize the battering ram using ropes to pull it upwards. Sometimes it was broken by means of two stones tied together and thrown down from the city wall. Each ram was about sixty cubits [30 metres] *long and suspended from ropes in the wooden tower. At the head of each was a heavy lump of iron.*

Round towers

Castle owners soon discovered that square keeps and towers were easier to undermine than round ones. Square keeps had other disadvantages as well. Their corners were easily damaged by stones from a trebuchet or mangonel. Rounded walls, on the other hand, did not have corners to smash. They were much stronger. This is why castle builders in the thirteenth century began to build round towers and curved walls like those you can see in the French castle (left).

They also built higher walls to make it more difficult for the enemy to use siege towers or catapults. They erected towers or turrets which stood out in front of the wall. Arrow slits in the walls of these towers now made it possible for archers in the castle to fire arrows from different angles if enemy soldiers tried to set up a battering ram or siege tower against the wall or the gates. 'Murder holes' like those in the photograph were used to drop heavy rocks, flaming pitch and boiling water on enemy soldiers below.

Curtain walls

As you can see, thirteenth-century castles were different from those built by the Normans 150 years earlier. As time went on, castle builders put more and more emphasis on the wall as a strong curtain protecting the people inside. This is why they were called *curtain wall* castles. Eventually they even did away with the keep in the middle. Instead, they made the towers along the wall into strongpoints. Now there were several buildings as strong as the keep instead of only one.

They also built massive gatehouses since, otherwise, the entrance was likely to be a weak point in the castle defences. Entrance to the castle was by lowering the *drawbridge* across a moat. The drawbridge was raised by massive chains operated by guards in the two huge towers on either side of the gatehouse. A massive sliding gate with iron spikes, called a *portcullis*, slid down inside two grooves behind the drawbridge. It was slammed down shut at the approach of an enemy.

Many castles also had an outer gatehouse as well. This was called the *barbican*.

Caerphilly Castle, which was begun by Gilbert de Clare, Lord of Glamorgan, in 1270 was the first and the largest concentric castle to be built in Britain

Concentric castles

The concentric castle you can see in the photograph above was an advance on the curtain wall castle. It had the same high wall with towers and turrets, but in addition it was surrounded by a lower wall a few yards in front. This could be manned by a front line of archers since they were below the line of fire of the archers defending the main curtain wall behind.

The most perfect examples of this type of castle were built by Edward I in North Wales, such as at Beaumaris and Harlech. These castles cost an enormous sum of money to build and employed many hundreds of workers, as you can find out on page 166.

Moat at Bodiam Castle in Sussex

29.17 What were the main differences between an Edwardian castle and a Norman castle? AT1C ■

29.18 Draw or trace an outline of Caerphilly Castle from the photograph (below). Use the information on these pages to draw in arrows and labels to show the castle features you can identify. AT1C/L5

29.19 How and why did the design of castles change between 1066 and 1300? What were the main changes? What things stayed much the same? AT1A ■

Drawbridge at Dover Castle in Kent

Portcullis at Hever Castle in Kent

The outer gatehouse, or barbican, guarding the approach to Lewes Castle in Sussex

Hever Castle, Kent

29.20 Make a list of words in Source 29.F which are opinions not facts. AT2/L3

29.21 Use the details in this description to draw a rough plan of the manor. How do they help you to know what a medieval manor house looked like? AT3/L5

The fortified manor house

As the danger of war passed, more and more people began to live in fortified manor houses such as Hever Castle (above) and Ightham Mote (page 107). Like a castle, the manor had battlements and other defences, but it was a much more comfortable place in which to live, as you can see from this description written in 1256.

Source 29.F

A sufficient and handsome hall with a ceiling made of oak. On the western side is a good bedroom, a garderobe [toilet], *and another room. At the eastern end is a pantry and a buttery. There is a suitable chapel covered with tiles, a portable altar and a small cross. There are four tables on trestles in the hall. Likewise too, there is a good kitchen, well covered with tiles, with a furnace and ovens, one large, the other small, for cakes, two tables, and alongside the kitchen a small house for baking. A new granary, too, covered with oak shingles, and a building in which the dairy is contained. Also a henhouse, a good stable and two barns. These buildings are enclosed with a moat, a wall and a hedge.*

Castles were becoming obsolete. Guns were used in siege warfare by the fifteenth century. The popularity of the large manor house (or mansion) and the Wars of the Roses also hastened their end. As you saw on page 158, many great lords were killed in the Wars of the Roses. The new king, Henry VII, stopped nobles keeping private armies. Without a garrison there was little point in building a castle.

How castles were built

The first thing the castle builders did was to clear the site. Then labourers dug trenches for the foundations. They filled them with rubble and stones and rammed them down hard to take the weight of the heavy walls above. Then the wall was laid, stone by stone, by the masons. It took them many years to complete.

The master mason in charge was assisted by a clerk and by a number of foremen, each in charge of a different type of work. Rough masons shaped the blocks of stone brought to the site from the quarry and cut the stone roughly to size. Other masons shaped the stone blocks exactly and laid them in a layer of mortar on the wall to set hard. Skilled craftsmen carved designs in harder stone and freemasons shaped softer stone to fit round the doors, arrow loops, merlons and embrasures. You can find out more about how they worked on pages 178–9.

We know how medieval castles were built from a number of sources such as pictures, account books, and letters recording the money spent on wages and building materials.

In Source 29.G you can read an extract from a letter sent by Master James of St George and Walter of Winchester to the Exchequer on 27 February 1296. Walter of Winchester was the royal official in charge of building works at Beaumaris Castle in North Wales, and Master James was the master craftsman.

They sent this letter because they needed £250 a week to pay the wages of the workmen and the garrison of 130 men (10 mounted soldiers, 20 crossbowmen and 100 foot soldiers).

Source 29.G

Some of it [the wall] *already stands about 28 feet* [8.5 metres] *high and even where it is lowest it is 20 feet* [6 metres]. *We have begun ten of the outer and four of the inner towers. Four gates have been hung and are shut and locked every night. Each gateway is to have three portcullises. So much have we been able to do in spite of all the Welshmen.*

In case you should wonder where so much money could go in a week, we would have you know that we have needed—and shall continue to need—400 masons, both cutters and layers, together with 2000 minor workmen, 100 carts, 60 waggons and 30 boats bringing stone and sea-coal, 200 quarrymen, 30 smiths, and carpenters for putting in the joists and floor-boards. All of this takes no account of the garrison nor of purchases of materials, of which there will have to be a great quantity.

P.S. And Sirs, for God's sake be quick with the money; otherwise everything done up till now will have been of no avail.

29.22 How many people worked on the site of Beaumaris castle in 1296? Who were the most important workers? AT3/L3

29.23 How many portcullises were planned for Beaumaris? What stage had the castle reached by February 1296? Was it secure from attack yet? AT3/L3

29.24 How do the clues in the letter help you to know how and why a castle was built in the Middle Ages? Write a paragraph summing up what you find out. AT3/L5

29.25 Look at the pictures. What types of scaffolding did workers use to build a medieval castle? Make a list of the tools and machines they used. AT3/L4

29.26 Where in these pictures can you see (a) a skilled mason carving stone (b) workmen operating a simple crane (c) tilers laying tiles on a roof? AT3/L3

Time Line

1066	First motte and bailey castle built at Pevensey
1078	First Norman stone keep begun at the Tower of London
1100–1200	Siege engines used in the Crusades
1200–1300	Round towers built
1270	First concentric castle begun at Caerphilly
1280–1300	Work in progress on Edwardian castles in Wales
1485	End of the Wars of the Roses

30 Living in a castle

FOCUS

► *WHAT was it like to live and work in a medieval castle?*

ATIC ■

The great hall

The main living room of the castle was the great hall. This was the largest room in the castle and the place where everyone ate. There was a huge fire there. At the start of the Middle Ages it was simply an open hearth in the centre of the room. The smoke escaped through the roof. By 1500 it had been replaced in most castles by a massive fireplace and a chimney.

Castles did not usually have glass windows until the end of the Middle Ages. Instead they had narrow openings in the wall which let in the sun, rain, snow and wind. After dark, wooden shutters were drawn across to keep out the cold night air. The hall was lit at night by candles or rushlights. They flickered in the draught and were fixed to spikes on the walls or to an iron ring hanging from the roof.

The top table was at one end of the hall on a raised platform, called a *dais*. The king and queen or the lord and lady sat here, together with their children, guests, leading knights and officials. The other tables were at right angles to this, and stretched the length of the hall.

The great hall at Castle Rising in Norfolk was on the first floor

Eating and cooking

People sat on wooden benches to eat. They used a knife and their hands. There were no forks. Most of the food was greasy. The meat dripped with fat. This was why they used thick slices of stale bread, called *trenchers*, as plates. These soaked up the spare fat.

We know what people ate at these meals from medieval account books. A country lady, for instance, served 120 meals to her visitors and family in three days in about 1350. During that time they consumed 160 loaves of bread, 270 litres of ale, 12 kg beef, 12 kg bacon and 130 herrings to say nothing of 16 pigeons and 2 chickens.

Fireplace at Warkworth Castle

The meat they ate was often old and tough. It was not easy to feed cattle in winter in the Middle Ages, so some beasts were killed off in the autumn and stored in salt barrels during the winter. This is why spices from the East were popular. They gave flavour to tasteless meat. Luckily for the castle residents, they sometimes ate fresh venison and game caught by the baron and his knights when hunting.

◄ *Banquet in the eleventh century*

Banquet in the fifteenth century

Meat was cooked over the fire—either roasted on a turnspit or boiled in a cauldron. The kitchen where bread and pastry were baked was usually in a detached building in the inner bailey. This was to avoid the risk of fire. The oven used by the baker was just a hole in a wall (see page 140). A fire was lit inside it. When the ashes were white hot, they were raked to one side and the dough inserted using a pole. Other foods were kept in store rooms nearby, such as wine and ale in the buttery and bread and butter in the pantry.

People often had complaints about the food or about the conditions they had to face in the great hall. Here are two of them.

Source 30.A At the court of King Henry II

A priest or a soldier attached to the court has bread put before him like lead, full of bran and unbaked. Wine is spoiled either by being sour or mouldy. I have seen noblemen drink it with their eyes shut and teeth closed. The tables are sometimes filled with putrid food, and were it not for the fact that those who eat it indulge in powerful exercise, many more deaths would result from it.

Source 30.B At the court of the French king, 20 June 1349

The next day, Monday [20 June 1349], *the great table of marble in the hall was made longer with a great plank board of oak, four inches* [10cm] *thick which was richly covered. The hall was so full of people a man could not turn without pain. A great number of minstrels played pleasantly. Then the king and the bishops and the queen and the ladies washed and sat down at the tables. People were sorely oppressed by the heat and put to much pain. The queen herself was on the point of ordering a back door to be broken up to get fresh air.*

30.1 Which parts of Source 30.A are opinions rather than facts which can be proved? Why would you need some other evidence as well if you wanted to prove that medieval food was often bad? AT2 ■

30.2 Use the Time Line on page 131 to say roughly how many years separate Sources 30.A and 30.B. What were the complaints of these writers? AT3/L4

30.3 What do the two pictures of banquets have in common? What changes took place between the eleventh and fifteenth centuries? Make a list of the similarities and differences. AT1A ■ AT1C ■

30.4 What do Source 30.A and Source 30.B tell us about banquets which we cannot find out from the medieval pictures? AT3 ■

Living in the castle

In the early Middle Ages, the lord and lady of a castle sometimes slept at one end of the great hall in an area partitioned off from the rest of the room by a wooden wall. In later castles, they had a number of private rooms. These included bedchambers and a private living room called a *solar* (because it caught the sun) on the first floor. This was the lady of the castle's private room. It was here that she could sit with her needlewomen and play with, or teach, her children.

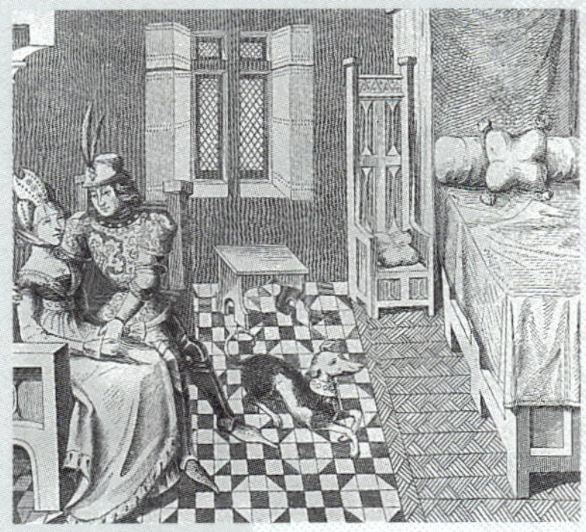

Solar in the fifteenth century

Most rooms in the castle had beds of one description or another. They were not confined to bedrooms. Important people, such as guests and officials, had chambers of their own. Others slept in the rooms where they worked. The armourer slept in the armoury, the cook in the kitchen, and the priest in the chapel. Some had straw mattresses or heaps of straw for bedding. Others slept on benches or on the floor.

Although water could be drawn from a well inside the keep or from the bailey, people usually drank ale or wine instead. It was safer. The lord and lady of the castle often had a stone washbasin in their solar. They bathed in a wooden tub which servants filled with hot water.

Sanitary arrangements were very primitive. Chamber pots were used and also small rooms built inside the thick walls with outlets into the moat. These were called *garderobes*. Servants used buckets of water to flush them out from time to time.

At work

Much of the daily work of a castle took place in the great hall. This was where the baron held his court to settle local disputes and to bring criminals to justice.

Many other people lived and worked in the castle as well. Ladies in waiting, knights and squires joined the baron and his family when they ate in the great hall. Chamberlains, stewards, marshals, clerks, bailiffs, reeves and other officials helped to run the castle. They organised the work on its estates. The priest took mass every morning in the chapel. Cooks and servants prepared meals and drew water from the well.

In the bailey, or courtyard, smiths, carpenters, armourers (armour), bowyers (bows) and fletchers (arrows) made and repaired armour and weapons in wooden workshops. In the later Middle Ages gunsmiths had their workshops here as well. All these workers and the other residents of the castle were expected to take up weapons and wear armour if the castle was attacked.

We can get some idea of the jobs done by these workers from medieval records. At Aberystwyth Castle in 1286–9, for instance, payments were made for the work listed in Source 30.C.

Source 30.C

Building a stable and bakehouse under one roof with carpentry
Repairing the wall of the kitchen
To John the smith and his assistant
To William the plumber for roofing the tower
To David the carpenter for making a new granary in the castle
To Thomas of Buildwas for deepening a well
For covering the well and for a rope for it
Mending a window and gutter in the king's garderobe

◀ *This fifteenth-century gun was found in the moat at Bodiam Castle in Sussex*

A castle bedroom

A medieval queen accompanied by attendants listening to a minstrel in her solar ▶

The well inside the keep at Castle Rising

30.5 Write two or three sentences describing the furniture, furnishings, floor covering and beds you can see in the pictures of the solar and the medieval bedroom. AT3/L4

30.6 Why was there a well inside the keep at Castle Rising? AT3/L3

30.7 Use Source 30.C to make a list of the craft workers who must have been employed at Aberystwyth Castle in 1286. AT1C/L5

30.8 What buildings and workshops would you have seen at Aberystwyth Castle at that time? AT1C/L5

30.9 Write a paragraph saying what these accounts tell you about everyday life and work in Aberystwyth Castle in 1286. AT3/L5

The life of a lady

When the baron or knight was away from the castle, his wife took charge. This could be a regular occurrence, since he might be away at Court on king's business, in the Holy Land as a pilgrim or as a Crusader, visiting a distant estate, or fighting a war in France, Wales or Scotland. This is why it was vital that the lady of the castle should know how to manage its affairs as well as her husband did.

She dealt with tenants, instructed the castle officials and listened to their advice. She entertained guests and took action if there were any emergencies (such as an armed raid). When Edward III was fighting the French at Calais, 'the queen of England sent for men of war and archers'. She did not take part in the actual battle, although women, such as Queen Matilda in the twelfth century and Joan of Arc in the fifteenth century, did participate in other wars.

The life of a knight

A knight in the thirteenth century was basically a professional soldier who owed about six weeks of military service a year to his lord. To become a knight, he had to serve a long apprenticeship as a squire.

The medieval idea of a knight was coloured by the romantic tales sung by minstrels. Stories about King Arthur, Queen Guinevere and Sir Lancelot gave the idea that knights were chivalrous and would come to a lady's rescue. Stories of courtly love and the knightly code of conduct led to the founding of the great orders of chivalry, such as the Order of the Garter in 1349.

Medieval painting of a tournament

In fact some knights, far from being romantic, were coarse and brutal. The behaviour of the Crusaders, for instance, did them little credit. Some treated their Muslim captives with barbarity and the utmost cruelty.

In Source 30.D you can read what Geoffrey Chaucer wrote about a knight in 1380.

Barons and knights each had their own coats of arms. This distinguished them from each other at a tournament. But there were so many, it could be confusing. This is why heralds were used to tell them apart. We know about knights and tournaments from writers like Geoffrey Chaucer (Sources 30.E and 30.F) and from colourful paintings like the one above.

Knights practised their tournament skills on the quintain on the village green at Offham in Kent. If they galloped fast enough and struck the flat studded area evenly with their lance it swung round and let them pass. If not, the weight on the other end of the pivot gave them a smack in the back! ▶

Source 30.D

A knight there was and that a worthy man. From the time that he first began to ride, he loved chivalry, truth, honour, generosity and courtesy. In his bearing he was as modest as a maid and he had never used foul language in all his life. In fact he was a very perfect gentle knight.

With him there was his son, a young squire. He was a pleasant young man about 20 years of age, with curly hair. He was about medium height, very agile and remarkably strong. In a short time he had acquitted himself well in campaigns in Flanders, Artois and Picardy. He was fancily dressed in a short gown with long wide sleeves. He was always singing or playing the flute and could compose songs, joust, dance well, draw and write. He sat well on a horse and could ride with skill. He was courteous, humble and always willing to serve.

30.10 What does the painting tell us about tournaments which is not covered by the extract in Source 30.F? AT3 ■

30.11 Use the information on these pages to write an imaginary description of the knight in the picture on page 88. AT3/L4

30.12 Make a list of the qualities of the knight and squire in Source 30.D. Do you think they were too good to be true? Why would it be silly to think every knight and squire was like this? AT2 ■

30.13 Look at Source 30.F. Was this a friendly tournament?

30.14 Look at the painting as well as at Sources 30.E and 30.F. How were the horses 'splendidly adorned'? What did the knights wear? Write a paragraph describing a medieval tournament, using the painting and the information in Sources 30.E and 30.F. AT3/L4

Source 30.E A tournament

At sunrise there was a great commotion and clattering as the horses were harnessed. The many lords riding up to the palace made a brilliant show with their bright shields, horse trappings, headpieces, gold helmets and coats of mail. They rode on splendidly adorned horses followed by a retinue of knights, squires and armourers busy with their files and hammers.

Source 30.F

A great shout from the crowd raised the sky and the trumpets sounded as the company rode out to the Lists. The gates to the tournament ground were shut and the heralds cried, 'Do now your duty, proud young knights.' Trumpets blared once more and at the clarion call the spears were held firmly in position and the knights advanced spurring their horses forward. It was easy to see who could ride and who could joust. Then came the clash as the lance shafts shivered on thick shields and some knights felt the sharp prick of the spear through the breast. Up sprang the spears six metres on high and out came the swords all silver and bright. The knights hacked away and shred to pieces the helmets of their opponents. Out flowed the blood in long streams of red, and bones broke as mighty maces were swung.

Hunting was a popular sport for the castle residents. It was good exercise and very good training for a knight on horseback. They hunted deer and wild pigs and also hunted birds using hawks and falcons.

31 How and why cathedrals were built

FOCUS

▶ WHY and WHERE were cathedrals built in Britain?

AT1B ■

▶ HOW and WHY did they change during the Middle Ages?

AT1A ■

▶ HOW were they built?

AT1C ■

Why cathedrals were built

Almost everyone went to church in the Middle Ages. It was important in most people's lives. This is why the leaders of the Church were powerful and influential men. Many were among the king's leading advisers. The Archbishop of Canterbury was one of the most powerful people in Britain. At that time the Church owned great estates. This meant that each bishop, abbot or abbess had tenants owing rents and labour services. The income from these estates provided some of the money needed to build new buildings. You can see how these estates were managed in Source 31.A. It was written by a monk at Bury St Edmunds Abbey in about 1200.

Lincoln Cathedral is shaped like a cross with the high altar at the east end (bottom right in the photograph)

31.1 Make a list of England's medieval cathedrals. Put ticks against those in county towns. Put a star against a monastic cathedral. Where were most cathedrals in England situated? Write down one or two sentences summing up what these facts tell you about cathedrals in the Middle Ages. AT1C ■

31.2 Look at Source 31.A. How did the abbot at Bury St Edmunds increase the abbey's income from the land? AT1B/L4

31.3 Trace an outline of Lincoln Cathedral from the photograph opposite. Use the plan on page 180 to mark in and name the chancel, nave, west front, east front and north and south transepts. AT1C/L5

31.4 Make a list of the reasons which help to explain why cathedrals were built in the Middle Ages. AT1B ■

31.5 Look at the photograph below. Why did Bishop Remigius choose this site for Lincoln Cathedral? AT1B ■

The West Front of Lincoln Cathedral. This is the only part of Bishop Remigius's cathedral still standing.

Source 31.A

The Abbot enquired what annual rents were paid by the free men in each manor and the names of the peasants and their holdings and the services due from each. He had them all set down in writing. He also brought many lands back into cultivation. Within four years from his election there was not one who could deceive him about the income of the Abbey to a single pennyworth.

In a way, a cathedral was the bishop's equivalent of a baron's castle. *Cathedra* was the Latin word for the bishop's throne. So a cathedral was simply a church which housed a bishop's throne. By 1066 there were already bishoprics at Canterbury, Durham, Rochester, Winchester and Worcester. These were *monastic* cathedrals run by monks. Exeter, Hereford, Lichfield, London, Wells and York were *secular* cathedrals. They were run by priests and laymen.

After the Norman Conquest, the king's council at Windsor made a decree in 1072. All cathedrals had to be built inside walled towns instead of in villages. As a result, the Bishop of Selsey moved to Chichester, Dorchester-on-Thames went to Lincoln, Sherborne to Salisbury and North Elmham to Norwich (with its Benedictine Priory). Four other monasteries—at Bath, Carlisle, Coventry and Ely—later became cathedrals in the Middle Ages.

Each bishop had many priests in his diocese. The Bishop of Lincoln's territory stretched from the Humber to the Thames. This meant that he had to travel a lot, since only a bishop could ordain a new priest.

This is one reason why the cathedral itself was managed by the prior or dean. He conducted the business affairs of the cathedral in the chapter house together with other senior monks and priests. They arranged the daily, weekly and holy day services. They also kept the building in good repair and guarded its treasures. They made arrangements for the pilgrims and visitors who came to see its sacred shrines. Above all, they made sure the cathedral was a worthy building 'for the living worship of Almighty God.' The greater the church, the greater the glory.

Choosing a site

In about 1073 William the Conqueror granted a charter to Bishop Remigius. It gave him the power to move the seat of his bishopric from Dorchester-on-Thames to Lincoln. He was also given

land sufficient to build a mother-church for the whole bishopric.

Bishop Remigius built his new cathedral in Lincoln on a ridge above the river Witham. It was at a meeting point of routes.

Durham Cathedral (see photograph on page 93) was also built on a hill. It was like a fortress surrounded on three sides by the river Wear. Durham Castle defended it on the fourth side facing the town.

By contrast, Ely Cathedral (see photograph on page 108) was built on an island of firm land in a marshland area which often flooded. As a result, it stood out above the flat fens and could be seen for miles.

Other cathedrals built on low-lying sites like this, such as Norwich and Salisbury, had extra-tall spires and towers. They were prominent landmarks. The sight of them alone must have had a magnetic effect on people living in the surrounding towns and villages.

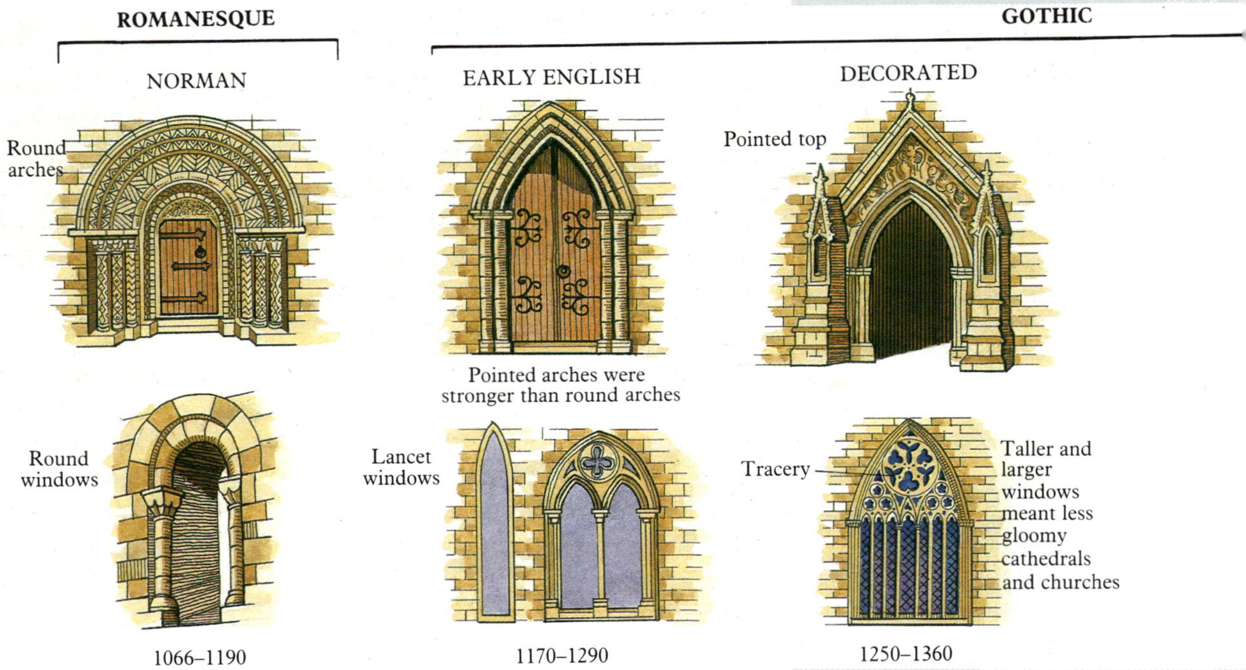

Arches, windows and doorways like these give a clue to the date when the different parts of a church or cathedral were built

How and why cathedrals changed

Most of England's cathedrals were rebuilt at some time or other. Some walls fell down because they were badly built. Some were damaged by lightning, fire or storm. Lincoln Cathedral suffered three disasters in a row with fires in 1124 and 1141 and an earthquake in 1185. Source 31.B tells what happened to Ely Cathedral on 22 February 1322.

In fact the tower, called the Octagon, which he built with the aid of his master mason and a carpenter called William Hurle, is one of the greatest buildings of the Middle Ages. It is octagonal in shape and roofed with timber. Huge windows in each of the eight walls, thirty metres above the floor, throw light down into the centre of the cathedral.

When part of a cathedral was rebuilt like this, the master masons and carpenters used the most uptodate building methods they knew. They did not rebuild the walls and windows in the style in which they had originally been built, as modern architects would do. They rebuilt them instead in the latest styles, using the newest methods. Since these changed frequently in the Middle Ages, it meant that most cathedrals today are now a mixture of different styles. Only a few, like Salisbury, date almost entirely from one period of building.

Stone buttresses (left), like these at Salisbury, gave extra support to the walls and corners of the building. Flying buttresses (right) were built a short distance away from the wall and supported it with an angled arch like this. They were more elegant to look at and gave even stronger support to the wall.

Source 31.B

As the brethren were returning to the dormitory, the central tower suddenly fell. Alan de Walsingham, our Sacrist [the monk in charge of building repairs], *was distraught. He didn't know which way to turn, or what means could be used to repair so vast a ruin.*

He first spent great labour and much money in removing from the Cathedral the fallen stones and beams. Then he measured out the place where he thought to build the new tower. He set the workmen to dig for the foundations of the eight columns which would support the whole building. When these had been firmly founded with stones and sand, at last he began to build those eight columns, with the stonework which they supported. This he completed in six years by 1328.

PERPENDICULAR

1330–1550

31.6 Look at the photographs below and at the diagram above. When do you think these doorways were built? When was the wall at Salisbury (photographs opposite) built? AT3/L4

31.7 How does Source 31.B help us to know how a medieval cathedral was planned and built? AT3/L5

31.8 What were the main differences between a Norman cathedral and a Perpendicular cathedral? AT1C ■

31.9 How and why did the design of cathedrals change during the Middle Ages? What were the main changes? What things stayed much the same? AT1A ■ AT1B ■

New ways of building made cathedrals stronger and safer to live and work in. They also made the interior lighter and more spacious. At the start of the Middle Ages the Normans built long, low, gloomy cathedrals with short stubby towers. Thick buttresses supported the massive walls. Doors and windows were small, with round arches. This style of architecture was called *Norman* or Romanesque. This was because the Norman arches looked like those built by the Romans (page 29). Round arches were also used to roof narrow corridors. These formed a solid arched roof called a *barrel vault*. Timber beams were used to roof the cathedral itself.

By about 1170 builders were beginning to erect a new type of window and doorway arch. It came to a point at the top. This made it stronger than a round Norman arch. This style of architecture was later called *Gothic*. The first arches like this to be built in England were long and thin *lancet* windows. This style is sometimes known as *Early English* or Early Pointed. Builders at this time were also beginning to build vaulted roofs with thin ribs of stone which crossed or met to form a vault (see photograph on page 185). Ribbed vaults were stronger than barrel vaults and made corridors seem deeper and lighter.

When two lancet windows were built next to each other, they made a wider window opening. This led eventually to an even bigger window. The stone around the edges of the windows was highly decorated with carved *tracery*. This style of architecture is known as *Decorated*.

By the end of the Middle Ages, master masons (the medieval architects) were building in the *Perpendicular* style. They built high, slender walls which were strong because they were supported by flying buttresses. This meant they could leave bigger windows without seriously weakening the walls. These tall windows threw more light into the church. The Perpendicular towers and spires they built were also tall and elegant.

How cathedrals were built

We know how cathedrals were built from medieval documents and pictures. They tell us about the craftsmen involved. We know how much they were paid and about some of the problems they had to solve.

Medieval painting of builders at work on a new cathedral

We know about the hours worked by masons on York Minster in 1370 from this agreement:

Source 31.C

It is ordained by the Chapter that all the masons shall from Michaelmas Day [29 September] *until the first Sunday of Lent, be each morning at their work as soon as they can reasonably see by daylight. And from the first Sunday of Lent to Michaelmas, they shall be at their work at the sun rising. They shall stand there truly and busily working until it be no more than a mileaway before sunset.*

◀ *A medieval carpenter at work*

Sources 31.D, 31.E and 31.F (opposite) come from a medieval chronicle. It tells us about the problems faced by Abbot John (1195–1214) when he began to rebuild the front of St Albans Abbey in the early thirteenth century. This building later became St Albans cathedral.

31.10 What stage had been reached by the builders of the medieval cathedral on the left? AT3/L3

31.11 What tools and implements did they use? How did they lift building materials up to the roof? AT1B/L3

31.12 Use the diagram on pages 176–77 to say roughly when you think this picture may have been painted. AT3/L4

31.13 Use the picture below to explain the work of a woodcarver. What tools did he use? What work is the child doing? Briefly describe his workshop. AT3/L5

31.14 Write down at least two reasons which help to explain why Abbot John did not finish building the front of the church at St Albans. AT1B ■

31.15 What different sources of money did Abbot John use to pay for the building work at St Albans? AT1C/L5

31.16 How did the church benefit from Abbot William's improvements in 1215–25? What type of window would you have expected to see there? AT3/L4

31.17 Describe the changes made to the abbey at St Albans between 1195 and 1225. Did they all improve the abbey? AT1A ■

31.18 What does Source 31.C tell us about the working hours of a mason in York (a) on 21 December (b) on 21 June? AT3/L5

31.19 Why do you think experts think the phrase 'a mileaway' in Source 31.C meant the masons had to work until about twenty minutes before sunset? How far is 'a mileaway'?

31.20 How many different churches are under construction in the picture on the right? What scaffolding, building materials and building methods did these workers use?

31.21 How does the scene in front resemble a modern building site? How does it differ? AT1C/L3

31.22 Write a paragraph summing up what these sources tell you about the building of a medieval cathedral. AT1C ■

This medieval painting shows a number of churches at various stages of completion ▶

Source 31.D

Abbot John had received from his predecessor one hundred marks [£66] for the work of the church. With it he pulled down the wall of the front of our church.

Then he began to haul wood and to pile up a lot of stones. He sent for a large number of specially chosen masons, over whom stood Master Hugh Goldcliff. He was a deceitful and lying man, indeed, but an excellent workman. They dug and extended the trench. But in a short time the hundred marks was spent and the wall still did not reach the level of its foundation.

Source 31.E

Work on the wall slowed down. Since they lay uncovered in the winter weather, the stones, being fragile, broke into bits. The wall, looking like a tumbled-down ruin, fell down under its own weight. This did not stop the abbot. He set aside one sheaf of corn from every acre of sown land on the abbey's estates to meet the cost of the work. He had it preached throughout all the lands of St Alban and collected quite a lot of money. But that unfortunate work took it all.

Abbot John, in despair, turned his attention to other works. He built a new refectory and a new dormitory. This pleased the monks. But the abbey chronicler said that in order to construct

these two noble buildings, the convent gave up its wine for fifteen years.

John's successor, Abbot William (1214–25), was better organised.

Source 31.F

He rebuilt the front of the church with a roof of selected material, with timbers, beams and rafters. He built glass windows perfectly made and suitably covered over with lead. He also repaired the stone work with glass panes in the great wall and in the wings of the church. As a result, the church, illuminated by the benefit of this new light, looked like new.

32 Life and work in the church

▶ *WHAT part did a cathedral play in everyday life in the Middle Ages?* ATIC ■
▶ *WHAT was it like to live in a religious community?* ATIC ■

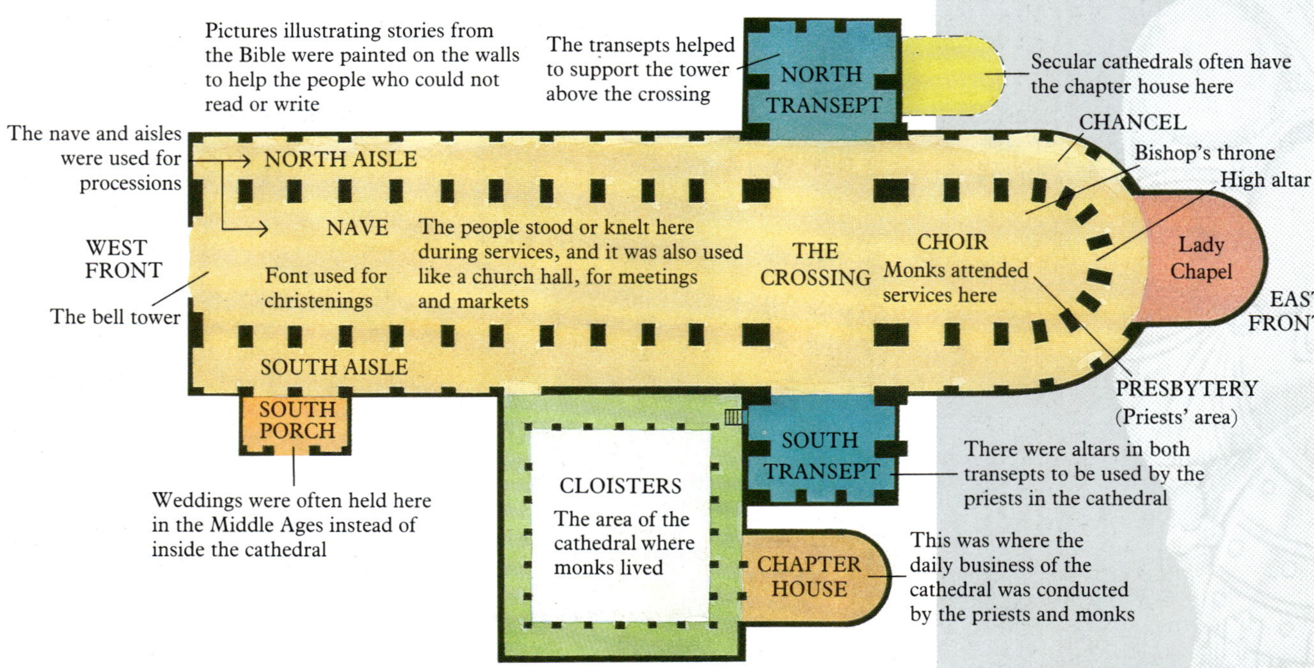

No two cathedrals were the same. This plan shows the approximate position of some of the features you can see if you visit a cathedral today. It also tells you how they were used in the Middle Ages.

Everyday life in a cathedral

A cathedral was a holy place. Much of the shock felt by people when Thomas Becket was murdered (pages 110–13) was simply because a crime had been committed inside the cathedral itself. This was sacrilegious. It made the crime even more terrible. Cathedrals, like churches, were places of sanctuary. Even criminals fleeing from justice could take refuge there (page 122). Cathedrals were also places of pilgrimage (page 113). Many, like Canterbury, had holy shrines which attracted Christians from all over Europe.

There were no seats or pews in the nave of a medieval cathedral. The people attending a service had to stand and kneel. There was straw on the floor but it was often wet and dirty from the boots of the peasants. Most worshippers were illiterate. They could not read English, let alone understand the service, which was always in Latin. However, there were paintings on the walls. Priests used these wall pictures to tell stories from the Bible.

Medieval cathedrals and churches were not looked upon as places for holding religious worship alone. Meetings of local people were often held in the nave. It was sometimes more like a church hall than a church. Traders even set up market stalls, and mystery and miracle plays were performed there in the early Middle Ages.

Medieval pictures and documents help us to know something of the part played by cathedrals in everyday life and about how people lived. However, we can also find out for ourselves, simply by looking at the medieval carvings and pictures in churches and cathedrals which survive to this day.

This medieval painting shows the Canterbury pilgrims on their way to pray at the tomb of Thomas Becket. This was one of the most visited holy shrines in Europe. The wealth the pilgrims brought to Canterbury helped to rebuild the cathedral after a great fire in 1174.

32.1 Look at these photographs and at the other church photographs in this book, such as those on pages 105, 107, 143, 145 and 149. Write one or two sentences saying what each photograph can tell you about everyday life and work in the Middle Ages.
AT3/L6

32.2 What do the carvings and stained glass windows in your nearest medieval church tell you about everyday life in the Middle Ages? AT3/L6

This is a carving on the underside of a seat called a misericorde *in the choir of Fairford Church in Gloucestershire. This was where monks and nuns stood during daily services. When the seat was lifted up, they could use the ledge to take the weight off their feet. Medieval woodcarvers often carved scenes of everyday life on the underside of misericordes. In this carving a woman is shown spinning wool. But what is her dog up to?*

Effigy (or statue) of a dead knight in Suffolk

Engraved memorial brass to a wealthy knight in Cornwall

Stained glass window depicting a wealthy lady whose family gave money to a church in Suffolk

This roof boss in Norwich Cathedral was the keystone in the arch at the point where the ribs in a ribbed vault met

A religious community

As you have seen, over half of England's cathedrals were linked to a monastery run by regular canons (priests who lived together in a community) or monks. By 1300 there were over 700 religious communities in England. About 20 000 monks, nuns or regular canons lived in abbeys, priories, monastic cathedrals and other religious houses. Women could not become priests, but they could become nuns. They lived in nunneries. Most of them came from well-to-do homes, like many of the monks.

Each community belonged to a religious order. The earliest of these was the Benedictine Order founded by St Benedict. However, by the end of the Middle Ages there were at least ten others, such as the Cistercians, Carthusians and Augustinians. The Cistercians built many great abbeys and priories like those you can see in the photograph and picture on these pages.

The members of a religious community carried out the main parts of the daily routine together. They slept in the same dormitory, ate together at long tables in the refectory and prayed together in church. Each individual gave up their personal wealth and possessions and could not own property. Everything was in common ownership. As you can see from the picture, their abbeys and priories were self-contained. They were surrounded by a wall and protected by a gatehouse (see page 109). Everything they needed to live a simple life could be found inside the abbey walls.

Each monk and nun had to take a vow of poverty, a vow of obedience and a vow of chastity. They lived according to a set of regulations called the Rule. This Rule varied from one religious order to another. A chapter from it was read out loud each morning at the daily meeting in the chapter house. If any member of the order committed an offence, they were punished. They could even be flogged in front of the rest of the community in the chapter house.

They could only leave the precincts of the abbey or priory if this was a necessary part of their work. They met outsiders only if they came in search of help, such as travellers, the poor, the sick or elderly and the children who attended the monastic school.

32.3 How did the chapter house get its name? AT3/L3

32.4 Draw a picture of Fountains Abbey from the photograph but show it as it might have looked 500 years ago from the same point of view. Mark and label the church, the cloisters, the chapter house, the refectory and the building for the *lay brothers*. These were peasant monks who worked on the abbey's farms. They took the monastic vows, but did not take part in the daily round of prayers and services. AT1C/L5

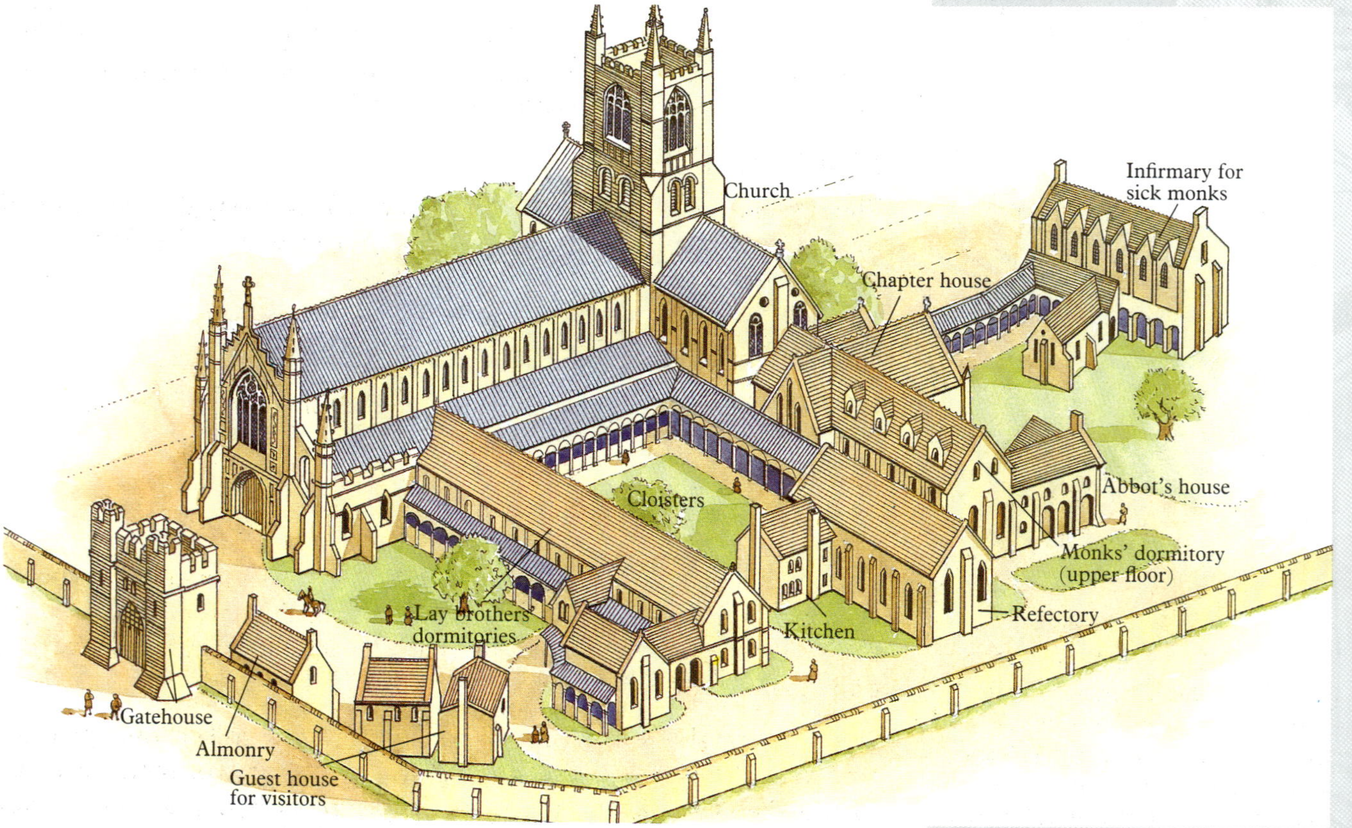

The buildings of a Cistercian abbey almost always followed the same basic plan

Fountains Abbey in Yorkshire, like every other monastery in Britain, fell into ruins after Henry VIII closed the monasteries in about 1540

Life in an abbey

The first duty of a monk or nun was prayer. This is why the members of the community went into church seven or eight times a day. These services were called the *Canonical Hours.*

Source 32.A The Canonical Hours

Matins	*2.00 a.m*	**Sext**	*12.00 noon*
Lauds	*First light*	**Nones**	*3.00 p.m.*
Prime	*Sunrise*	**Vespers**	*Early evening*
Terce	*9.00 a.m.*	**Compline**	*At sunset*

Every day was much the same. They went to the daily meeting in the chapter house in the morning. They ate their main meal in the afternoon in the refectory. They went to bed early. In addition they all had work to do in the abbey or on its estates.

The abbot or abbess in charge of an abbey was normally chosen by the members of the community. They usually picked a senior monk or nun, such as the *prior* (deputy abbot) or the *prioress* (deputy abbess). Duties of other monks and nuns are listed in Source 32.B on the next page.

The toilet block, called the reredorter *or* necessarium, *was close to the river. It was usually built downstream from the abbey buildings. Rows of cubicles were built over a drain like those you can see here at Fountains Abbey.*

◀ *Much of what we know about medieval history comes from the chronicles written by monks. They worked in a study like this, called a* carrel. *They invented and brought to perfection the art of decorating and illuminating manuscripts. The illustrations they painted tell us a lot about everyday life in the Middle Ages.*

Nuns wore a habit *and a special piece of cloth framing the face, called* a wimple. *Monks wore a long, coarse woollen gown called a* cassock. *Their hair was shaved in the middle to form* a tonsure.

Source 32.B

Position	Duty
Almoner	*Distributed alms to the poor in the almonry*
Cellarer	*In charge of supplies of food and drink*
Chamberlain	*In charge of monks' clothing and the dormitory*
Fraterer	*In charge of meals in the refectory or frater*
Hosteller	*Looked after visitors in the guest house*
Infirmarian	*Looked after the sick in the infirmary*
Kitchener	*Head cook in the kitchen*
Precentor	*In charge of services in church*
Sacristan	*Kept the abbey buildings in good repair*

Much of the wealth of an abbey was spent on charitable work. They provided travellers, especially pilgrims, with food and shelter (see also page 109). They cared for sick people at a time when there were few doctors and nurses (pages 150–1). They gave money and food (called *alms*) to the poor. They also ran schools like the one on pages 136–7. Some were song schools which trained poor boys in music as well as teaching them Latin. Some nunneries were like boarding schools and taught the daughters of nobles and knights.

Monks and nuns washed their hands in the basins in the laver. This was outside the refectory where they ate their meals.

The night stairs at Hexham Abbey in Northumberland made it easier for the monks to attend Matins in winter. They got up at about 2.00 a.m. and went into the church down this flight of steps.

32.5 How can modern photographs help us to find out about life in an abbey in the Middle Ages? AT3/L5

32.6 Which of the complaints in Source 32.C was against the Rule of the abbey? AT1C/L5

32.7 How was the reredorter an advance on the toilet facilities in a castle (page 170) or town (page 141)? Why was it built downstream from the abbey? AT1C/L5

32.8 What do you think this sign in the refectory meant: *Bow thy right forefinger and put it on thy lower lip?*

32.9 Imagine you are living in the Middle Ages. Use the information on these pages to write a paragraph describing a day in your life as a monk or nun about 600 years ago. AT1C ■

Source 32.C Complaints at Godstow Abbey, 29 May 1445

Elizabeth Felmersham, the abbess, says she cannot stop students from Oxford having access to the monastery and cloisters. The nuns talk with the folk that come to visit the monastery, without asking any leave from the abbess.

Alice Lumley, the prioress, says the nuns often go to Oxford saying they are going to visit friends.

Most of the monastic buildings could be reached from the cloisters. These were corridors which surrounded a central square. Monks or nuns talked, studied and thought here. Cloisters were usually situated to the south of the church to take advantage of the sun.

Food from the kitchen was passed into the refectory through a serving hatch like this one at Tintern Abbey. Meals were eaten in silence while a fellow monk or nun read aloud from the Bible. This is why the monks and nuns used a sign language. Holding the 'right hand flatways in the palm of the left' was the sign for cheese. To ask for the fish, they wagged a 'hand displayed sideways in manner of a fish tail.'

Teacher's Notes

Flexibility

The three books in this series have been designed to be as flexible in use as possible. Each book can be used by individual pupils working on their own, by pupils working in small groups, or by pupils working together in class. Taken together, these books offer a wide variety of choice in selecting which combinations of options to teach. Yet they still provide coverage similar in depth and extent to that available otherwise from twelve separate topic books covering all five *core* study units and seven *optional* topics. They also provide the opportunity, not available otherwise, to cross-refer, to compare the Roman and Islamic Empires, for instance, and to set the study of castles and cathedrals firmly within the context of the Middle Ages and the work pupils do on Medieval Realms.

Choice of Optional Study Units

The choice of options offered by the series is as follows:

From Group A, a choice of:

either Castles and Cathedrals 1066 to 1500 (Book 1)
or The impact of the Industrial Revolution on a local area (Book 3)
or Britain and the Great War 1914 to 1918 (Book 3)

From Group B, a choice of:

either Reformation and Counter-Reformation in the sixteenth century (Book 2)
or The French Revolution and the Napoleonic era (Book 2)

From Group C, a choice of:

either Islamic Civilisations: seventh to sixteenth centuries (Book 1)
or India from the Mughal Empire to the coming of the British (Book 2)

In accordance with the requirements of the National Curriculum, each optional study unit makes demands comparable to those of a core study unit, in historical knowledge, understanding and skills. Nonetheless, it has been assumed that, in general, rather more time in class will be needed to cover the five core study units.

Choice of Option Routes

As this table shows, the series makes possible a total combination of twelve different option routes.

Option routes		1	2	3	4	5	6	7	8	9	10	11	12
Book One:	**Old World**												
CORE	THE ROMAN EMPIRE	1	1	1	1	1	1	1	1	1	1	1	1
Option C	Islamic Civilisations	2	2	2	2	2	2						
CORE	MEDIEVAL REALMS	3	3	3	3	3	3	2	2	2	2	2	2
Option A	Castles and Cathedrals	4			4			3			3		
Book Two:	**Changing World**												
Option B	The Reformation	5	4	4				4	3	3			
CORE	MAKING OF THE UNITED KINGDOM	6	5	5	5	4	4	5	4	4	4	3	3
Option C	Mughal India							6	5	5	5	4	4
Option B	French Revolution				6	5	5				6	5	5
Book Three:	**Expanding World**												
CORE	EXPANSION, TRADE AND INDUSTRY	7	6	6	7	6	6	7	6	6	7	6	6
Option A	Impact of Industrial Revolution		7			7			7			7	
Option A	Britain and the Great War			7			7			7			7
CORE	ERA OF THE SECOND WORLD WAR	8	8	8	8	8	8	8	8	8	8	8	8

These different option routes make it possible to use the same sets of books with classes following very different courses. Not only can the different teachers in a school use them to teach the options they prefer, but option changes can also be made easily from year to year (such as when new staff are appointed) without incurring the extra cost of purchasing new books and materials.

Expansion

As envisaged in the National Curriculum, the work done on each topic can be expanded or modified to take account of pupils' interests; to make use of original documents, artefacts, pictures and music; and to take advantage of local study opportunities in the vicinity of the school. This is why colour photographs have been used in the text to focus on historical features which not only relate the past to the present but can be used, as well, to stimulate local study work in history and to draw attention to local buildings and sites. In particular, much of the work on Castles and Cathedrals could well be centred round visits to good local examples. Few schools are far from a great medieval castle, cathedral or abbey.

Attainment Targets and Statements of Attainment
Questions, assignments and tasks have been set in the text. They test comprehension, expand historical ideas and concepts and can be used progressively to develop historical skills. Most have been tagged with a simple, unobtrusive code to indicate the relevant National Curriculum attainment target and level of attainment.

The different statements of attainment lettered (a), (b) and (c) in Attainment Target 1: *Knowledge and understanding of history* are shown by the codes **AT1A** (change), **AT1B** (causation and consequence), and **AT1C** (analysis of historical situations). **AT2** indicates Attainment Target 2: *Interpretations of history* and **AT3** indicates Attainment Target 3: *The use of historical sources.*

Similarly, the relevant Key Stage 3 statements of attainment are coded **L3**, **L4**, **L5**, **L6** and **L7**. Thus **AT1A/L3** is the abbreviation for Attainment Target 1: *Knowledge and understanding of history*, Level Three: 'Describe changes over a period of time'.

Each tagged question has a unique reference indicated by its chapter number and question number, such as 1.1 (chapter 1, question 1) and 18.23 (chapter 18, question 23). Tagged questions like these can be located in the relevant attainment level boxes on the Assessment Charts which follow (pages 188–91).

Differentiation by Outcome
Some tasks differentiate between different levels of attainment by outcome. In other words they differentiate according to the varying responses of pupils to the question which has been set. Levels of attainment can sometimes extend in theory, if not always in practice, across the entire range of attainment envisaged for pupils at Key Stage 3. Thus one pupil asked to explain the reasons for the Norman invasion in 1066 might give only a single simple reason (**AT1B/L3**); another might 'identify different types of cause and consequence' (**AT1B/L5**); while a third might 'show how the different causes are connected' (**AT1B/L7**).

Questions like these have been tagged in the text by the code for the Attainment Target only (**AT1A ■**). They are shown underlined in the Assessment Charts on pages 188–91 (**20.8**) and always appear in at least two or more adjacent attainment level boxes.

Please bear in mind, however, that the levels of attainment indicated in the text can only suggest. They cannot prescribe. The actual level of attainment will depend on the learning situation and the supplementary resources available in class. Accurate assessment of individual performance will always depend on the judgement of the teacher setting the task and on the level of interest and assiduity shown by the pupil or pupils.

Some questions carry two attainment target references. This is token recognition of the fact that many assignments can be classified under two or more attainment target headings. For instance, describing 'changes over a period of time' (**AT1A/L3**) will often mean much the same thing as identifying 'differences between times in the past' (**AT1C/L3**).

Many questions do not carry tags, even when it is obvious to which attainment target they are directed. This is partly to avoid further overcrowding the Assessment Charts and partly because, in some cases, appropriate questions and assignments do not fit obviously into any of the existing statements of attainment.

Assessment Charts
The Assessment Charts which follow (pages 188–91) can be photo-copied. When clipped together they will provide a continuous record of the pupil's achievements in history at Key Stage 3 and make it possible to identify at a glance the level of attainment reached in each attainment target.

Space has been provided to insert the pupil's name at the top of each sheet. It is suggested that the relevant question reference number be circled, struck out, ticked or highlighted whenever a pupil satisfactorily completes an assignment or question.

The blank panel in the bottom right-hand corner of each box can later be used to insert the date when the overall performance of the pupil is judged satisfactory at that level of attainment. These boxes can also be used, of course, to record satisfactory achievement in exercises based on local investigations or other assignments set independently of the books in this series.

It is suggested that at the end of a study unit, a record of the highest level of attainment reached by a pupil in each attainment target be transferred to the assessment chart for the next study unit. This can be done quickly by simply recording the date of achievement or highlighting or ticking the relevant box.

The acceptable completion of a single question or assignment will not in itself normally signify that a specific level of attainment has been achieved. Some questions are much more demanding than others. It will depend very much on circumstances – the nature and width of the assignment and the depth of understanding shown by the pupil.

Continuous Assessment
Opportunities for making valid assessments as part of an integral continuous process abound. They encompass every conceivable classroom learning situation—from the formal written exercise for every student in class to the informal, off-the-cuff question put to an individual pupil working on her own or in a group. Suitable opportunities may also occur during work on group or individual projects; during a visit to a local castle, cathedral or museum; in a group or class discussion; during a simulation; and so on.

Although a large number of questions have been tagged, this has only been done to ensure that as wide a range of assessment opportunities is provided as possible. This should be of particular value when making individual and informal assessments.

It is not anticipated, however, that every tagged question will be needed for assessment. Far from it! Indeed, most of these questions will typically be used in a non-assessment mode and the tags will be ignored.

Attainment targets and statements of attainment references are taken from *History in the National Curriculum* (England, DES, March 1991).

Name:

Assessment chart: The Roman Empire

Level	Attainment target 1A	Attainment target 1B	Attainment target 1C	Attainment target 2	Attainment target 3
	Knowledge and understanding of history: Change	Knowledge and understanding of history: Causation and consequence	Knowledge and understanding of history: Analysis of historical situations	Interpretations of history	The use of historical sources
3	Describe changes over a period of time. 1.11 1.20 3.4 3.7 3.8 8.9 8.25 9.12 10.5	Give a reason for an historical event or development. 1.7 1.10 1.21 4.10 6.12 8.19 9.18	Identify differences between times in the past. 1.11 1.20. 3.4 3.9	Distinguish between a fact and a point of view. 1.8 7.13 7.14	Make deductions from historical sources. 1.1 1.6 1.14 1.17 1.19 2.1 2.4 4.13 4.14 4.15 5.2 5.9 6.4 6.10 6.11 7.5 8.16 9.1 9.2
4	Recognise that over time some things changed and others stayed the same. 1.20 3.5 3.7 3.8 5.12 6.17 6.21 8.9 8.24 8.25 9.12 10.5	Show an awareness that historical events usually have more than one cause and consequence. 1.7 1.10 1.21 4.10 9.18	Describe different features of an historical period. 2.13 3.9 6.7 7.1 8.1 8.20 9.3	Show an understanding that deficiencies in evidence may lead to different interpretations of the past. 2.2 2.9 2.11 7.15 8.14 9.5	Put together information drawn from different historical sources. 1.15 4.11 4.16 5.3 5.4 5.6 5.10 6.5 6.6 6.16 6.18 6.19 7.16 8.1 8.10 8.11 8.17 9.3 9.9
5	Distinguish between different kinds of historical change. 3.7 3.8 5.12 8.25 10.5	Identify different types of cause and consequence. 1.7 1.10 1.21 4.10 9.17 9.18	Show how different features in an historical situation relate to each other. 1.9 3.9 5.14 7.1 7.7 7.11 8.2 8.20 8.23	Recognise that interpretations of the past, including popular accounts, may differ from what is known to have happened. 2.2 4.6 7.10 7.15 8.14	Comment on the usefulness of an historical source by reference to its content, as evidence for a particular enquiry. 2.2 2.6 2.14 4.7 6.20 7.8 8.3 8.22 9.15
6	Show an understanding that change and progress are not the same. 3.8 5.12 6.22 8.26 10.5	Recognise that causes and consequences can vary in importance. 1.7 1.10 1.21 4.10 9.18	Describe the different ideas and attitudes of people in an historical situation. 2.12 3.9 4.2 6.14 7.17 8.21 9.6 9.16	Demonstrate how historical interpretations depend on the selection of sources. 7.15 8.14	Compare the usefulness of different historical sources as evidence for a particular enquiry. 4.8 6.15 9.15
7	Show an awareness that patterns of change can be complex. 3.8 10.5	Show how the different causes of an historical event are connected. 1.7 1.21 4.10	Show an awareness that different people's ideas and attitudes are often related to their circumstances. 9.16	Describe the strengths and weaknesses of different interpretations of an historical event or development. 7.15 8.14	Make judgements about the reliability and value of historical sources by reference to the circumstances in which they were produced. 9.15

Name:

Assessment chart: The Islamic Civilisations

Level	Attainment target 1A	Attainment target 1B	Attainment target 1C	Attainment target 2	Attainment target 3
	Knowledge and understanding of history: Change	Knowledge and understanding of history: Causation and consequence	Knowledge and understanding of history: Analysis of historical situations	Interpretations of history	The use of historical sources
3	Describe changes over a period of time. 12.3 12.7 12.8 13.15 16.6 16.7 16.9	Give a reason for an historical event or development. 12.4 12.7 13.14 14.3	Identify differences between times in the past. 12.3 12.8 16.6	Distinguish between a fact and a point of view. 13.3 13.5 13.8	Make deductions from historical sources. 11.6 12.5 12.9 12.11 13.10 14.1 14.5 14.6
4	Recognise that over time some things changed and others stayed the same. 12.3 12.7 12.8 13.7 13.15 15.6 16.6 16.7	Show an awareness that historical events usually have more than one cause and consequence. 12.4 12.7 13.7 13.14 14.3 16.7	Describe different features of an historical period. 11.5 11.7 11.8 13.13 15.7	Show an understanding that deficiencies in evidence may lead to different interpretations of the past. 13.3 13.5 13.8 13.11	Put together information drawn from different historical sources. 11.9 11.10 12.10 12.11 13.12 14.4 14.8 14.11 16.1 16.4 16.8
5	Distinguish between different kinds of historical change. 12.3 12.7 13.15 15.7 16.3 16.7	Identify different types of cause and consequence. 12.4 12.7 13.14 14.3 16.7	Show how different features in an historical situation relate to each other. 11.1 11.5 11.7 11.8 11.13 12.1 13.1 13.13 14.2 14.10 14.12 15.7	Recognise that interpretations of the past, including popular accounts, may differ from what is known to have happened. 13.3 13.4 13.5 13.8 13.11	Comment on the usefulness of an historical source by reference to its content, as evidence for a particular enquiry. 11.2 11.11 12.11 13.2 14.7 14.9 15.5
6	Show an understanding that change and progress are not the same. 12.7 13.15 16.7	Recognise that causes and consequences can vary in importance. 12.4 12.7 13.14 16.7	Describe the different ideas and attitudes of people in an historical situation. 11.5 11.8 13.9	Demonstrate how historical interpretations depend on the selection of sources. 13.3 13.5 13.6 13.8 13.11	Compare the usefulness of different historical sources as evidence for a particular enquiry. 12.11 12.12 13.6
7	Show an awareness that patterns of change can be complex. 12.7 13.15 16.7	Show how the different causes of an historical event are connected. 12.4 12.7 13.14	Show an awareness that different people's ideas and attitudes are often related to their circumstances. 11.8	Describe the strengths and weaknesses of different interpretations of an historical event or development. 13.3 13.5 13.8	Make judgements about the reliability and value of historical sources by reference to the circumstances in which they were produced. 12.11

Assessment chart: Medieval Realms

Name:

Level	Attainment target 1A	Attainment target 1B	Attainment target 1C	Attainment target 2	Attainment target 3
	Knowledge and understanding of history: Change	Knowledge and understanding of history: Causation and consequence	Knowledge and understanding of history: Analysis of historical situations	Interpretations of history	The use of historical sources
3	Describe changes over a period of time. 18.5 18.22 18.23 20.6 20.8 20.13 20.15 20.17 20.18 21.4 23.15 25.4 25.22 25.23 25.32	Give a reason for an historical event or development. 19.10 20.12 20.21 23.3 24.7 24.8 24.13 24.15 24.17 25.2 25.3 26.8 27.14 27.16 28.10 28.13	Identify differences between times in the past. 18.3 18.18 18.22 23.1 23.9 23.15 25.1 28.16	Distinguish between a fact and a point of view. 17.2 18.11 20.16 24.11 25.10 25.13 27.4 27.10 28.7	Make deductions from historical sources. 18.1 18.2 18.15 19.2 19.3 19.7 19.8 19.9 21.8 22.6 23.1 23.2 23.6 23.7 23.10 23.14 25.12 25.17 25.18 25.19 25.25 26.7 27.1
4	Recognise that over time some things changed and others stayed the same. 18.22 20.6 20.8 20.13 20.15 20.17 20.18 23.15 25.4 25.6 25.22 25.23 26.12 26.15 26.24 27.6	Show an awareness that historical events usually have more than one cause and consequence. 18.6 18.17 19.10 20.12 20.21 22.2 22.7 23.3 23.12 24.7 24.8 24.13 24.15 24.17 25.2 25.3 26.21 27.8 27.14 27.16 28.10	Describe different features of an historical period. 18.7 18.18 18.19 18.20 19.5 23.15 25.1 25.5 25.19 25.31 26.4 28.4 28.16	Show an understanding that deficiencies in evidence may lead to different interpretations of the past. 17.1 17.2 17.5 18.11 19.6 20.9 20.16 21.10 22.9 24.11 27.4 27.10 28.6 28.7	Put together information drawn from different historical sources. 17.3 17.6 17.8 17.9 18.13 20.7 20.10 21.3 21.7 21.8 21.10 22.10 24.10 25.11 25.12 25.14 25.17 25.18 25.19 25.20 25.21 26.18 26.19 26.20 26.25
5	Distinguish between different kinds of historical change. 18.21 19.4 20.6 20.8 20.13 20.15 20.22 23.15 25.9 25.22 25.23	Identify different types of cause and consequence. 18.17 19.10 20.12 20.21 22.2 22.7 24.8 24.13 24.15 24.17 25.3 27.14 27.16 28.10 28.11 28.12	Show how different features in an historical situation relate to each other. 17.10 18.4 18.9 19.1 19.5 20.11 20.19 20.20 23.8 23.11 24.9 24.12 25.1 25.5 25.7 25.16 25.19 25.31 26.4 26.5 26.9 26.14 27.15 28.4 28.8 28.15 28.16	Recognise that interpretations of the past, including popular accounts, may differ from what is known to have happened. 17.2 17.5 19.6 20.9 20.16 21.10 22.9 22.11 24.11 26.2 27.4 27.10 28.1 28.6 28.7	Comment on the usefulness of an historical source by reference to its content, as evidence for a particular enquiry. 18.14 19.11 20.4 20.16 21.8 21.9 21.10 22.5 22.9 23.4 24.3 24.11 24.16 25.8 25.12 25.27 25.29 25.30 26.2 26.13 26.22 26.23 27.2 27.7 28.1 28.5 28.6
6	Show an understanding that change and progress are not the same. 20.13 25.22 25.23	Recognise that causes and consequences can vary in importance. 18.17 19.10 20.12 20.21 22.2 22.7 24.8 24.13 24.17 27.14 27.16 28.10	Describe the different ideas and attitudes of people in an historical situation. 17.11 18.9 18.10 19.1 21.2 21.5 21.11 22.2 22.12 23.11 24.14 26.10 27.15 28.3 28.4 28.8 28.9 28.16	Demonstrate how historical interpretations depend on the selection of sources. 17.2 17.5 17.11 17.13 19.6 20.16 21.10 24.11 27.4 27.11 28.6 28.7	Compare the usefulness of different historical sources as evidence for a particular enquiry. 18.12 20.5 21.9 21.10 24.4 24.11 25.12 25.29 25.30 27.3 27.13 28.6 28.14
7	Show an awareness that patterns of change can be complex. 20.13 25.22 25.23 27.9	Show how the different causes of an historical event are connected. 19.10 20.12 22.7 24.8 24.13 24.17 27.14	Show an awareness that different people's ideas and attitudes are often related to their circumstances. 18.9 19.1 27.15 28.3 28.4 28.8 28.16 27.16 28.10	Describe the strengths and weaknesses of different interpretations of an historical event or development. 17.5 19.6 20.16 21.10 27.4 28.6 28.7	Make judgements about the reliability and value of historical sources by reference to the circumstances in which they were produced. 18.12 21.10 24.11 28.6

Name:

Assessment chart: Castles and Cathedrals

Level	Attainment target 1A	Attainment target 1B	Attainment target 1C	Attainment target 2	Attainment target 3
	Knowledge and understanding of history: Change	Knowledge and understanding of history: Causation and consequence	Knowledge and understanding of history: Analysis of historical situations	Interpretations of history	The use of historical sources
3	Describe changes over a period of time. 29.7 29.19 30.3 31.9 31.17	Give a reason for an historical event or development. 29.1 29.2 29.4 29.5 29.6 31.4 31.5 31.9 31.11	Identify differences between times in the past. 29.7 29.17 30.3 31.8 31.21	Distinguish between a fact and a point of view. 29.11 29.20 30.1	Make deductions from historical sources. 29.13 29.22 29.23 29.26 30.4 30.6 30.10 31.10 32.3
4	Recognise that over time some things changed and others stayed the same. 29.7 29.19 30.3 31.9 31.17	Show an awareness that historical events usually have more than one cause and consequence. 29.1 29.2 29.4 29.5 29.6 31.2 31.4 31.5 31.9 31.14	Describe different features of an historical period. 29.7 29.17 30.3 31.1 31.8 31.22 32.9	Show an understanding that deficiencies in evidence may lead to different interpretations of the past. 30.1 30.12	Put together information drawn from different historical sources. 29.8 29.3 29.13 29.16 29.25 30.2 30.4 30.5 30.10 30.11 30.14 31.6 31.12 31.16
5	Distinguish between different kinds of historical change. 29.7 29.19 30.3 31.9 31.17	Identify different types of cause and consequence. 29.1 29.2 29.5 29.6 31.4 31.9 31.14	Show how different features in an historical situation relate to each other. 29.7 29.10 29.15 29.17 29.18 30.3 30.7 30.8 31.1 31.3 31.15 31.22 32.4 32.6 32.7 32.9	Recognise that interpretations of the past, including popular accounts, may differ from what is known to have happened. 30.1 30.12	Comment on the usefulness of an historical source by reference to its content, as evidence for a particular enquiry. 29.9 29.13 29.14 29.21 29.24 30.4 30.9 30.10 31.7 31.13 31.18 32.5
6	Show an understanding that change and progress are not the same. 31.9 31.17	Recognise that causes and consequences can vary in importance. 29.1 29.2 29.5 29.6 31.4 31.9 31.14	Describe the different ideas and attitudes of people in an historical situation. 32.9	Demonstrate how historical interpretations depend on the selection of sources. 30.1 30.12	Compare the usefulness of different historical sources as evidence for a particular enquiry. 30.4 30.10 32.1 32.2
7	Show an awareness that patterns of change can be complex. 31.9 31.17	Show how the different causes of an historical event are connected. 29.6 31.4 31.9 31.14	Show an awareness that different people's ideas and attitudes are often related to their circumstances. 32.9	Describe the strengths and weaknesses of different interpretations of an historical event or development.	Make judgements about the reliability and value of historical sources by reference to the circumstances in which they were produced.

Index